W9-COT-471

AKÉ
The Years
of Childhood

OTHER BOOKS BY WOLE SOYINKA

Collected Plays
The Interpreters
Myth, Literature and the African World
Opera Wonyosi
The Man Died

AKÉ
The Years of Childhood

Wole Soyinka

Random House · New York

Copyright © 1981 by Wole Soyinka

All rights reserved under International and Pan-American Copyright
Conventions. Published in the United States by Random House, Inc.,
New York, and simultaneously in Canada by Random House of Canada Limited,
Toronto. Originally published in the United Kingdom by Rex Collings Ltd., London

Library of Congress Cataloging in Publication Data
Soyinka, Wole.
Aké: the years of childhood.
1. Soyinka, Wole – Biography – Youth. 2. Authors, Nigerian – 20th century –
Biography. 3. Nigeria – Social life and customs. I. Title.
PR9387.9.S6Z462   1982   822 [B]   82-40148
ISBN 0-394-52807-7

Manufactured in the United States of America

First American Edition

PR
9387.9
.S6
Z462
1981

12782

DEDICATION

For Eniola (the 'Wild Christian'), and to the memory of 'Essay'. Also for Yeside, Koyọde and Fọlabọ, who do not inhabit the memory span of the years recounted in these pages.

I

The sprawling, undulating terrain is all of Aké. More than mere
loyalty to the parsonage gave birth to a puzzle, and a resentment,
that God should choose to look down on his own pious station, the
parsonage compound, from the profane heights of Itoko. There was
of course the mystery of the Chief's stable with live horses near the
crest of the hill, but beyond that, this dizzying road only sheered
upwards from one noisy market to the other, looking down across
Ibàràpa and Ita Aké into the most secret recesses of the parsonage
itself.

On a misty day, the steep rise towards Itoko would join the sky. If
God did not actually live there, there was little doubt that he
descended first on its crest, then took his one gigantic stride over
those babbling markets—which dared to sell on Sundays—into St
Peter's Church, afterwards visiting the parsonage for tea with the
Canon. There was the small consolation that, in spite of the temp-
tation to arrive on horseback, he never stopped first at the Chief's,
who was known to be a pagan; certainly the Chief was never seen
at a church service except at the anniversaries of the Alake's
coronation. Instead God strode straight into St Peter's for morning
service, paused briefly at the afternoon service, but reserved his most
formal, exotic presence for the evening service which, in his honour,
was always held in the English tongue. The organ took on a dark,
smoky sonority at evening service, and there was no doubt that the
organ was adapting its normal sounds to accompany God's own
sepulchral responses, with its timbre of the *egúngún*,* to those
prayers that were offered to him.

Only the Canon's residence could have housed the weekly Guest.
For one thing, it was the only storey-building in the parsonage.
square and stolid as the Canon himself, riddled with black wooden-
framed windows. BishopsCourt was also a storey-building but only
pupils lived in it, so it was not a house. From the upper floor of the

*Ancestral masquerade.

Canon's home one *almost* looked the top of Itókò straight in its pagan eye. It stood at the highest lived-in point of the parsonage, just missing overlooking the gate. Its back was turned to the world of spirits and ghommids who inhabited the thick woods and chased home children who had wandered too deeply in them for firewood, mushrooms and snails. The Canon's square, white building was a bulwark against the menace and the siege of the wood spirits. Its rear wall demarcated their territory, stopped them from taking liberties with the world of humans.

Only the school-rooms of the primary school shared this closeness to the woods, and they were empty at night. Fenced by rough plastered walls, by the windowless rear walls of its houses, by tumuli of rocks which the giant trees tried vainly to obscure, Aké parsonage with its corrugated roofs gave off an air of fortifications. Secure within it, we descended or climbed at will into overlapping, inter-leaved planes, sheer rock-face drops, undergrowths and sudden hide-outs of cultivated fruit groves. The hibiscus was rampant. The air hung heavy with the perfumes of lemon leaves, guavas, mangoes, sticky with the sap of *boum-boum* and the secretions of the rain-tree. The school-compounds were lined with these rain-trees with wide-spread shade filled branches. Needle-pines rose above the acacia and forests of bamboos kept us permanently nervous; if monster snakes had a choice, the bamboo clumps would be their ideal habitation.

Between the left flank of the Canon's house and the School playing-fields was—the Orchard. It was too varied, much too profuse to be called a garden, even a fruit-garden. And there were plants and fruits in it which made the orchard an extension of scripture classes, church lessons or sermons. A leaf-plant, mottled white-and-red was called the Cana lily. As Christ was nailed to the Cross and his wounds spurted blood, a few drops stuck to the leaves of the lily stigmatizing it for ever. No one bothered to explain the cause of the abundant white spots which also appeared on every leaf. Perhaps it had to do with the washing of sins in the blood of Christ, leaving even the most mottled spots in a person's soul, snow-white. There was the Passion fruit also, born of another part of that same history, not however a favourite of any of us children. Its lush green skin was pleasant to fondle in one's palm, but it ripened into a dessicated yellow, collapsing like the faces of the old men and women we knew. And it barely managed to be sweet, thus failing the infallible test of a real fruit. But the queen of the orchard was the pomegranate which grew, not so much from a seed of the stone church, as of the lyrical Sunday School. For it was at the Sunday School that the real stories were told, stories that lived in the events themselves, crossed the time-border of Sundays or leaves of the Bible and entered the world of fabled lands, men and women. The pomegranate was most niggardly in producing. It yielded its outwardly hardy fruit only once in a while, tended with patience by the thick-veined hands and face which belonged to someone we only knew as Gardener. Only Gardener could be trusted to share the occasional fruit among the small, dedicated band of pomegranate watchers, yet even the tiniest wedge transported us to the illustrated world of the Biblical Tales Retold. The pomegranate was the Queen of Sheba, rebellions and wars, the passion of Salome, the siege of Troy, the Praise of beauty in the Song of Solomon. This fruit, with its stone-hearted look and feel unlocked the cellars of Ali Baba, extracted the genie from Aladdin s lamp, plucked the strings of the harp that restored David to sanity, parted the waters of the Nile and filled our parsonage with incense from the dim temple of Jerusalem.

It grew only in the Orchard, Gardener said. The pomegranate was foreign to the black man's soil, but some previous bishop, a white man had brought the seeds and planted them in the Orchard. We asked if it was *the* apple but Gardener only laughed and said No. Nor, he added, would that apple be found on the black man's soil. Gardener was adjudged ignorant. It was clear that only the pomegranate could be the apple that lost Adam and Eve the joys of paradise. There existed yet another fruit that was locally called apple, soft yet crisp, a soft pink skin and reasonably juicy. Before the advent of the pomegranate it had assumed the identity of the apple that undid the naked pair. The first taste of the pomegranate unmasked that impostor and took its place.

Swarms of bats inhabited the fig tree, their seed-pocked droppings would cake the stones, lawns, paths and bushes before dawn. An evergreen tree, soft and rampant bordered the playing-field on the side of the bookseller's compound, defying the Harmattan; it filled the parsonage with a tireless concert of weaver-birds.

An evil thing has happened to Aké parsonage. The land is eroded, the lawns are bared and mystery driven from its once secretive combs. Once, each new day opened up an unseen closure, a pocket of rocks, a clump of bush and a colony of snails. The motor-hulk has not moved from its staging-point where children clambered into it for journeys to fabled places; now it is only a derelict, its eyes rusted sockets, its dragon face collapsed with a progressive loss of teeth. The abandoned incinerator with its lush weeds and glistening snakes is marked by a mound of mud. The surviving houses, houses which formed the battlements of Aké parsonage are now packing cases on a depleted landscape, full of creaks, exposed and nerveless.

And the moods are gone. Even the open lawns and broad paths, bordered with whitewashed stones, lilies and lemon grass clumps, changed nature from season to season, from weekday to Sunday and between noon and nightfall. And the echoes off the walls in lower Parsonage acquired new tonalities with the seasons, changed with the emptying of the lawns as the schools dispersed for holidays.

If I lay across the lawn before our house, face upwards to the sky, my head towards BishopsCourt, each spread-out leg would point to the inner compounds of Lower Parsonage. Half of the Anglican Girls' School occupied one of these lower spaces, the other half had taken over BishopsCourt. The lower area contained the school's junior classrooms, a dormitory, a small fruit-garden of pawpaws, guava, some bamboo and wild undergrowth. There were always snails to be found in the rainy season. In the other lower compound was the mission bookseller, a shrivelled man with a serene wife on whose ample back we all, at one time or the other slept, or reviewed the world. His compound became a short cut to the road that led to Ibará, Lafenwá or Igbèin and its Grammar School over which Ransome-Kuti presided and lived with his family. The bookseller's compound contained the only well in the parsonage; in the dry season, his place was never empty. And his soil appeared to produce the only coconut trees.

BishopsCourt, of Upper Parsonage, is no more. Bishop Ajayi Crowther would sometimes emerge from the cluster of hydrangea and bougainvillaea, a gnomic face with popping eyes whose formal photograph had first stared at us from the frontispiece of his life history. He had lived, the teacher said, in BishopsCourt and from that moment, he peered out from among the creeping plants whenever I passed by the house on an errand to our Great Aunt, Mrs Lijadu. BishopsCourt had become a boarding house for the girls' school and an extra playground for us during the holidays. The Bishop sat, silently, on the bench beneath the wooden porch over the entrance, his robes twined through and through with the

4

lengthening tendrils of the bougainvillea. I moved closer when his eyes turned to sockets. My mind wandered then to another photograph in which he wore a clerical suit with waistcoat and I wondered what he really kept at the end of the silver chain that vanished into the pocket. He grinned and said, Come nearer, I'll show you. As I moved towards the porch he drew on the chain until he had lifted out a wholly round pocket-watch that gleamed of solid silver. He pressed a button and the lid opened, revealing, not the glass and the face-dial but a deep cloud-filled space. Then he winked one eye, and it fell from his face into the bowl of the watch. He winked the other and this joined its partner in the watch. He snapped back the lid, nodded again and his head went bald, his teeth disappeared and the skin pulled backward till the whitened cheekbones were exposed. Then he stood up and, tucking the watch back into the waistcoat pocket, moved a step towards me. I fled homewards.

BishopsCourt appeared sometimes to want to rival the Canon's house. It looked a house-boat despite its guard of whitewashed stones and luxuriant flowers, its wooden fretwork frontage almost wholly immersed in bougainvillaea. And it was shadowed also by those omnipresent rocks from whose clefts tall, stout-boled trees miraculously grew. Clouds gathered and the rocks merged into their accustomed grey turbulence, then the trees were carried to and fro until they stayed suspended over BishopsCourt. This happened only in heavy storms. BishopsCourt, unlike the Canon's house, did not actually border the rocks or the woods. The girls' playing fields separated them and we knew that this buffer had always been there. Obviously bishops were not inclined to challenge the spirits. Only the vicars could. That Bishop Ajayi Crowther frightened me out of that compound by his strange transformations only confirmed that the Bishops, once they were dead, joined the world of spirits and ghosts. I could not see the Canon decaying like that in front of my eyes, nor the Rev J. J. who had once occupied that house, many years before, when my mother was still like us. J. J. Ransome-Kuti had actually ordered back several ghommids in his life-time; my mother confirmed it. She was his grand niece and, before she came to live at our house, she had lived in the Rev J.J.'s household. Her brother Sanya also lived there and he was acknowledged by all to be an *òrò*, which made him at home in the woods, even at night. On one

---

*A kind of tree daemon.

5

occasion however, he must have gone too far.

'They had visited us before,' she said, 'to complain. Mind you, they wouldn't actually come into the compound, they stood far off at the edge, where the woods ended. Their leader, the one who spoke emitted wild sparks from a head that seemed to be an entire ball of embers—no, I'm mixing up two occasions—that was the second time when he chased us home. The first time, they had merely sent an emissary. He was quite dark, short and swarthy. He came right to the backyard and stood there while he ordered us to call the Reverend.

'It was as if Uncle had been expecting the visit. He came out of the house and asked him what he wanted. We all huddled in the kitchen, peeping out.'

'What was his voice like? Did he speak like an *egúngún*?'

'I'm coming to it. This man, well, I suppose one should call him a man. He wasn't quite human, we could see that. Much too large a head, and he kept his eyes on the ground. So, he said he had come to report us. They didn't mind our coming to the woods, even at night, but we were to stay off any area beyond the rocks and that clump of bamboo by the stream.'

'Well, what did Uncle say? And you haven't said what his voice was like.'

Tinu turned her elder sister's eye on me. 'Let Mama finish the story.'

'You want to know everything. All right, he spoke just like your father. Are you satisfied?'

I did not believe that but I let it pass. 'Go on. What did Grand Uncle do?'

'He called everyone together and warned us to keep away from the place.'

'And yet you went back!'

'Well, you know your Uncle Sanya. He was angry. For one thing the best snails are on the other side of that stream. So he continued to complain that those *òrò* were just being selfish, and he was going to show them who he was. Well, he did. About a week later he led us back. And he was right you know. We gathered a full basket and a half of the biggest snails you ever saw. Well, by this time we had all forgotten about the warning, there was plenty of moonlight and anyway, I've told you Sanya is an *òrò* himself. . . .'

'But why? He looks normal like you and us.'

'You won't understand yet. Anyway, he is *òrò*. So with him we felt

6

quite safe. Until suddenly this sort of light, like a ball of fire began to glow in the distance. Even while it was still far we kept hearing voices, as if a lot of people around us were grumbling the same words together. They were saying something like, "You stubborn, stiff-necked children, we've warned you and warned you but you just won't listen. . . ."'

Wild Christian looked above our heads, frowning to recollect the better. 'One can't even say, "they". It was only this figure of fire that I saw and he was still very distant. Yet I heard him distinctly, as if he had many mouths which were pressed against my ears. Every moment, the fireball loomed larger and larger.'

'What did Uncle Sanya do? Did he fight him?'

'Sanya wo ni yen? He was the first to break and run. Bo o ló o yă mi, o di kítìpà kítìpà!* No one remembered all those fat snails. That iwin** followed us all the way to the house. Our screams had arrived long before us and the whole household was—well, you can imagine the turmoil. Uncle had already dashed down the stairs and was in the backyard. We ran past him while he went out to meet the creature. This time that iwin actually passed the line of the woods, he continued as if he meant to chase us right into the house, you know, he wasn't running, just pursuing us steadily.' We waited. This was it! Wild Christian mused while we remained in suspense. Then she breathed deeply and shook her head with a strange sadness.

'The period of faith is gone. There was faith among our early christians, real faith, not just church-going and hymn-singing. Faith. Igbàgbó. And it is out of that faith that real power comes. Uncle stood there like a rock, he held out his Bible and ordered, "Go back! Go back to that forest which is your home. Back I said, in the name of God". Hm. And that was it. The creature simply turned and fled, those sparks falling off faster and faster until there was just a faint glow receding into the woods.' She sighed. 'Of course, after prayers that evening, there was the price to be paid. Six of the best on every one's back. Sanya got twelve. And we all cut grass every day for the next week.'

I could not help feeling that the fright should have sufficed as punishment. Her eyes gazing in the direction of the square house,

*If you aren't moving, get out of my way!
**A 'ghommid'; a wood sprite which is also believed to live in the ground.

7

Wild Christian nonetheless appeared to sense what was going on in my mind. She added, 'Faith and—Discipline. That is what made those early believers. Psheeaw! God doesn't make them like that any more. When I think of that one who now occupies that house . . .'

Then she appeared to recall herself to our presence. 'What are you both still sitting here for? Isn't it time for your evening bath? Lawanle!' 'Auntie' Lawanle replied 'Ma' from a distant part of the house. Before she appeared I reminded Wild Christian, 'But you haven't told us why Uncle Sanya is òrò.'

She shrugged, 'He is. I saw it with my own eyes.'

We both clamoured. 'When? When?'

She smiled. 'You won't understand. But I'll tell you about it some other time. Or let him tell you himself next time he is here.'

'You mean you saw him turn into an òrò?'

Lawanle came in just then and she prepared to hand us over, 'Isn't it time for these children's bath?'

I pleaded, 'No, wait Auntie Lawanle', knowing it was a waste of time. She had already gripped us both, one arm each. I shouted back, 'Was Bishop Crowther an òrò?'

Wild Christian laughed. 'What next are you going to ask? Oh I see. They have taught you about him in Sunday school have they?'

'I saw him.' I pulled back at the door, forcing Lawanle to stop. 'I see him all the time. He comes and sits under the porch of the Girls School. I've seen him when crossing the compound to Auntie Mrs Lijadu.'

'All right,' sighed Wild Christian. 'Go and have your bath.'

'He hides among the bougainvillaea. . . .' Lawanle dragged me out of hearing.

Later that evening, she told us the rest of the story. On that occasion, Rev J.J. was away on one of his many mission tours. He travelled a lot, on foot and on bicycle, keeping in touch with all the branches of his diocese and spreading the Word of God. There was frequent opposition but nothing deterred him. One frightening experience occurred in one of the villages in Ijebu. He had been warned not to preach on a particular day, which was the day for an egúngún outing, but he persisted and held a service. The egúngún procession passed while the service was in progress and, using his ancestral voice, called on the preacher to stop at once, disperse his people and come out to pay obeisance. Rev J.J. ignored him. The egúngún then left, taking his followers with him but, on passing the

8

main door, he tapped on it with his wand, three times. Hardly had the last member of his procession left the church premises than the building collapsed. The walls simply fell down and the roof disintegrated. Miraculously however, the walls fell outwards while the roof supports fell among the aisles or flew outwards—anywhere but on the congregation itself. Rev J.J. calmed the worshippers, paused in his preaching to render a thanksgiving prayer, then continued his sermon.

Perhaps this was what Wild Christian meant by Faith. And this tended to confuse things because, after all, the *egúngún* did make the church building collapse. Wild Christian made no attempt to explain how that happened, so that feat tended to be of the same order of Faith which moved mountains or enabled Wild Christian to pour ground-nut oil from a broad-rimmed bowl into an empty bottle without spilling a drop. She had the strange habit of sighing with a kind of rapture, crediting her steadiness of hand to Faith and thanking God. If however the basin slipped and she lost a drop or two, she murmured that her sins had become heavy and that she needed to pray more.

If Rev J.J. had Faith however, he also appeared to have Stubborness in common with our Uncle Sanya. Stubborness was one of the earliest sins we easily recognized, and no matter how much Wild Christian tried to explain the Rev J.J. preaching on the *egúngún's* outing day, despite warnings, it sounded much like stubborness. As for Uncle Sanya there was no doubt about his own case; hardly did the Rev J.J. pedal out of sight on his pastoral duties than he was off into the woods on one pretext or the other, and making for the very areas which the *òrò* had declared out of bounds. Mushrooms and snails were the real goals, with the gathering of firewood used as the dutiful excuse.

Even Sanya had however stopped venturing into the woods at night, accepting the fact that it was far too risky; daytime and early dusk carried little danger as most wood spirits only came out at night. Mother told us that on this occasion she and Sanya had been picking mushrooms, separated by only a few clumps of bushes. She could hear his movements quite clearly, indeed, they took the precaution of staying very close together.

Suddenly, she said, she heard Sanya's voice talking animatedly with someone. After listening for some time she called out his name but he did not respond. There was no voice apart from his, yet he

9

appeared to be chatting in friendly, excited tones with some other person. So she peeped through the bushes and there was Uncle Sanya seated on the ground chattering away to no one that she could see. She tried to penetrate the surrounding bushes with her gaze but the woods remained empty except for the two of them. And then her eyes came to rest on his basket.

It was something she had observed before, she said. It was the same, no matter how many of the children in the household went to gather snails, berries or whatever, Sanya would spend most of the time playing and climbing rocks and trees. He would wander off by himself, leaving his basket anywhere. And yet, whenever they prepared to return home, his basket was always fuller than the others'. This time was no different. She came closer, startling our Uncle who snapped off his chatter and pretended to be hunting snails in the undergrowth.

Mother said that she was frightened. The basket was filled to the brim, impossibly bursting. She was also discouraged, so she picked up her near empty basket and insisted that they return home at once. She led the way but after some distance, when she looked back, Sanya appeared to be trying to follow her but was being prevented, as if he was being pulled back by invisible hands. From time to time he would snatch forward his arm and snap,

'Leave me alone. Can't you see I have to go home? I said I have to go.'

She broke into a run and Sanya did the same. They ran all the way home.

That evening, Sanya took ill. He broke into a sweat, tossed on his mat all night and muttered to himself. By the following day the household was thoroughly frightened. His forehead was burning to the touch and no one could get a coherent word out of him. Finally, an elderly woman, one of J.J.'s converts, turned up at the house on a routine visit. When she learnt of Sanya's condition, she nodded wisely and acted like one who knew exactly what to do. Having first found out what things he last did before his illness, she summoned my mother and questioned her. She told her everything while the old woman kept on nodding with understanding. Then she gave instructions:

'I want a basket of *àgìdí*, containing 50 wraps. Then prepare some *èkuru* in a large bowl. Make sure the *èkuru* stew is prepared with plenty of locust bean and crayfish. It must smell as appetizing as possible.'

10

The children were dispersed in various directions, some to the market to obtain the *àgìdì*, others to begin grinding the beans for the amount of *èkuru* which was needed to accompany 50 wraps of *àgìdì*. The children's mouths watered, assuming at once that this was to be an appeasement feast, a *sàarà** for some offended spirits.

When all was prepared however, the old woman took everything to Sanya's sick-room, plus a pot of cold water and cups, locked the door on him and ordered everybody away.

'Just go about your normal business and don't go anywhere near the room. If you want your brother to recover, do as I say. Don't attempt to speak to him and don't peep through the keyhole.'

She locked the windows too and went herself to a distant end of the courtyard where she could monitor the movements of the children. She dozed off soon after however, so that mother and the other children were able to glue their ears to the door and windows, even if they could not see the invalid himself. Uncle Sanya sounded as if he was no longer alone. They heard him saying things like:

'Behave yourself, there is enough for everybody. All right you take this, have an extra wrap . . . Open your mouth . . . here . . . you don't have to fight over that bit, here's another piece of crayfish . . . behave, I said . . .'

And they would hear what sounded like the slapping of wrists, a scrape of dishes on the ground or water slopping into a cup.

When the woman judged it was time, which was well after dusk, nearly six hours after Sanya was first locked up, she went and opened the door. There was Sanya fast asleep but, this time, very peacefully. She touched his forehead and appeared to be satisfied by the change. The household who had crowded in with her had no interest in Sanya however. All they could see, with astonished faces, were the scattered leaves of 50 wraps of *àgìdì*, with the contents gone, a large empty dish which was earlier filled with *èkuru*, and a water-pot nearly empty.

No, there was no question about it, our Uncle Sanya was an *òrò*; Wild Christian had seen and heard proofs of it many times over. His companions were obviously the more benevolent type or he would have come to serious harm on more than one occasion, J.J.'s protecting Faith notwithstanding. Uncle Sanya was very rarely with us at this time, so we could not ask him any of the questions which Wild Christian refused to answer. When he next visited us at the parsonage, I noticed his strange eyes which hardly ever seemed to

*An offering, food shared out as offering.

11

blink but looked straight over our heads even when he talked to us. But he seemed far too active to be an *òrò*; indeed for a long time I confused him with a local scoutmaster who was nicknamed Activity. So I began to watch the Wolf Cubs who seemed nearest to the kind of secret company which our Uncle Sanya may have kept as a child. As their tight little faces formed circles on the lawns of Aké, building little fires, exchanging secret signs with hands and twigs, with stones specially placed against one another during their jamboree, I felt I had detected the hidden companions who crept in unseen through chinks in the door and even from the ground, right under the aggrieved noses of Wild Christian and the other children in J.J.'s household, and feasted on 50 wraps of *àgìdi* and a huge bowl of *èkuru*.

The Mission left the parsonage just a vicar and his catechist; Aké was no longer worth a bishop. But even the Vicar's 'court' is a mere shell of itself. The orchard has vanished, the rows of lemon grass have long been eaten by goats. Lemon grass, the cure of fevers and headaches— an aspirin or two, a cup of hot lemon grass tea and bed. But its effusion was really fragrant and we drank it normally as a variant of the common tea. Stark, shrunk with time is that white square monument which, framed against the rocks dominated the parsonage, focussing the eye on itself as a visitor entered the parsonage gate. The master of that house was a chunk from those rocks, black, huge, granite head and enormous feet.

Mostly, they called him Pastor. Or Vicar, Canon, Reverend. Or, like my mother, simply Pa Delumo. Father's choice was Canon and this also became my own, but only because of a visit to Ibara. We made several of those outings; visit to relations, accompanying Wild Christian on her shopping expeditions or for some other purpose which we could never grasp. At the end of such outings however, we were left with a vague notion of having been taken out to see something, to experience something. We were left with exhilaration—and of course exhaustion, since we walked most of the way. But sometimes it was difficult to recall what concrete things we had seen, what had been the purpose of our setting out, specially dressed and neatly combed. And with much bustle and preparation.

We had climbed a steep road and come on the imposing entrance—the white pillars and plaque which said: THE RESIDENCY. Some white man clearly lived there, the gate was patrolled by a

12

policeman in baggy shorts who stared over our heads. The house itself was set well back up a hill, part hidden by trees. But the objects on which my eyes were fastened were two black heavy-snouted tubes mounted on wooden wheels. They stood against the pillars, pointed at us, and beside each one was a pile of round metallic balls, nearly as big as footballs. They are guns, my mother said, they are called cannons, and they are used to fight wars.

'But why does Papa call Pa Delumo a cannon?'

She explained the difference but I had already found my own answer. It was the head, Pa Delumo's head was like a cannon ball, that was why father called him Canon. Everything about the guns recalled the man's presence, his strength and solidity. The cannons looked immobile, indestructible, and so did he. He seemed to overwhelm everything; when he came to visit us he filled the front room completely. Only the parlour appeared to suit him, once he was sunk in one of the armchairs he became easier to contain. I felt sorry for his catechists, junior vicar or curate—his assistants seemed to have different names also—they appeared insipid, starved parodies of himself, so seemingly poor in spirit that I would later think of them as church mice. Of the men who came to our house wearing a round collar, only our uncle Ransome-Kuti—whom everyone called Daodu—matched and even exceeded his personality. Pa Delumo's presence awed me, he dominated not merely the parsonage but Aké itself, and did this more effectively than Kabiyesi, our Oba at whose feet I often saw men fall prostrate. Occasionally I met far more mysterious clerics, elusive, with their own very private awesomeness, such as Bishop Howells who lived in retirement not far from our house. But the Canon was the vicar of St Peter's and he filled the paths and lawns completely as he strode downhill to visit his flock or deliver his booming sermons.

The Canon came often for discussions with father. Sometimes the talk was serious, other times his laughter resounded throughout the house. But they never argued. Certainly I never heard them argue about God the way my father carried on with the bookseller or his other friends. It was frightening at first to hear them discuss God in this way. The bookseller especially, with his shrill voice and turkey neck, he seemed to be poorly equipped, physically, for such flippant statements about such a Power. The Canon sometimes seemed to be that Power, so the contest, conducted though it was indirectly, seemed very unequal and risky for the bookseller. My father of course

I assumed to be specially invulnerable. Once, the Canon was walking across the parsonage while they argued on something which had to do with the birth of Christ. They spoke at the top of their voices, sometimes all at once. The Canon was separated from them by no further than the lawn outside and I wondered, when he stopped suddenly, if he had overheard and was about to come and rebuke them.

But he had only stopped to talk to a little boy held by the hand by a woman, perhaps his mother. He stooped to pat him on the head, his large mouth opened in an endless smile and the corners of his eyes broke into wrinkles. His forehead creased—sometimes it was difficult to tell whether he was pleased at something or he had a sudden headache. His jacket was far too small, the trousers stopped some distance above his ankles and his round collar seemed about to choke him. The broad-brimmed clerical hat squashed his giant figure—I glanced quickly to see if he had suddenly diminished in size and was reassured by his enormous shoes which, I learnt from a cousin, were called No-Size-in-London. I obtained a last flash of his vast bottom before he straightened up and the woman's hand vanished totally from sight as he encased it in his own. These alternations between superhuman possibilities and ordinary ill-fitting clothes unsettled me, I wished he would remain constantly in his cassock and surplice.

Essay's favourite position in all arguments was the devil's advocate—he was called S.A. from his inititials, HM or Headmaster, or Es-Ay-Sho by his more rumbustious friends. For some reason, few called him by his own name and, for a long time, I wondered if he had any. It did not take long for him to enter my consciousness simply as Essay, as one of those careful stylistic exercises in prose which follow set rules of composition, are products of fastidiousness and elegance, set down in beautiful calligraphy that would be the envy of most copyists of any age. His despair was real that he should give birth to a son who, from the beginning, showed clearly that he had inherited nothing of his own handwriting. He displayed the same elegance in his dressing. His eating habits were a source of marvel to mother, who by contrast I soon named The Wild Christian. When Essay dissected a piece of yam, weighed it carefully, transferred it to his plate, paused, turned it around, sliced off a piece and returned it to the dish, then commenced the same ritual with the meat and stew, she would shake her head and ask,

'Does that extra piece really matter?'

Essay merely smiled, proceeded to chew methodically, slicing off each piece of meat, yam, like a geometric exercise, lifting a scoop of stew with the edge of his knife and plastering the slice of yam like a master mason. He never drank between mouthfuls, not even a sip. At debate time however, he soon grew as excitable as the bookseller, the shrillest of them all with his tiny twinkling eyes. He appeared to have the sun permanently beamed in his eyes. The bookseller brought into the house that aura of guinea-fowl, turkeys, sheep and goats all of which he raised in his abundant compound. The sheep were always being rounded up; either the gates bad been left carelessly open by a visitor or the stubborn animals had found yet another gap in the stone-and-mud walls. Thin and peppery, leather-taut cheekbones thrust out restlessly, he punctuated his discourse with bird-like gestures. Even at his most aggressive his shoulders slouched, his fingers refused to release the cloth-cap which, outside, never left his head, perhaps because he was completely bald. We could tell his laughter apart, shrill and raspy, revealing gapped teeth which imparted to his face, finally, the look of an old wicker-chair.

The bookseller's wife was one of our many mothers; if we had taken a vote on the question, she would be in the forefront of all the others, including our real one. With a bovine beauty, jet-black skin and inexhaustible goodness, she nevertheless put disquieting thoughts in my head, and all because of her husband. By contrast to him, she was ample, and sometimes when the bookseller disappeared for days, I felt certain that she had just swallowed him up. It was with great relief that I would encounter his bald head bobbing about in animation somewhere in his house or in the bookshop. Of all the women on whose backs I was carried, none was as secure and comfortable as Mrs B's. It was capacious, soft and reassuring, it radiated the same repose and kindliness that we had observed in her face.

We slept often at the bookseller's. Mrs B would send a maid to inform our house that we would eat and sleep at their own house for the night, and that was that. When we got into trouble we ran behind her and she shielded us:

'No no, I take the beating on myself. . . .'

Wild Christian tried to reach round her with the stick, but there was simply too much of her. Unless the offence was particularly serious, that was the end of the matter.

Her only daughter, Bukola, was not of our world. When we threw

15

our voices against the school walls of Lower Parsonage and listened to them echo from a long distance, it seemed to me that Bukola was one of the denizens of that other world where the voice was caught, sieved, re-spun and cast back in diminishing copies. Amulets, bangles, tiny rattles and dark copper-twist rings earthed her through ankles, fingers, wrists and waist. She knew she was *àbíkú*.* The two tiny cicatrices on her face were also part of the many counters to enticements by her companions in the other world. Like all *àbíkú* she was privileged, apart. Her parents dared not scold her for long or earnestly.

Suddenly her eyes would turn inwards, showing nothing but the whites. She would do it for our benefit whenever we asked her. Tinu stood at a distance ready to run away, somehow she expected terrible things to follow. I asked Bukola:

'Can you see when you do that with your eyes?'

'Only darkness.'

'Do you remember anything of the other world?'

'No. But that is where I go when I fall in a trance.'

'Can you fall into a trance now?'

From her safe distance Tinu threatened to report to our parents if I encouraged her. Bukola merely replied that she could, but only if I was sure I could call her back.

I was not very sure I could do that. Looking at her, I wondered how Mrs B. coped with such a supernatural being who died, was re-born, died again and kept going and coming as often as she pleased. As we walked, the bells on her anklets jingled, driving off her companions from the other world who pestered her incessantly, pleading that she should rejoin them.

'Do you actually hear them?'

'Often.'

'What do they say?'

'Simply that I should come and play with them.'

'Haven't they got anyone to play with? Why do they bother you?'

She shrugged. I felt resentful. Bukola was after all our own playmate. Then I had an idea.

'Why don't you bring them over here? Next time they call you, invite them to come and play with us in our own compound.'

She shook her head. 'They can't do that.'

*A child which is born, dies, is born again and dies in a repetitive cycle.

16

'Why not?'

'They cannot move as we do. Just as you cannot go over there.'

She was so rare, this privileged being who, unlike Tinu and me, and even her companions in that other place, could pass easily from one sphere to another. I had seen her once during her fainting spell, her eyes rolled upwards, teeth tightly clenched while her body went limp. Mrs B. kept wailing:

'Egbà mi, ara è ma ntutu! Ara è ma ntutu!'* desperately chafing her limbs to bring her back to life. The bookseller ran from the shop through the adjoining door and forced her teeth open. The maid had already snatched a bottle from a cupboard and together some liquid was forced down her throat. The *àbikú* did not immediately regain consciousness but I could tell, after a little while, that the danger had passed. The household grew less tense, they stretched her on the bed and she relaxed totally, her face suffused with an unnatural beauty. We sat beside her, Tinu and I, watching until she woke. Her mother then made her drink some light fish-soup which she had busied herself preparing while she slept. Normally we would all eat from the same bowl but this time, Mrs B. transferred some of the soup to a smaller pot to which she then added some thick liquid from a bottle. It was brackish and had a pungent smell. While we spooned up our soup from a separate bowl, Mrs B. held her daughter's head back and made her drink her own soup in one go. Bukola evidently expected it; she drank her potion without any complaint.

Afterwards, we went out to play. The crisis was completely over. Mrs B. however insisted that we remain within their compound. I reminded Bukola of that spell. 'Was it your other playmates who called you then?'

'I don't remember.'

'But you can do it any time you want.'

'Yes, especially if my parents do something to annoy me. Or the maid.'

'But how do you do it? How do you actually *do* it? I know your eyes first of all turn white. . . .'

'Do they? All I know is that if . . . let us say I want something, and my mother says No. It isn't all the time mind you, but sometimes my father and mother will deny me something. So then I may hear my other companions saying, ''You see, they don't want you there, that

*Help me, she is getting cold all over!

17

is what we've been telling you.'' They may say that and then I get a feeling of wanting to go away. I really *want* to go away. I always tell my parents, I will go, I will go if you don't do so and so. If they don't, I just faint.'

'What happens if you don't come back.'

'But I always come back.'

It made me uneasy. Mrs B. was too kind a woman to be plagued with such an awkward child. Yet we knew she was not being cruel; an *abiku* was that way, they could not help their nature. I thought of all the things Bukola could ask for, things which would be beyond the power of her parents to grant.

'Suppose one day you ask something they cannot give you. Like the Alake's motor-car.'

'They have to give me what I ask,' she insisted.

'But there are things they don't have. Even a king doesn't have everything.'

'The last time it happened I only asked for a *sàarà*. My father refused. He said I had one not so long ago, so I fainted. I was really going.'

Tinu protested, 'But one cannot have a *sàarà* every day.'

'I don't have a *sàarà* every day.' she persisted. 'And the *sàarà* I asked for that time was not for me, it was for my companions. They told me that if I couldn't come to play with them just yet, I should make them *sàarà*. I told my mother and she agreed, but father refused.' She shrugged. 'That is what happens when the grown-ups refuse to understand. Papa had to kill an extra fowl because it took longer than usual for me to come back.'

Her oval, solemn face changed from innocence to authority as she spoke. I watched her intently, wondering if she was scheming another departure. Natural as it all seemed, there was also a vague disquiet that this was too much power for a child to wield over her parents. I went over all the faces at the *sàarà*, the movement of food and drinks, the sudden disputes that rose as we ate, and the peace-making voices of the grown-ups; nothing unusual appeared to have happened. It had been a *sàarà* like any other. We sat in groups on mats spread out in the garden, all in outing dresses, Bukola especially gorgeously dressed. Her eyes were deeply marked in antimony and her face powdered. She ate at our mat, from the same dish, there was nothing other-wordly about her; certainly I had not seen her giving food secretly to unseen companions, yet the *sàarà* was for them.

18

I wondered sometimes if Mr B. took refuge in our house to escape the tyranny of this child. Fond of arguments as father was, on any subject on earth or in heaven, it was the bookseller who usually prolonged their disputations far into the night. He would worry the dead flesh of an argument with hawk-like talons, conceding a point with the greatest reluctance, only to return to a position long discarded or overtaken by new arguments. Even I could tell that, and the exaggerated patience in Essay's voice only served to confirm it.

And sometimes their arguments took frightening turns. One day the bookseller, Fowokan the junior headmaster of the primary school, the catechist and one other of Essay's cronies followed him home from church service. Osibo the pharmacist enjoyed sitting on these sessions but took little part in them. Their voices had long preceded them into the house, they were all hotly wrapped in the debate, talking all at once and refusing to yield a point. It went on right through bottles of warm beer and soft drinks, exhausted Wild Christian's stock of chin-chin and sweet biscuits and carried over into lunch. Even as she shook her head in despair at 'these friends of your father', wondering why he always managed to attract to himself friends with such stomachs for arguments and food, it was obvious that Wild Christian enjoyed the rôle played by the Headmaster's house as the intellectual watering-hole of Aké and its environs.

Towards late afternoon, tea and sandwiches or cakes refuelled their vocal powers for the final rally, for by then it was approaching the hour of evening service and they all had to return home for a change of clothing. It was usually at this time that Bukola's father seemed in the greatest danger. The arguments would take a physical turn with the bookseller, always the bookseller, about to be made the sacrificial proof of some point of disagreement. My loyalty to his wife created a terrible dilemma. I felt it was my duty to run and warn her that her husband was about to be sold into slavery, banished from Abeokuta, dropped from an aeroplane, hurled from the church tower, tied to a tree in the dead of night alone with evil spirits, sent on an investigatory mission to hell or on a peace mission to Hitler . . . always some dangerous consequence of a going argument, and the only way, they would all decide, in which it could be resolved. That day, these friends actually wanted to cut off one of Mr B's limbs.

'All right, shall I tell Joseph to sharpen the cutlass?'

The argument had started from that morning's sermon. It had gone a hundred different ways at different times and, as usual, the bookseller's gesticulating arms had fanned the embers back to life when every point had been exhausted. Now he seemed about to lose the arm. Still, he fought back. He always did.

'Did I tell you that my right arm had offended me?'

Amidst laughter—and this was the strangest part, they always laughed—Essay called out to Joseph to bring the cutlass.

Mr Fowokan offered. 'Or an axe. Whichever is sharper.'

Mr B's hands flapped about even more desperately, 'Wait, wait. Did I tell you that my arm had offended me?'

'Are you now saying that you are without sin?' the Catechist countered.

'No, but who is to say definitely that it was my hand which committed the sin? And which arm are you going to cut off, left or right?'

'Well . . .' My father gave the matter some thought. 'You are left-handed. So the probability is that your left hand committed the sin. Joseph!'

'Not so fast. Let's go over God's injunction again . . . if thine right hand offendeth thee . . . note, *offended thee* . . . it says nothing about committing a sin. My right hand may commit a sin, or my left. That makes it an offence against God. But that does not mean that *I* am offended. God may be offended, but it is up to him to take whatever action he pleases.'

Essay looked shocked. 'You are now claiming that an offence against God is not to be regarded as an offence against man? You refuse to take God's side against sin?'

Hastily, the bookseller reassured God. 'No, don't put words into my mouth. I never said such a thing. . . .'

With one accord they shouted, 'Good. In that case let's waste no more time.'

Joseph had already arrived and was waiting in the wings. My father took the cutlass, the others seized the bookseller.

'Wait, wait,' the man pleaded. I turned to Tinu with whom I eavesdropped from the corner of the parlour: 'One of us had better run and fetch Mrs B'. But then she was never really interested in the discussions, so she could not see when an argument had to be put to a dangerous test.

Essay tested the edge of the cutlass with the tip of his thumb. The bookseller shouted: 'But I tell you neither my left nor right hand has offended me.'

20

My father sighed. 'Today is a Sunday, God's own day. Imagine you are standing before him. You are his servant, a respected sidesman in his church at St Peter's. You insist that Christ's injunctions are meant to be taken literally. All right, God is now asking you, has your right hand *ever* offended thee? Yes or no.'

It was the sort of language which frightened me even more than the violence about to be visited on the bookseller. My father had the habit of speaking as if he was on first-name terms with God. Why should he suggest that God would come into our front-room just to prosecute the bookseller! I expected any moment a Visitation worse than the bookseller would ever experience from this unequal contest.

Tinu slipped away. The crowd in the front room were laughing at the bookseller who struggled furiously, especially with his voice. Their laughter made it all the more wicked. Essay scraped the cutlass along the concrete floor and advanced one step. The bookseller suddenly wriggled free, flung open the door and escaped. Yelling 'After him! Catch him' they all dispersed, remembering to fling back their thanks to Wild Christian for the Sunday feast. I dashed through the dining-room and the backyard to our gate so I could watch the chase through the parsonage. It ended where the paths separated, one towards the bookseller's compound, the other to the parsonage gate through which the others would regain their own homes. Their laughter rang through the compound as they waved good-bye to one another. I did not appreciate their levity in the least, feeling too deeply thankful that Mrs B. would not have to cope with a one-armed husband in addition to that wilful *àbíkú*.

II

Every morning before I woke up, Tinu was gone. She returned about midday carrying a slate with its marker attached to it. And she was dressed in the same khaki uniform as the hordes of children, of different sizes, who milled around the compound from morning till afternoon, occupied in a hundred ways.

At a set hour in the morning one of the bigger ones seized the chain which dangled from the bell-house, tugged at it with a motion which gave the appearance of a dance and the bell began pealing. Instantly, the various jostling, tumbling, racing and fighting pupils rushed in different directions around the school buildings, the smaller in size towards the schoolroom at the further end of the compound where I could no longer see them. The bigger pupils remained within sight, near the main building. They split into several groups, each group lined up under the watchful eye of a teacher. When all was orderly, I saw father appear from nowhere at the top of the steps. He made a speech to the assembly, then stood aside. One member of the very biggest group stepped forward and raised a song. The others took it up and they marched into the school-building in twos, to the rhythm of the song.

The song changed every day, chosen from the constant group of five or six. That I came to have a favourite among them was because this was the same one which they sang with more zest than others. I noticed that on the days when it was the turn of this tune, they danced rather than marched. Even the teachers seemed affected, they had an indulgent smile on their faces and would even point out a pupil who on a certain charged beat in the tune would dip his shoulders in a most curious way, yet march without breaking the rhythm. It was an unusual song too, since the main song was in English but the chorus was sung in Yoruba; I could only catch the words of the latter:

> B'ina njo ma je'ko
> B'ole nja, ma je'ko

22

Eni ebi npa, ọmọ wi ti'rẹ*

I never heard any such lively singing from the other school, indeed that group simply vanished from sight, yet this was where my sister went. I never saw her anywhere among the marching group; in any case, there was nobody her size in that section. My curiosity grew every day. She sensed this and played on it, refusing to answer my questions or else throwing off incomplete fragments which only fed my curiosity.

'I am going to school', I announced one day. It became a joke to be passed from mouth to mouth, producing instant guffaws. Mother appeasingly said. 'Wait till you are as old as your sister.'

The hum of voices, once the pupils were within the buildings, took mysterious overtones. Through the open windows of the school-room I saw heads in concentration, the majestic figure of a teacher who passed in and out of vision, mumbling incantations over the heads of his attentive audience. Different chants broke out from different parts of each building, sometimes there was even direct singing, accompanied by a harmonium. When the indoor rites were over, they came out in different groups, played games, ran races, they spread over the compound picking up litter, sweeping the paths, clipping lawns and weeding flower-beds. They roamed about with hoes, cutlasses, brooms and sticks, retired into open workshop sheds where they wove baskets, carved bits of wood and bamboo, kneaded clay and transformed them into odd-shaped objects.

Under the anxious eyes of 'Auntie' Lawanle, I played by myself on the pavement of our house and observed these varied activities. The tools of the open air were again transformed into books, exercise books, slates, books under armpits, in little tin or wooden boxes, books in raffia bags, tied together with string and carried on the head, slung over shoulders in cloth pouches. Directly in front of our home was the lawn which was used exclusively by girls from the other school. They formed circles, chased one another in and out of the circles, struggled for a ball and tossed it through an iron hoop stuck on a board. Then they also vanished into classrooms, books were produced and they commenced their own observances of the mystery rites.

    *If the house is on fire, I must eat
    If the house is being robbed, I must eat
    The child who is hungry, let him speak.

Tinu became even more smug. My erstwhile playmate had entered a new world and, though we still played together, she now had a new terrain to draw upon. Every morning she was woken earlier than I, scrubbed, fed and led to school by one of the older children of the house. My toys and games soon palled but the laughter still rankled, so I no longer demanded that I join Tinu in school.

Instead, I got up one morning as she was being woken up, demanded my bath at the same time, ate, selected the clothing which I thought came closest to the uniforms I had seen, and insisted on being dressed in them. I had marked down a number of books on father's table but did not yet remove them. I waited in the front-room. When Tinu passed through with her escort, I let them leave the house, waited a few moments, then seized the books I had earlier selected and followed them. Both parents were still in the dining-room. I followed at a discreet distance, so I was not noticed until we arrived at the infant school. I waited at the door, watched where Tinu was seated, then went and climbed on to the bench beside her.

Only then did Lawanle, Tinu's escort that day, see me. She let out a cry of alarm and asked me what I thought I was doing. I ignored her. The teachers heard the commotion and came into the room. I appeared to be everybody's object of fun. They looked at me, pointed and they held their sides, rocked forwards and backwards with laughter. A man who appeared to be in charge of the infant section next came in, he was also our father's friend and came often to the house. I recognized him, and I was pleased that he was not laughing with the others. Instead he stood in front of me and asked,

'Have you come to keep your sister company?'

'No. I have come to school'.

Then he looked down at the books I had plucked from father's table.

'Aren't these your father's books?'

'Yes. I want to learn them.'

'But you are not old enough, Wole.'

'I am three years old.'

Lawanle cut in, 'Three years old *wo*? Don't mind him sir, he won't be three until July.'

'I am nearly three. Anyway, I have come to school. I have books.'

He turned to the class-teacher and said, 'Enter his name in the register.' He then turned to me and said, 'Of course you needn't come to school everyday—come only when you feel like it. You may wake up tomorrow morning and feel that you would prefer to play at home. . . .'

I looked at him in some astonishment. Not feel like coming to school! The coloured maps, pictures and other hangings on the walls, the coloured counters, markers, slates, inkwells in neat round holes, crayons and drawing-books, a shelf laden with modelled objects— animals, human beings, implements—raffia and basket-work in various stages of completion, even the blackboards, chalk and duster. . . . I had yet to see a more inviting playroom! In addition, I had made some vague, intuitive connection between school and the piles of books with which my father appeared to commune so religiously in the front room, and which had constantly to be snatched from me as soon as my hands grew long enough to reach them on the table.

'I shall come everyday' I confidently declared.

Mr Olagbaju's bachelor house behind the school became a second lunch-hour home. His favourite food appeared to be the pounded yam, *iyan*, at which I soon became his keen accomplice. Through the same *iyan*, I made my first close school friend, Osiki, simply by discovering that he was an even more ardent lover of the pounded yam than either Mr Olagbaju or I. It seemed a simple matter of course that I should take him home or to Mr Olagbaju's whenever the meal was *iyan*; moreover, Mr Olagbaju was also teaching me to play *ayo*,* and this required a partner to play with. It was with some surprise that I heard my mother remark:

'This one is going to be like his father. He brings home friends at meal-times without any notice.'

I saw nothing to remark in it at all; it was the most natural thing in the world to bring a friend home at his favourite meal-time. So Osiki became an inseparable companion and a regular feature of the house, especially on *iyan* days. One of the house helps composed a song on him:

> Osiki oko oniyan
> A ti nwa e, a ko ri e**

which she began singing as soon as we appeared, hand in hand, on

---

*A game played on a wooden board with dug-out holes, and seeds.
**Osiki, lord of the pounded-yam seller
we have sought you everywhere but failed to find you.

25

the path leading from the school. But the pounded yam was also to provide the first test of our friendship.

There were far too many aspects of the schoolroom and the compound to absorb in the regular school hours, moreover, an empty schoolroom appeared to acquire a totally different character which changed from day to day. And so, new discoveries began to keep me behind at lunch-time after everyone had gone. I began to stay longer and longer, pausing over objects which became endowed with new meanings, forms, even dimensions as soon as silence descended on their environment. Sometimes I simply wandered off among the rocks intending merely to climb a challenging surface when no one was around. Finally, Osiki lost patience. He would usually wait for me at home even while Tinu had her own food. On this day however, being perhaps more hungry than usual, Osiki decided not to wait. Afterwards he tried to explain that he had only meant to eat half of the food but had been unable to stop himself. I returned home to encounter empty dishes and was just in time to see Osiki disappearing behind the croton bush in the backyard, meaning no doubt to escape through the rear gate. I rushed through the parlour and the front room, empty dishes in hand, hid behind the door until he came past, then pelted him with the dishes. A chase followed, with Osiki instantly in front by almost the full length of the school compound while I followed doggedly, inconsolable at the sight of the increasing gap, yet unable to make my legs emulate Osiki's pace.

Finally, I stopped. I no longer saw Osiki but—Speed, Swiftness! I had not given any thought before then to the phenomenon of human swiftness and Osiki's passage through the compound seemed little short of the magical. The effect of his *dansiki* which flowed like wings from his sides also added to the illusion of him flying over the ground. This, more than anything else, made it easy enough for the quarrel to be settled by my mother. It was very difficult to cut oneself off from a school friend who could fly at will from one end of the compound to the other. Even so, some weeks elapsed before he returned to the pounded-yam table, only to follow up his perfidy by putting me out of school for the first time in my career.

There was a birthday party for one of the Canon's children. Only the children of the parsonage were expected but I passed the secret to Osiki and he turned up at the party in his best *buba*. The entertainments had been set up out of doors in front of the house. I noticed that one of the benches was not properly placed, so that it acted like a

26

see-saw when we sat on it close to the two ends. It was an obvious idea for a game, so, with the help of some of the other children, we carried it to an even more uneven ground, rested its middle leg on a low rock outcrop and turned it into a proper see-saw. We all took turns to ride on it.

For a long time it all went without mishap. Then Osiki got carried away. He was a bigger boy than I, so that I had to exert a lot of energy to raise him up, lifting myself on both hands and landing with all possible weight on my seat. Suddenly, while he was up in his turn, it entered his head to do the same. The result was that I was catapulted up very sharply while he landed with such force that the leg of the bench broke on his side. I was flung in the air, sailed over his head and saw, for one long moment, the Canon's square residence rushing out to meet me.

It was only after I had landed that I took much notice of what I had worn to the party. It was a yellow silk *dansiki*, and I now saw with some surprise that it had turned a bright crimson, though not yet entirely. But the remaining yellow was rapidly taking on the new colour. My hair on the left side was matted with blood and dirt and, just before the afternoon was shut out and I fell asleep, I wondered if it was going to be possible to squeeze the blood out of the *dansiki* and pump it back through the gash which I had located beneath my hair.

The house was still and quiet when I woke up. One moment there had been the noise, the shouts and laughter and the bumpy ride of the see-saw, now silence and semi-darkness and the familiar walls of mother's bedroom. Despite mishaps, I reflected that there was something to be said for birthdays and began to look forward to mine. My only worry now was whether I would have recovered sufficiently to go to school and invite all my friends. Sending Tinu seemed a risky business, she might choose to invite all her friends and pack my birthday with girls I hardly even knew or played with. Then there was another worry. I had noticed that some of the pupils had been kept back in my earlier class and were still going through the same lessons as we had all learnt during my first year in school. I developed a fear that if I remained too long at home, I would also be sent back to join them. When I thought again of all the blood I had lost, it seemed to me that I might actually be bed-ridden for the rest of the year. Everything depended on whether or not the blood on my *dansiki* had been saved up and restored to my head. I raised it now and turned towards

27

the mirror; it was difficult to tell because of the heavy bandage but, I felt quite certain that my head had not shrunk to any alarming degree.

The bedroom door opened and mother peeped in. Seeing me awake she entered, and was followed in by father. When I asked for Osiki, she gave me a peculiar look and turned to say something to father. I was not too sure, but it sounded as if she wanted father to tell Osiki that killing me was not going to guarantee him my share of *iyan*. I studied their faces intently as they asked me how I felt, if I had a headache or a fever and if I would like some tea. Neither would touch on the crucial question, so finally I decided to put an end to my suspense. I asked them what they had done with my *dansiki*.

'It's going to be washed,' mother said, and began to crush a half-tablet in a spoon for me to take.

'What did you do with the blood?'

She stopped, they looked at each other. Father frowned a little and reached forward to place his hand on my forehead. I shook my head anxiously, ignoring the throb of pain this provoked.

'Have you washed it away?' I persisted.

Again they looked at each other. Mother seemed about to speak but fell silent as my father raised his hand and sat on the bed, close to my head. Keeping his eyes on me he drew out a long, 'No-o-o-o-o.'

I sank back in relief. 'Because, you see, you mustn't. It wouldn't matter if I had merely cut my hand or stubbed my toe or something like that—not much blood comes out when that happens. But I saw this one, it was too much. And it comes from my head. So you must squeeze it out and pump it back into my head. That way I can go back to school at once.'

My father nodded agreement, smiling. 'How did you know that was the right thing to do?'

I looked at him in some surprise, 'But everybody knows.'

Then he wagged his finger at me, 'Ah-ha, but what you don't know is that we have already done it. It's all back in there, while you were asleep. I used Dipo's feeding-bottle to pour it back.'

I was satisfied. 'I'll be ready for school tomorrow' I announced.

I was kept home another three days. I resumed classes with my head still swathed in a bandage and proceeded to inform my favourite classmates that the next important event in the parsonage was going to be my birthday, still some months away. Birthdays were not new. I had shared one with Tinu the previous year and even little

Dipo had had his first year of existence confirmed a few weeks before the fateful one at the Canon's house. But now, with the daily dressing of my head prolonging the aura of the last, the Birthday acquired a new status, a special and personal significance which I assumed was recognized by everyone. Indeed I thought that this was a routine knowledge into which one entered in the normal way of growing up. Understanding the functioning of the calendar became part of the order of birthdays and I dutifully watched Essay cancel one date after the other on the IBUKUN OLU STORES 1938 Almanac alias The Blessed Jacob, the alias of which was printed, for some reason, in a slanting form, rather like my father's handwriting.

All was ready on the thirteenth of July. I headed home after school with about a dozen of the favoured friends, led by Osiki. They all stacked their slates in the front room and took over the parlour. On the faces of the guests, everyone on his best behaviour, was a keen anticipation of food and drinks, of some music from the gramophone and games and excitement. Now that they were home, I became a little uncertain of my rôle as celebrant and host; still, I took my place among the others and awaited the parade of good things.

We had settled down for a while before I noticed the silence of the house. Essay was still at school, mother was obviously at her shop with Dipo who would probably be strapped to the back of Auntie Lawanle. But where were the others? Come to think of it I had expected mother to be home to welcome my friends even if she had to go back to the shop to attend to her customers. It occurred to me also that Tinu had not come home at all, perhaps she went straight to the shop—she was considered old enough by now to do this on her own. That looked promising; any moment now I expected our mother to rush through the doors, making up for the delay with all sorts of unexpected delights.

I went out to the backyard, expecting to find at least one of our cousins or detect signs of preparations for the Birthday. There was nobody. The kitchen was empty and there was no aroma from recent cooking. I called out, announcing that I was home with guests and where was everybody? Really puzzled now, I returned to the dining-room, inspected the cupboards, the table—beyond the usual items there was nothing at all, no jars of *chin-chin*, no *akara*, no glasses or mugs obviously set aside, no pan-cakes, jollof rice . . . there was simply nothing out of the ordinary. This was not how Birthdays normally behaved but, there did not seem to be any cause for alarm.

29

I checked the date on Ibukun Olu Stores once more, satisfied myself that there was no mistake, then settled down with my guests to wait for Birthday to happen.

My mother rushed in not long afterwards, Dipo strapped to her back, Auntie Lawanle and others following, carrying the usual assorted items which accompanied them to the shop every morning. This was impressive because it meant that the shop had been closed for the day and it was still early afternoon—obviously Birthday was really about to happen in earnest. But she came in shaking her head and casting up her eyes in a rather strange manner. She stopped in the parlour, took a long look at my friends, looked at me again, shook her head repeatedly and passed through to the kitchen from where I heard her giving rapid orders to the welcome ring of pots and pans and the creak of the kitchen door. I nodded with satisfaction to the guests and assured them,

'The Birthday is beginning to come.'

A moment later Tinu came in to say I was wanted by mother in the kitchen. I found her with her arms elbow deep in flour which she was kneading as if possessed. Without taking her eye off the dough she began,

'Now Wole, tell me, what have your friends come for?'

It was a strange question but I replied, 'We've come to eat Birthday.'

'You came to eat Birthday' she repeated. For some reason, Lawanle and the others had already burst out laughing. Mother continued, 'Do you realize that you and your friends would still be sitting in that parlour, waiting to "eat your birthday" if Tinu hadn't come and told me?'

'But today is my birthday' I pointed out to her.

Patiently she explained, 'No one is denying that. I had planned to cook something special tonight but . . . look, you just don't invite people home without letting us know. How was I to know you were bringing friends? Now look at us rushing around, your friends have been sitting there, nearly starving to death, and you say you've brought them to eat birthday. You see, you have to let people know. . . .'

The Birthday proved to be all that was expected once it had got over the one disappointing limitation—Birthday did not just happen but needed to be reminded to happen. That aspect of its character bothered me for a while, it was a shortcoming for which I tried to

30

find excuses, without success. The Birthday lost a lot in stature after this, almost as if it had slid down from the raised end of that fateful see-saw to the lower end and landed in a heap, among other humdrum incidents in the parsonage. Still, it had added the calendar to my repertoire of knowledge. When it came to my turn to entertain the gathering, I sang:

> Ogbon'jo ni September
> April, June ati November
> February ni meji din l'ogbon
> Awon iyoku le okan l'ogbon

The others took it up, Osiki supplying a ko-ko-ti-ko-ko . . . ko-ko-ti-ko-ko beat on the table so fluently that my mother asked him jokingly if he had been drumming for the masqueraders. To everybody's surprise he said, Yes. Their *agbole*,* he revealed, even possessed its own mask which paraded the town with others at the yearly festival of the *egúngún*. When Osiki promised to lead their *egúngún* on a visit to our house at the next festival, I could not help feeling that the Birthday had more than made up for its earlier shortcoming. I had watched them before over the wall of the backyard, seated on Joseph's shoulders. I knew that the *egúngún* were spirits of the dead. They spoke in guttural voices and were to be feared even more than kidnappers. And yet I had noticed that many of them were also playful and would joke with children. I had very nearly been startled off Joseph's shoulders once when one of them passed directly beneath the wall, looked up and waved, calling out in the familiar throaty manner,

'Nle o, omo Tisa Agba.'**

But Joseph explained that it was only natural that the dead should know all about the living ones. After all, they once lived like us and that friendly one might even have been in the compound before. Now, discovering that Osiki had an *egúngún* which emerged from their compound every year was almost the same as if we also had one of our own. We crowded round him and I asked if he knew which of his dead ancestors it was.

He shook his head. 'I only know it is one of our ancient people.'

'Are you actually there when he emerges from the bottom of the earth?'

*Family compound.
**Greetings, son of the Senior Teacher.

31

He nodded yes. 'Any of us can watch. As long as you are male of course. Women mustn't come near.'

'Then you must come and call me the next time' I said. 'I want to watch.'

'You want to what?' It was mother, her voice raised in alarm. 'Did I hear you say you want to go and watch *egúngún* in his compound?'

'Osiki will take me' I said.

'Osiki is taking you nowhere. Better not even let your father hear you.'

'Why not?' I said, 'he can come too. Osiki, we can take him can't we? He is not like Mama, he is a man too.'

My mother gave a sigh, shook her head and left us to listen to Osiki's tales of the different kinds of *egúngún*, the dangerous ones with bad charms who could strike a man with epilepsy and worse, the violent ones who had to be restrained with powerful ropes, the *opidan* with their magical tricks. They would transform themselves into alligators, snakes, tigers and rams and turn back again into *egúngún*. Then there were the acrobats—I had seen those myself over the wall, performing in a circle of spectators near the cenotaph. They did forward and backward somersaults, doubled up their limbs in the strangest manner, squeezed their lower trunks into mortars and then bounced up and down in the mortar along short distances as if they were doing a mortar race. Apart from Giro, the crippled contortionist to whose performance we had once been taken in the palace compound, only these *egúngún* appeared to be able to tie up their limbs in any manner they pleased.

'Can I come back as an *egúngún* if I die?' I asked Osiki.

'I don't think so' he said. 'I've never heard of any Christian becoming an *egúngún*.'

'Do they speak English in the *egúngún* world?' I now wanted to know.

Osiki shrugged. 'I don't know. Our own *egúngún* doesn't speak English.'

It seemed important to find out. The stained-glass windows behind the altar of St Peter's church displayed the figures of three white men, dressed in robes which were very clearly *egúngún* robes. Their faces were exposed, which was very unlike our own *egúngún*, but I felt that this was something peculiar to the country from which those white people came. After all, Osiki had explained that there were many different kinds of *egúngún*. I sought his opinion on the

32

three figures only to have Tinu interrupt.

'They are not *egúngún*' she said, 'those are pictures of two missionaries and one of St Peter himself.'

'Then why are they wearing dresses like *egúngún*?'

'They are Christians, not masqueraders. Just let Mama hear you.'

'They are dead aren't they; They've become *egúngún*, that is why they are wearing those robes. Let's ask Osiki.'

Osiki continued to look uncertain. 'I still haven't heard of any Christian becoming *egúngún*. I've never heard of it.' Then he suddenly brightened. 'Wait a minute, I've just remembered. My father told me that some years ago, they carried the *egúngún* of an *ajele*, you know, the District Officer who was here before.'

I rounded on Tinu triumphantly. 'You see. Now I can speak to those *egúngún* in the church window whenever they come. I am sure they only speak English.'

'You don't know what you are talking about. You are just a child.' She turned scornfully away and left us alone.

'Don't mind her' I told Osiki. 'She knows I've always liked the one in the middle, the St Peter. I've told her before that he is my special *egúngún*. If I come first to your compound, perhaps we can go next to the church cemetery and make him come out of the ground in the same way.'

'With his face bared like that?' Osiki sounded scandalized.

'Of course not' I assured him. 'That is only his picture. When he comes out of the ground he will be properly dressed. And I'll be able to talk to him.'

Osiki looked troubled. 'I don't know. I don't really know if he will be a real *egúngún*.'

'But you've just said that the *egúngún* of the District Officer came out in procession before.'

'It is not the same thing. . . .' Osiki tried to explain, but finally admitted that he did not really understand. Somehow, it was not going to be possible but, why it should be that way, he didn't know. I reminded him that the District Officer was both white and Christian, that St Peter's had the advantage because he was near a cemetery. In addition, anyone with eyes could see that he was already in his *egungun* robes, which meant that he had joined in such festivals before. Osiki continued to be undecided, to my intense disappointment. Without his experience, I did not even know how to begin to bring out *egúngún* St Peter without whom, from then on, the parade of ancestral masquerades at Aké would always seem incomplete.

When I again lay bleeding on the lawns of the infant school, barely a year later, I tried to see myself as a one-eyed masquerade, led by Osiki along the paths of the parsonage to visit my old home and surprise Tinu and Dipo by calling out their names. The accident occurred during a grass-cutting session by the bigger boys. The rest of us simply played around the school grounds or went home for the rest of the day. Osiki should have been cutting grass with the others but he had become my unofficial guardian, taking me home or to Mr Olagbaju's house after school or fetching me from home, as if I had not walked to school all by myself nearly two years before. On that afternoon we were playing together, he chasing me round and round the infant school building. I was already developing a sense of speed, nothing to match his, but could dodge faster than he could turn whenever his arms reached out to grab me. I had just rounded the corner of the schoolroom when I saw, through the corner of my eye, the upward flash of a blade. Beneath it was a crouching form, its back turned towards me. That was all I had time to see. The next instant I felt the blade bite deep into the corner of my eye, the day was blotted out in a flush of redness and I collapsed forward on my face, blinded. I heard screams from everywhere. When I rolled over and put my hands to my face they were instantly drenched in the same warm thick flood which had accompanied my somersault in the Canon's garden.

I lay still, unaware of any pain. My only thought was that if I did not remain like that, on my back, my eye would fall out on to the ground. Then I thought perhaps I would actually die this time; since I had obviously lost an eye, I tried to recall if I had ever seen a one-eyed masquerade among the *egúngún* whom we watched over the wall. There were sounds of heavier feet running towards me. I recognized the voices of teachers, felt myself raised up and carried into the schoolroom, then laid on a table. I heard Mr Olagbaju send someone to fetch my father.

Through the noise and confusion I gathered that I had run straight into the upward stroke of a cutlass wielded by a pupil who was busy cutting grass, his back turned to me. I heard the confused boy calling on God to save him from the stigma of becoming a murderer in his lifetime. One of the teachers told him to shut up and eventually pushed him out. When I heard my father's voice, it occurred to me to

34

open the undamaged eye—I had not, until then, acted on the fact that I was only hit in one eye, not both. Wiping the blood from the left eye, I blinked it open. Standing round the table was a semi-circle of teachers, looking at me as if I was already a masquerade, the *opidan* type, about to transform himself into something else. I touched myself to ensure that this had not already happened, so strangely watchful were all the pairs of eyes.

'How did it happen?' my father demanded even as he examined the wound. A babble of voices rose in explanation.

I asked him, 'Am I blind?'

Everyone shouted at once, 'Keep still, Wole. Don't move!'

I repeated my question, feeling now that I was not dying but wondering if I would be obliged to become a beggar like those blind men who sometimes came into the parsonage, led by a small child, sometimes no bigger than I. It occurred to me then that I had never seen a small child leading a blind child.

Someone asked, 'Where is that Osiki?'

But Osiki was gone. Osiki, when I was struck down, had simply continued running in the direction which he was facing at the time. He ran, I was sure, at a speed which surpassed even his usual phenomenal swiftness. Some of the bigger boys had tried to catch him—why, I did not know—but Osiki outstripped them running lean and light in the wind. I could see him, and the sight brought a smile to my face. It also made me open the injured eye and, to my surprise, I could see with it. There were loud gasps from the anxious faces who now crowded closer to see for themselves. The skin was split right into the corner of the eye but the eyeball itself was unscathed. Even the bleeding appeared to have stopped. I heard one teacher breathe 'Impossible!' while another shouted, 'Olorun ku ise!'.* My father simply stood back and stared, his mouth agape in disbelief.

And then I felt very tired, a mist appeared to cover my eyes, and I fell asleep.

*God's work be praised!

III

I could not climb the ladder by myself, but I already knew where it was. Simply by following the rush of feet, I knew where to go whenever the sounds from an event carried into the house of Aké. It was an iron ladder and sometimes four or five of the household would stand on it at once gazing out, throwing off comments on the event. They ignored my efforts to come on the ladder with them, claiming it was dangerous.

Then one day Joseph relented and hoisted me up on his shoulders and I obtained my first look over the wall of our yard. I followed the group of dancers from the road which went past the cenotaph, behind the church, then disappeared in the direction, Joseph said, of the palace. I had recognized the church and the cenotaph. I had also recognized another feature of the landscape, and this was the large gate of the parsonage itself. I understood then that the outer walls of the parsonage were joined continuously, giving way in places to gates or windows. Seated on Joseph's shoulder, I traced the wall against which our bodies were pressed leftwards, saw it melt into the wall of the storeroom where the pots—both for cooking and for father's gardening—were kept, then vanish into the wall of the barn for firewood and chicken, after which it became the wall of a small recess which served as father's garden nursery, then the wall of the bathroom, and finally the kitchen. From there it moved to encase the catechist's compound, wrapped round the rest of his house, then changed back into a plain wall until it was broken into by the parsonage gate. It then ran into the wall of the lower Girls' School before sheering off at the corner into the frontage of the bookshop, the only building in the parsonage which faced outwards on to the street.

Along the way, there were a few windows here and there, token ventilations, set high in the wall, almost against the iron sheet roof. Mostly however, the walls ran smoothly, varied in places by overflowing banana leaves, guava, or the bitter-leaf plant such as the luxuriant one whose leaves brushed my face at that moment. It

36

became clear then that we in the parsonage were living in a separate town by ourselves, and that Aké was the rest of what I could see. That other town, Aké, was linked by rusted roofs just as ours was joined by walls. Only special buildings like the church or the cenotaph stood by themselves. Everything else was joined in one continuous seam.

And so the next time that the sounds came, I did not bother to contest a place on the ladder, which I could not climb anyway. I had recognized now where that gate was, through which I passed on the way to church, clutching Lawanle's, Joseph's or Mama's hand. I had realized also that one would obtain a much clearer view simply by going outside the gates and watching from there. On reaching the gate, I was surprised to find it latched; it was even more annoying that I could not reach the wooden peg which would release the latch. Then I heard excited voices on the outside, obviously there were others before me who had the same idea. I banged on the gate and someone opened it.

They were all strangers. I had seen none of the faces before. I wondered if they were passers-by who had climbed the steps leading up to the gate for an even clearer view. I thought they looked at me in some rather uncertain way, but, they made way for me to come to the front and we ignored each other's presence at the sight of the police band, the cause of the excitement. They had on bright sashes, bright red fez caps with dangling tassels and what looked like embroidered waistcoats. The drum which was strapped to the man in front was unbelievable in its size; at every step I expected him to topple over, but he pounded its white skin with complete mastery, his gaze set rigidly to the front. His arms made flourishes in the air, giving the heavy-ended drumsticks a twirl, then dashing them against the sides. The man in the lead juggled an enormous mace, threw it in the air, spun around and caught it as it descended. Once, he even caught it backwards, earning a roar from the crowd. A gleaming brass funnel rose between the players; the face which blew into it looked as if it would burst. It gave off notes which were nearly as deep as the big drum but the strain on the player's face far exceeded that of the drummers.

I had a strange sensation. Each time the big drum was hit, it seemed that the vibrations entered my stomach, echoed around its walls, then went out again to re-join the drum. I listened and *felt* each time the *boom* came and I was left in no doubt about it; obviously it was the way of the big drum, I had no doubt that it affected

37

everyone the same way. I noticed little boys following the band, some walked directly behind, imitating the march of the policemen, others walked alongside, at the extreme edges of the road. They seemed not much bigger than I, and I soon joined them. Unlike the strangers at the gate, none of them seemed to notice me. I stayed with the group at the back, taking care however not to mimic the swagger of the others. It did not seem a decorous thing to do and the policemen looked stern enough to take offence.

We marched past the bookshop and I felt vindicated. The frontage was exactly where I had gauged it while seated on Joseph's shoulder. But then the curious thing happened; after the bookseller's, the wall rolled away into a different area I had never seen before. Soon it moved away altogether, was covered up by houses and shops and disappeared for ever. It upset my previous understanding of the close relationship between the parsonage and Aké. I expected the wall to be everywhere; by now I should have been on the outside of the walls of the school playing fields, the roofs of the primary school should be visible, then the infant, the corn-field of the school farms and perhaps the cemetery. None of this happened. Instead there were shops and storey-buildings. And there were inscriptions everywhere: AKINS PHOTO STUDIO: LONDON TRAINED PORTRAITIST, then, in smaller letters: A Trial Will Convince You. Photos lined the two halves of the open door of the studio, while the photographer himself sat outside on a bench with crossed legs, a scarf around his neck, smoking a pipe. I recognized him because he had been in our house before to take photographs of Dipo when he was born. I thought that photographers did all their work in people's homes and was surprised to discover that they also ran their own shops.

I made a note to start learning how to ride a bicycle as we marched past a bicycle hirer, busy mending a tube. A learner whose feet barely touched the pedals was just taking off, supported by a teacher who was no bigger but who appeared very full of instructions. The parsonage wall had vanished for ever but it no longer mattered. Those token bits and pieces of Aké which had entered our home on occasions, or which gave off hints of their nature in those Sunday encounters at church, were beginning to emerge in their proper shapes and sizes.

Every week, sometimes more often, Lawanle or Joseph would go off with a large basin of corn and return with it crushed, a layer

38

of water over it. Then would begin a series of operations with calabashes, strainers, baskets and huge pots. It ended with those pots being placed in a dark corner of the kitchen, covered. As the days passed they would give off an ever ripening smell of fermentation. A week would pass and after several tests, tasting and sniffing, one pot would emerge from the darkness, and from it was scooped the smooth white paste which in turn was stirred in hot water to provide the morning *ogi*, a neutral mixture which everyone seemed to enjoy but I. The *akara** which went with it, the *jogi,** *moinmoin** or *leki** was a different matter. My mouth was watering even as I thought of it. But I could not understand how *ogi* which took so much mysterious labour, could appeal to any taste.

Now I saw that the labour involved was even much greater than I knew, which only made matters worse for *ogi*, in my estimate of its pretensions. We were passing by a small shop in which a machine whirled, propelling a belt with enough noise to match the music of the police band. A cluster of women waited by the door with their corn-filled basins and I realized that this was where Joseph or Lawanle came on those weekly excursions. There was a basin placed under a wide funnel which opened downwards. Suddenly the thitish mixture was flushed through into the basin, of the same coarse mix that Lawanle would bring home. Then they would all commence the task of refining it and leaving it for some days to settle. Mother loved the 'omi'kan, the sour, fermented liquid which formed at the top after its period of rest. It had some curative powers, she claimed, a suggestion which I found unappealing. Medicine and food led separate lives and should never be mixed up.

The starched, cowled, white lady who visited us sometimes with bags of lozenges apparently also lived in a compound. For there, boldly etched on the gates in a stone-fenced wall were the words: Miss McCutter's Maternity Clinic. This was the first word that day to give me any trouble. We knew her simply as Miss Makota, and there had been no previous hint that her name might be spelt differently. Nevertheless the 'Maternity Clinic' left me in no doubt that this was where the lady lived. I wondered if I should surprise her with a visit, but decided against it, fearful that I might not be able to catch up with the band.

Once or twice I did wonder if I was not being carried too far from

*Delicacies made from black-eyed beans.

39

home. There was however the reassurance that one part of my observation about the town remained intact—the houses remained linked together. We encountered more and more houses which stood on their own, like the church and the cenotaph, but they continued to be linked, if not along the roofs, then by the fences which surrounded them. At one point or the other, they touched. Why this should prove so reassuring, I did not know, but I continued to feel much at home with every step.

We came on the police station not far from McCutter's and I expected the band to stop there. They did not even glance in the direction of the station but marched straight past, trumpets blaring and the trombones flashing in the sun. The composition of the group of children around me appeared to change all the time. Suddenly one face or group disappeared, only to be replaced by a new crop which surfaced along the way, as if by pre-arrangement. It crossed my mind that I was perhaps depriving someone of his place in the procession by remaining, but no one said anything; on the contrary every face appeared wrapped up in the music, the marching, in simply enjoying themselves. I marched along with the rest.

Near the first road-junction we came to yet another sign over which I pored. It read: MRS T. BANJOKO. LONDON-TRAINED SEWING MISTRESS. I looked for 'A Trial Will Convince You' in vain. In its place was an invitation to 'Enquire Within for the Proprietress, Banjoko Sewing Academy'. It seemed unnecessary to enquire 'within', since the sewing school was taking place right before us, on the pavement. The girls all wore uniforms of blue, shapeless dresses which made me think that the first task of the pupils was to sew their own dresses before they learnt how. Mama made dresses for us, and I could not remember seeing anything so shapeless on Tinu. The lady who sat at the machine appeared to fit the role of the Proprietress, at whose meaning I could only guess. I had not encountered such a difficult word before and I made a note to ask my father how it differed from the simpler one of a school-mistress.

There were quite a number of them. The proprietress had her back stolidly turned on the passing excitement and the girls sensed that they were obliged to do the same. Just the same, I caught them all, without exception, dart excited glances towards the road. Their obedient faces flashed a momentary conspiracy with the band of us marching behind and beside the column, I felt I was lifted in the air, secretively bonded to those poor slaves of the sewing machine. The termagant at the instruction desk knew nothing of our furtive contacts; I knew however that she must have sensed a loss of attention because she turned round, appeared to see the procession for the first time, then rounded on her pupils in a manner which was clearly angry and reprimanding. The girls clustered together, giggling but attentive. One, who had giggled the most, waved her hand at us behind her back and most of us waved back, some of the bolder even shouting a greeting or a mild abuse at the tyrant who would not let them join the troupe. The band remained impervious to the goings-on around them and behind their back. They blew and drummed stolidly ahead, the brass cymbals flashed and clashed, sweat covered the unfortunate one who was encased in the fat network of tubes which curved skywards and opened flat-lipped and wide-mouthed over the player's shoulder.

I knew now where I had encountered such a funnel. It was the same as the picture on our gramophone into which a dog barked, below which was written: HIS MASTER'S VOICE. Tinu and I had long rejected the story that the music which came from the gramophone was made by a special singing dog locked in the machine. We never saw it fed, so it would have long starved to death. I had not yet found a means of opening up the machine, so the mystery remained.

At the road-junction one arm of the signpost read: To LAFENWA; the other—IGBEIN, IBARA. The procession followed the latter. There was a market before we got to Ibara. There, women were waiting by the road, more were flocking from their stalls by the time we got there. Their stalls stretched endlessly from the right side of the road, goods piled up on low stools or on specially laid trestles. I hesitated; it did not seem possible that there was so much *thing* in the world! I moved to the side of the band so that I could see beyond them—there were no crossroads in sight and anyway, I reasoned that if I did not stay too long in the market, I could find my way back to the procession by the sound. I turned into the market, wide-eyed. Peppers of all shapes and sizes rose in profusion from wooden and enamel trays. There were mounds of gari which beggared those cupfuls that were brought out at cooking-time to be turned to *eba* in hot water. The earthy smell of yam powder assailed my nostrils long before I came on it, piled high in calabash trays. And SALT! Nobody surely, not even the whole of Aké could eat so much salt in a hundred

41

years, yet I came on the piles stall after stall. It gave way to a variety of tubers, vegetables, dried fish and crayfish, then the stalls of meat with men flashing long, two-edged knives among slabs of meat, brushing away flies with one hand or hitting a small boy on the head for dozing off while flies landed on the meat. The butcher was as magical in his own field as the policeman who performed the juggling with the mace. Each moment he looked as if he would cut his fingers but no, the knife flashed just between two fingers and down on the table landed two neatly sliced pieces of meat.

It seemed a long time before the foods stopped altogether, giving way to clothes, sewing materials, toys, even small bookstalls with pens, rubbers, inkwells and notebooks neatly laid out.

And then I came to a sudden stop and backed away. Staring me in the eye was a shrunken head of an animal, dangling from a low wooden shelf beneath a stall. Only then did I notice that it was still attached to the body. It had been dried and preserved. And there were more. My eyes continued along the shelf, dropped to the trestle-table below and encountered skulls, just the plain, whitened skull, without any skin or flesh, large empty sockets and holes for noses. And there were dried barks, leaves. It was the strangest line of stalls in the entire market, with its assortment of stones, beads, pieces of iron, coloured powders in little heaps, small parcels tied up in leaves, bottles filled with the strangest liquids, and barks and leaves visible within the bottles. There were also the dried snakes and mice. The women were much older in these stalls, they sat impassively, obviously unmoved by the music of the band which had driven the younger ones on to the street. From time to time, a wizened hand rose from the dark interior of the stalls, fly-whisk in hand, and described in a slow circle through the stall. I experienced shock at their flat, emptied breasts and remembered suddenly that it was wrong to stare. I looked away.

Were these the witches we heard so much about? No breast that I had seen before had appeared so flat, it did not seem human. Yet when I looked in the trays again I recognized barks and roots similar to those which were bought by father, stuffed into bottles and jars where they were left to soak for days. They were given to us for some ailments. Some we simply drank at periods mysteriously communicated to either parent. And there were other barks bred in huge pots. Once, after a fever, I broke out in a rash. I remembered being washed every day with the contents from such pots. The herbs and roots were brought home in baskets, boiled and allowed to cool, I was scrubbed in them, given pungent liquids from other stuffed jars to drink, and put to bed. Or there were pills from Miss McCutter's, Oke Padi or some other place, and teaspoonfuls of unpleasant fluids from neatly labelled bottles. Often both forms of remedies were administered together, or took turns from day to day. It did not seem to matter if one was ill or not, we always had to take something or the other, only the intervals varied. I was not reassured by the appearance of these women who appeared every bit as crinkled as the herbs and roots on their trays. The potions seemed now to be fluids from their own bodies since I could not conceive of blood flowing in them, certainly not blood of the same colour as I saw when I cut my feet on a stone.

The nearest looked up suddenly at me and I returned her gaze. Then she smiled. If she hadn't, I may have asked her the questions which were racing through my mind. But her face, which did not look like the face of the living while it was at rest, suddenly turned into the face of the shrunken heads which dangled just above her head. I turned and fled, running all the way until I caught up with the band. My head was pounding more from fright than from the exertion, for the thought had occurred to me that there was no certainty whatsoever that the skulls were really the skulls of animals. They could have been the skulls of young children who had been foolish enough to wander too close to the witches' stalls. I reflected that I had never liked those potions we were made to drink anyway; now I had a good reason for refusing them.

To my surprise, the signpost that we next encountered also read, LAFENWA: It was at a cross-roads, not a fork like the last one. Two other hands read IGBEIN, IBARA, then LANTORO, while AKÉ pointed the way we had marched from. We had already passed the road to Lafenwa; I did not know what to make of such misleading signposting but it was something else to ask my father when I returned home.

It was only appropriate that the Ransome-Kuti should live in a school compound like my father. Kuti was a principal and I recognized from the sign ABEOKUTA GRAMMAR SCHOOL that we were passing the compound where he taught. I tried now to recollect how my father had explained the difference between Principal and Headmaster, but the only fact that remained with me was that I would go to the Grammar School after I had finished in St

Peter's. Marching past the stone walls of the compound, I saw no reason why I should wait. The main building was set back into the compound and a wide path swept towards this stone mansion which stood on wide, arched pillars and was profusely covered in bougainvillaea like BishopsCourt of the parsonage. But it was far more imposing that that building, more imposing than BishopsCourt and Pa Delumo's own residence joined together. I pressed my face against the iron gates and wondered if I should not go in at once and resume my schooling there. Then I remembered it was a Saturday, so there would be no schooling. Monday however was a different matter, I would find my way back without difficulty.

As I rejoined the procession however, I thought I now understood the difference between a principal and a headmaster. Only a principal could preside over a school as huge and imposing as the one which I had just seen. Still, I hoped that the fact that I was only the son of a headmaster would not prevent me from obtaining a place there; in any case the principal was a frequent guest at our house. Mother called him Uncle and we were encouraged to do the same. I preferred his other name, Daodu. It fitted the man's appearance, his deep voice and energetic gestures. He rode about on the only motorized bicycle I had ever seen, his agbada billowing on either side of him.

One day, he fell off, right near us, at Aké. If we had been peeping over the wall at the time we would have seen it happen. He was brought into our house where I heard someone explaining that his agbada had billowed out as usual until the sleeve was caught in the spokes of the wheel. They all disappeared into father's room while mother flew all over the house. Water was boiled, bandages and lints prepared but then a nurse arrived, disappeared into the room and came out again with my father.

'We must take him to the hospital. The burn at the thigh is quite bad.'

I heard father mutter something about the machine falling on top of him, so that the hot exhaust must have done the damage. The nurse said my father had done the right thing by smearing the injury in vaseline. The nurse left the house again, we were herded into the back of the house and the parlour door locked on us. There were heavy movements, doors opening and shutting, then silence. When we emerged, the patient had gone, father and mother with him. When Daodu emerged from hospital he bought a car and never rode

44

on the motorped again. Koye, his first son whom we were told to call Cousin Koye because he was much older than Tinu and I, soon began to turn up on it at our house on errands or visits. Daodu's car, we learnt, was the third in the whole town. The first was owned by the Alake himself, another belonged to a wealthy Chief who lived in Itoku. Even the English District Officer did not appear to own one; he rode a motor-cycle or went on horseback.

I felt rather uplifted as I marched away from the Grammar School; I was going there, that was settled. But I also discovered that I liked the Kutis. Schooling under Daodu promised to be an adventure. This light-headed feeling helped me up the road towards Ibara which was so steep that my legs, for the first time, gave a hint of tiring. I had begun to think that I would have to sit down beside the road and rest when we came to yet another compound with neat rows of houses, small hut-like houses which were however built with concrete and roofed with iron sheets. The sergeant at the top of the column barked out an order and the band wheeled into the compound and entered. They marched straight towards the longest of these buildings, on to the grounds in front of it and re-grouped themselves to different orders from the sergeant. They were still in two lines, but now they stood shoulder to shoulder and marked time on one spot. I kept the same distance from them as I was when they began to line the grounds, indeed, I had slowed down when they entered the compound so that I was not really far from the gate. An order was given, the music stopped with a final drum-roll and a violent clash of cymbals. The air was very still.

And then I made a discovery. I was alone. The ragged, motley group of children who had followed, clowning, mimicking, even calling out orders had fallen off one by one. It occurred to me now that I had seen no one nor heard any of their festive voices for a while. They had all vanished, leaving no one but me. And then I made another discovery. In a matter-of-fact way, I realized that I did not know where I was.

The sergeant spun round on his heels, barked out some sentences in a very strange language to somebody hidden within the building. That person now came out, smartly uniformed. The first thing that struck me about him was that he was albino. Then the next moment I realized that he was not an albino at all but a white man. Also that, unlike the marching policemen, he wore shoes. He was dressed simply in khaki, so I knew that he was also a policeman. His appearance however bore very little resemblance to that of the band. He stood on the steps of his office while the sergeant called out yet another order which made the lines stiffen up. Another was called and they appeared to relax. The sergeant then continued in the same language within which I succeeded in catching a few English words and name-places. He appeared to be 'reporting' something, the 'Oba's palace' was involved in it, and it all ended with 'all correct' and 'further orders'. The white man spoke a few words, the Sergeant gave two more barks and the parade broke up and went their different ways, all except the sergeant. He stayed with the white officer and they spoke some more; it was during this dialogue that the white man looked up and saw me.

I was tired, I was sure of that now. The thought of running away at once when the man looked up, saw me, pointed and said something to the sergeant therefore remained just a thought. I had no idea in which direction to run. The sergeant also looked up, turned and began to march towards me. I probably would have run then, tiredness and all, but the white officer restrained him and came forward himself, the sergeant following close. Instinctively I backed one step towards the gate, but the man smiled, held out both hands in a gesture I did not quite understand, and approached. When he had come quite close, he bent down and, using the most unlikely accent I had ever heard asked,

'Kini o fe nibi yen?' *

I knew the words were supposed to be in my own language but they made no sense to me, so I looked at the sergeant helplessly and said,

'I don't understand. What is he saying?'

The officer's eyes opened wide. 'Oh, you speak English.'

I nodded.

'Good. That is venhrry clenver. I was asking, what do you want? What can I doon for you?'

'I want to go home.'

He exchanged looks with the Sergeant. 'Well, that seems vum-vum-vum. And where is home?'

I could not understand why he should choose to speak through his nose. It made it difficult to understand him all the time but by straining hard, I could make sense of his questions. I told him that I lived in Aké.

*Literally: what do you want there?

'It has a big church,' I added, 'just outside our walls.'

'Ah-ah, near the church. Tell me, whaznname?' I guessed that he was asking what my name was, so I told him, 'My name is Wole.'

'Wonlay. Good. And your father's name?'

'My father's name is Headmaster.'

'What?'

'My father's name is Headmaster. Sometimes his name is Essay.'

For some reason this amused him immensely, which I found offensive. There was no reason why my father's names should be the cause for such laughter. But the Sergeant had reacted differently. His eyes nearly popped out of his head. I noticed then that he was very different from the grown-ups whom I had seen around. He had long marks on his face, quite different from the usual kind we encountered in Aké. And when he spoke, his voice sounded like that of the Hausa traders who brought wares to our house for bartering with old clothes and strange assortments of items. It was a strange procedure, one which made little sense to me. They spread their wares in front of the house and I had to be prised off them. There were brass figures, horses, camels, trays, bowls, ornaments. Human figures spun on a podium, balanced by weights at the end of curved light metal rods. We spun them round and round, yet they never fell off their narrow perch. The smell of fresh leather filled the house as pouffes, handbags, slippers and worked scabbards were unpacked. There were bottles encased in leather, with leather stoppers, amulets on leather thongs, scrolls, glass beads, bottles of scent with exotic names—I never forgot, from the first moment I read it on the label— Bint el Sudan, with its picture of a turbanned warrior by a kneeling camel. A veiled maiden offered him a bowl of fruits. They looked unlike anything in the Orchard and Essay said they were called dates. I did not believe him; dates were the figures which appeared on a calendar on the wall, so I took it as one of his jokes.

Once or twice my father tried to offer money but the trader proved difficult. 'No, I can like to take changey-changey.' Out came old shirts, trousers, discarded jackets with holes under the armpit, yet Changey-changey—as we now called him—actually received these clothing derelicts in return for his genuine 'morocco' leather. 'Look'am master, a no be lie. Look, genuine morocco leather. 'E fit you, big man like you must have leather brief-case for carry file. 'E be genuine. Put 'am one more shirt. Or torosa.'

Their voices were so similar that they could only be brothers. I was

47

even more convinced of it when I heard him say, 'If na headmaster of
Aké be in father, I sabbe the place. But what 'im doing here?'

They both turned to me. I had no answer to the question. Then
the white man asked, 'Are you lost?'

'I followed the band,' I replied.

The officer nodded sagely, as if everything had fallen in place. He
turned to the sergeant and asked him to get his bicycle. The man
saluted and went off. Something continued to puzzle the officer
however. He put his hand on my shoulder and guided me towards
the office.

'How old are you?'

'I am four years and a half.'

He let out a loud 'What!', stopped, and looked at me again. 'Are
you sure?' I nodded. He looked at me more closely, said, 'Yes of
course. Of course. And you walked from Aké? Where did you start
from?'

'At the cenotaph. There were other children, but they left me.'

We reached his office and he lifted me on to a chair. 'Are you
thirsty?' already producing a bottle of orange squash. There was a jar
of water on the table and he mixed me a drink in a glass. I drank it to
the last drop.

'Do you want another glass?' He did not wait for a reply before
mixing another and handing it to me. It followed its predecessor just
as rapidly. I began to feel better. I looked round the office for the
first time, stretched my legs and took an interest in the papers on the
table. I recognized a journal on it which came every week to my
father. I looked at the man with greater interest.

'You are reading my father's paper.'

He looked startled. 'Which one?'

'That one. In Leisure Hours.'

'Really! You say it's your father's paper?'

'Yes. He has a new one every week.'

He opened it rapidly, looking for something on its pages. 'You
mean he is the editor?'

I could not understand him. I repeated, 'He has it every week.'

And then the man grinned and nodded. 'I see, I see.'

I was feeling drowsy. The Sergeant arrived with his bicycle. Half-
awake, I felt myself lifted on to the cross-bar and the bumpy ride
began. I barely sensed the arrival back home, hands lifting me up,
passing me to other arms. My head appeared to weigh a ton when I

48

tried to come awake and respond to the babble of voices I heard around me. I felt the immense expanse of the bed in mother's bedroom coming up to meet me, the room easily recognized by the smell of *òrí**-and-camphor. Then I dropped into oblivion.

I woke up in a hazy semi-darkness. A short while later, I realized where I was. I also felt a huge pit in my stomach and climbed down from the bed, heading for the kitchen to see what hour of meal it was. When I opened the door, a wave of human voices engulfed me. The entire front room was crowded with grown-ups and they all seemed to be speaking with excitement. So I turned and walked towards the sound. As I came through the parlour I pushed open the curtain in the intervening door and suddenly everything went silent. A hundred pairs of eyes were turned on me, and I wondered what the matter was. In the silence I spoke out the only thing on my mind:

'I am hungry.'

Mouths opened wide. Then the silence was broken by the bookseller's wife. She struck her palms together in a gesture of amazement and exclaimed, 'E-eh! Omo nla! Did you hear him? He is hungry.'

A babble of voices ensued, mostly echoing the bookseller's wife. I could not understand that there should be such excitement over the fact of my hunger. It looked like evening in any case, and I had not eaten all day. Then I heard my father's voice cutting in, and he appeared to be smiling.

'Well, it seems only natural that he should be hungry. Wouldn't you be, after a walk from Aké to Ibara?'

I heard someone say, 'Yes, but the way he said it!' before I was swept up by the bookseller's wife, and nearly smothered against her ample breasts. 'Give my child food!' she shouted. 'Mama, why are you starving him? My lord and husband says he is hungry and you haven't jumped to give him food. All right, I'll take him home and feed him.'

And before I knew what was happening, she had swung me on to her back, slipped her wrapper round to secure me tightly and was singing and dancing. And suddenly everyone was singing with her, laughing and shouting at the top of their voices. Only one person sat in her chair, seemingly unmoved by it all, this was mother, sitting

*Shea-butter.

49

with her chin rested on her palm, staring at me. From time to time she shook her head, sighed deeply and nodded to herself. Mrs Bookseller said,

'Look at her. I suppose she would still prefer him to be wandering through the wilds of Abeokuta. HM, please give me a stick. I think a dose of her favourite medicine will do her good.'

Father laughed and said, 'Good idea. I'll get the stick.' He whipped it out from its corner by his chair and handed it to the bookseller's wife. The next moment, Mama was up and bounding through the parlour. Everybody seemed in such high spirits, it was strange to see grown-up men and women prancing through the house like the urchins who had marched to the music of the police band until they chose to abandon me. I never knew when the meal was set out at last because I had again fallen asleep on the back of the bookseller's wife. I woke up in her bed the following morning, lightheaded and strangely exhilarated. At the back of my mind, even as I sat down to the biggest breakfast I had ever set eyes on, was a feeling that I had somehow been the cause of the excitement of the previous night and had, in some way, become markedly different from whatever I was before the march.

IV

I spluttered, grabbed Nubi's hand and fought for the sponge with all
my strength. At first I had merely pushed her hand away, again and
again, only to find her yet again suffocating me with water, soapsuds
and gritty strands of fibre. Nubi would not yield. Now if it had been
Joseph . . .

I wiped one eye free of soapsuds and found Nubi standing back,
looking at me.

'Are you going to let me wash you or not?'

'Let me do the face myself.'

'You!' Her laughter was scornful. 'Put your hand over your head
let me see.'

I obeyed her. It appeared to be some kind of test. Perhaps if I
passed she would leave my face alone.

'Right over. Like this.'

I placed my arm right over the top of my head, doing my best
to follow her. Now her fingers were playing with the lobe of her
left ear, she covered the ear completely, made it disappear in her
palm.

'Now, do you see a difference?'

I asked, 'Am I not doing it right?'

More scornful laughter. 'Don't you notice any difference?'

'What am I not doing right?'

'It is not what you are not doing right. It is what you are not doing
at all. Look at my hand. It reaches over my head and covers this ear
completely. See? Now look at yours. It hardly reaches over the top of
your head.'

It sounded very significant, but I could not see what she was
getting at. I kept staring at her hand, and the ear that kept appearing
and disappearing under it.

'That difference explains why I have to bathe you. If you think
because they allowed you in school you are now a big boy in the
house you still have a lot to learn. There are things they can't teach
you in school. Now, come on.'

51

She advanced, sponge in hand. 'Joseph lets me do my face,' I persisted.

'Mama says I should bathe you, that is all I know. She didn't divide your body into bits, some for you and some for me.'

Her left hand now dipped the bowl into the bucket, scooped up the water and moved to douse my head. I ducked.

'Look at you! You are wasting water. You know what Mama is going to do to you when I tell her?'

I moved to the corner of the bathroom. Too late, I realized I was trapped.

Even so, I fought for my life. As the bowl looped over my head with its contents, I reached out and deflected it. Nubi was drenched and it seemed to make her angry.

'Now you see what you have done!' The movemenr was so fast, I had no time to protect my face. From out of nowhere a huge wad of moistness slammed into my face, traversing every pore rapidly but most especially blocking my nostrils.

Her fingers dug into my skull, pressing it down while she scrubbed my face without once letting in air. When I tried to bite I only got a mouthful of the sponge, so I did my desperate routine, let my knee buckle and, in that brief respite, butted her in the stomach. I heard her scream. 'O pa mi o'* and the next moment there were cries of 'Tani yen?'* from all over the house.

'Tani lo' gun nbe yen? Tani?'* And then there were running feet.

Hastily wiping off soapsuds with both hands, I blinked my eyes open and saw Wild Christian framed against the opening. She shook her head from side to side, baffled as always. Now I was really scared that she was going to take over.

'She has finished,' I said. 'I've had my bath.'

'He butted me with his head,' Nubi complained, clutching her stomach.

'Stop exaggerating,' Mama snapped.

'Yes Ma.' And Nubi straightened up at once.

'Screaming down the whole house. Are you trying to scare everybody?'

'No Ma. But he wouldn't let me scrub his face.'

'You've scrubbed it,' I reminded everyone at large. 'You've done

*Murder!
 Who is that?
 Who screamed just now? Who?

52

nothing but scrub it since I came to have my bath. You've nearly scrubbed it to death, what more do you want to scrub? Tinu is still waiting for her bath.'

Suddenly I felt secure; there was a smile on Wild Christian's face. She said to Nubi, 'All right, call Tinu. In any case they are both old enough to start bathing themselves now.'

'Yes, yes. I've said it before. I don't need her or Joseph.'

'But you must bathe in their presence, so they can make sure you do a proper job.'

I nodded. It seemed a little enough concession to make. Just the same, I added, 'I don't really need them. In fact I have scrubbed myself before when Joseph was too busy. Joseph inspects me afterwards and he says I am quite clean.'

'All right then. Although I can never understand how you come to be so afraid of water, you, a July-born.'

I was now rinsing off the rest of the soap. 'But I am not afraid of water,' I protested.

'No? Just look at the way you are rinsing yourself. There is soap all over your face but you haven't even touched it.'

I quickly threw the next bowlful over my head. As usual, something went wrong. It usually did when water was cast over my head or face. The next moment I was spluttering and fisting the stinging rivulets off my face, fighting for breath.

Even through the wasps' nest that had erupted about my ears as the water commenced its habitual torture of my senses I heard Wild Christian laughing as she walked away.

At breakfast they discussed it. 'That son of yours . . .' she began, 'I don't know what he has done to water, but they don't appear to get on very well. Do you know what happened this morning?'

They discussed it as if I was not present. It was another of their strange habits, but I had also noticed that it seemed peculiar to most grown-ups; they would discuss their children as if the children were not there. We never discussed them when they were within hearing. As I listened to them from our own table I shook my head in strong denial. Yes, they had missed the point; I was confident, as usual, that I had discovered the loophole in their argument.

'Wole is shaking his head,' Essay observed.

My mother laughed. 'Are you going to deny that even when you yourself poured water on your head . . .'

'No, but I am not afraid of water. If I were, how is it I like to go

53

out and bathe in the rain?' I slapped my spoon into the bowl of *eko* making it send up a small splash.

'Be careful Mr Lawyer. Don't waste your food,' my mother admonished.

'I am not going to be a lawyer. I am going to marry Mrs Odufuwa and be a pastor.'

'Oh, it is Mrs Odufuwa now is it? What happened to Auntie Gbosere?'

'She hasn't come to visit us,' I explained. 'Mrs Odufuwa spent plenty of time with us at Easter. She is very fine.'

Essay took some time pondering the challenge. 'Well,' he said at last, 'maybe you are not afraid of rain. But it doesn't mean you are not afraid of water.'

Mother looked from one to the other, said, 'To ò,'* and prepared to leave for her shop. Her attitude indicated that she knew just how long the see-saw argument would take and that she had better things to do.

'Is rain not the same as water?' I demanded.

'Rain means water, but water does not necessarily mean rain.'

With suitably solemn nods, Wild Christian sighed, 'Ngh-hunnh!', called for her wosi-wosi** bag to be brought to her bedroom in preparation for the shop.

'But there can be no rain without water,' I protested.

Father nodded. 'True. But there can be water without rain.'

'The water came from rain in the first place didn't it?'

'Ah, that is where you are wrong. Rain actually comes from water. It is because of the water that rain is caused.'

I was getting in deep waters. My early triumph had long dissipated; then I remembered the Bible. 'What happened in the Bible?' I asked 'Didn't God create them both separately?'

'Well, let's see. Go and bring the Bible from the parlour.'

I climbed down from the bench, my mind tried to race ahead to what the Bible had to say on the subject. The choice of passage picked for us to learn by rote had not included verses from Genesis, at least, none surfaced.

I picked up the Bible and returned to the dining room. After handing it to him I returned to my table to pick up my bowl of eko, then joined him at his table, sitting in mother's chair. My *akara* was

*Well, well!
**Odds-and-ends.

54

long finished and I eyed the corracle-shaped dish which still contained four or five of his *akara*. He caught the glance and smiled, pushing the dish towards me.

'Mind you,' he continued, 'you will find that the Bible tells only one part of the story. After God created this and that, he still left them to react with one another in their own ways. There are what we call the laws of nature, that is where the question of how rain is formed comes in.'

It seemed an unnecessary complication. I sucked air through my lips as I bit into fresh green *atarodo** that the Wild Christian had fried into the *akara*. The entire issue should have been resolved by the order in which rain and water were created. Then I remembered:

'All right. Why has the whole town been saying prayers for rain? Does that not mean God is still creating rain when he likes?'

He reflected briefly. 'Remember this. Even after he has created things on earth and given them their own working laws, as the Creator he can still interfere; for instance he can quicken up the processes or slow them down.'

The Wild Christian came out of her bedroom into the parlour just then to say good-bye and heard what Essay had just said. She came out shaking her head with that perpetual wonder at the infinite patience of Essay. 'But dear, are you sure he can understand all these arguments you indulge him in?'

She came in then fully into view, saw that I had changed tables and also appropriated Essay's left-over *akara*. In one swift movement she had snatched up the dish, closed it and placed it in the basket now on the maid's head. As I knew only too well, that would form part of her 'elevenses'

'I did think the argument was getting rather lively. I didn't know that akaralogics and atarodimensis were making his tongue dance.' She hauled me off the chair. 'Carry this!' She plunked a bag in my hand and I knew what it meant. It was Saturday. Since there was no school, she meant to make me do my share at the shop.

'I have some homework,' I protested.

'Bring it to the shop with you.'

I put down the bag, disappeared into the 'pantry' for my books.

'You shouldn't encourage him too much dear. He is too argumentative. You know what he said to the sexton? Last Sunday,

---

*Fresh peppers, a round type.

55

during afternoon service. He was chattering away, he and that new friend of his, Edun's son. So the sexton went over and rebuked them. Do you know what this your son replied?'

'What did he say?'

'He said, of all the crowd in the church who were singing and praying, how could the sexton prove that he was talking? Can you imagine? Asking the sexton to prove that he was talking! I'm sure if the sexton had obliged they would still be in the pews arguing it out, that's the sort of child he is.'

I paused behind the door, horrified. Essay did not trifle with reports of mischief in church or Sunday school. How could the sexton have done this to me? Telling the Wild Christian was simply making sure that Essay got to hear it sooner or later. I remained motionless, glued my eye to the gap in the door, listening.

'We-e-ell,' I heard him say, 'it would be a rather difficult thing to prove you know . . .'

Wild Christian sighed. 'I knew it. I knew you would defend him when it came to a matter of argument. I don't know why I even bothered to tell you. After all, he got it from you. Where is he? Has he taken my bag?'

'That's it on your chair.'

'O ya, let's go.' She pushed the maid forward. 'I'll leave him to plague you with his arguments. In any case he only embarrasses me at the shop with all his foolish questions. Why is your stomach bigger than my father's? Are you pregnant like the organist? Yes, that's the sort of thing he asks, in case no one has told you.'

'Really.' His mouth opened wide with laughter. 'When was this?'

'Ask him. He's your son. Ọmọ,* let's go. My customers are waiting.' She gave the maid a shove and was gone from the house.

I stayed on the spot. Essay's laughter did not mean that there was definitely no reprimand to come. He remained in his chair, very still. I felt him listening. Through the crack in the door I could only see a thin line of his back, yet I knew he was listening for sounds of my movement in the 'pantry'. We both knew the game. Why, I could not tell, but Essay would make no move until I made mine. A footfall, cough, something knocked over, a creak in the door. Until I announced my existence, he would simply sit still, probably reach out a hand for a toothpick and, with a faraway look, long distanced

*Child.

56

from his surround, commence picking his teeth. Elegantly. I glued myself to the ground, hardly breathing.

And of course, the prayers began. There was one other way the contest could end, and that was with the arrival of a visitor. Essay had a long, even deliberately spun-out memory. It was part of his wicked patience. Days, weeks after the culprit had forgotten his misdemeanour, after many weeks in which Essay had even patted him on the back for some especial conduct, some achievement or initiative, an errand delivered accurately in spite of the complexity, high marks in school etc. etc., Essay would summon the oblivious one:

'Er . . . oh yes, Bunmi.'

'Sir?'

'Mm. You were sent to Itoku three weeks ago, not so? You remember?'

'Yes sir.'

'Mm-hm. And the road to Itoku passes these days through the bookseller's compound, not so?'

Silence. Resignation or the commencement of sweat.

'Have you lost your tongue? I said, to get to Itoku, you now have to pass through the bookseller's compound, and of course one is not allowed to leave the bookseller's compound without spending some time plucking his mangoes?'

Silently I tried to work out the scale of my offence, measuring talking during a church service to taking time off on an errand to pluck mangoes. The graduation was not reassuring. I prayed harder for a visitor, aware though I was that this might prove to be no more than a postponement of a painful reckoning. And then I had to sneeze!

'Wole!'

'Sir.'

And at that moment came the sound of a heavy step on the outside pavement. The voice of Wild Christian followed through. 'Dear, are you still home?'

'Yes, I'm here.'

She spoke to someone outside. 'Come in, come in. Take a seat, I'll call him for you.' She came through the parlour while I squeezed myself back behind the door, doubtful that this was exactly the respite I had prayed for. Not for the first time, I noticed that God had a habit of either not answering one's prayers at all, or answering them in a way that was not straightforward.

'God so good, I met Mr Adesina on the way. He was asking if you would be in this evening because he wanted to see you . . . I thought he might as well see you now, is that all right?'

'Is it about his job with the Synod?'

'What else does he ever think about? He keeps pestering me at the shop and I always tell him to see you. Is he scared to come? This time I dragged him back with me. If I had left him to come by himself he would be circling the parsonage till dark.'

'Why did you bring him? The answer is still the same—I won't plead for him. He cannot be trusted with funds.'

'All right, you tell him dear. I have told him a hundred times but he won't accept it. Let him hear it from your own mouth.'

They both went to the front room. I followed after all was silent in the dining-room, paused to flick a crumb of *akara* off Essay's plate into my mouth.

In the same practised move my hand swept to the wash-basin which stood on the left wall, facing into the dining-room. The hand dived smoothly into the basin, flicked up a tiny amount of water and brushed my lips in one fluid movement. Almost at once a powerful blow landed on the side of my head knocking me almost into Essay's chair.

'Good.'

She stood glowering over me. 'I thought we had cured you of that habit.'

Wild Christian had a habit of levitating from nowhere. For a moment I dwelt on the unfairness of it. I had cured the habit. My movement was, admittedly, the same as when it was a 'problem', but this time, I had merely rinsed my fingers of the *akara*, a movement which was normally completed by also wiping the mouth. Then, on a moment's reflection, I felt relieved. The blow could easily have been for eating that crumb of *akara* which, for her, could have meant GREED and would call for something more than a mere blow to the head. I did not even whimper as she proceeded to seize my right hand between hers and squeeze the fingers together until they hurt.

'Just let me catch you at it again.'

She then set about the purpose which had brought her back, got out a tea-mug for the visitor and removed the tea-cosy. I quietly reminded myself never again to give the appearance of reviving the ritual which I once repeatedly enacted with the Wash-Hand Basin, driving the household mad.

I also admonished the Wash-Hand Basin by kicking it; after all, it was the source of the 'habit' that took the entire household to cure. This basin was yet another of the mysterious presences in the house, full of myriad recesses, shelves and ledges. Amidst the scampering of cockroaches, salt sachets, tablets, mini-bottles, soaps and chipped china jostled with packets of potassium permanganate, pieces of alum, glucose and a variety of yeasts. Like every other item of furniture, it served more than the purpose for which it was known. And more than all other items, it was—a LANDMARK. The interior of the house was defined by its location . . . it's in the corner of the Wash-Hand Basin . . . underneath the Wash-Hand Basin . . . I was going past the Wash-Hand Basin when . . . go and fetch me the stick by the Wash-Hand Basin . . . he pushed me against the Wash-Hand Basin . . . I was polishing the Wash-Hand Basin . . .

Even the mice had picked up the habit of escaping from the pantry by one undeviating path which took them behind or under the Wash-Hand Basin.

It was higher behind than in front, so that when Essay raised the lid on the few occasions when it was closed, lifting it backwards on its hinges, it rose and rose to his height, then exceeded it—and Essay to us was a very tall man. I thought it was fortunate that the stand was where it was. If there were no wall for the lid to rest against, nothing would have saved the rest of the stand from toppling over backwards from the sheer weight of the lid.

The basin itself sat in a big hole on the flat shelf which formed the cover of the interior, below the main lid, and it always seemed to me, frowning into the darkness of the lower cupboard, that the view of cockroaches looking up at this big, white enamel protrusion, must be quite like the view of the rats which scuppered about in the big dug-out latrine whenever any grown-up buttocks filled the hole in the box above them. Both holes appeared about the same in size, but beyond that, there were no further similarities. The lower cupboard had a separate door which opened along a horizontal axis and was secured by a flimsy, metallic hook. Its two shelves housed every object that was missing from the pantry or which could not find space on the dining-table, the dresser in Wild Christian's bedroom, the window-sill by my father's place at the dining table, or the small cupboard behind his head where he kept his Epsom Salts, tooth-brush, a bottle of the mysterious 'Alcool' which he occasionally substituted for a chewing stick when cleaning his teeth, and cotton wads. Every other item of that domestic family of objects resided in the Wash-Hand Basin.

After a lot of pondering over the peculiar angle of the lid, I came to the conclusion that the extra inches at the back were to allow for that extra ledge on which were placed, in addition to the cake of soap, all other objects which could find no room in the lower cupboard. The search for any member of a particular family of objects, objects such as a bottle of aspirin or an exotic cake of soap usually began and ended in the Wash-Hand Basin.

The 'habit' had developed unnoticed by me. As for Essay—nothing escaped him. One day I was walking from the front room to the pantry, a course which took me between the Wash-Hand Basin and his dining-table when he shouted:

'Stop!'

I froze.

'Why did you do that?'

I did not know what I had done.

He studied me intently. 'All right. Where did you just come from?'

'Iwaju-ile.'*

'And you were going to the pantry, not so?'

'Yes sir. I needed to fetch a book.'

'I see.' He thought for a moment. 'Now go back. Sit at your desk for a minute. At the end of a minute, walk to the pantry exactly as you normally do.'

At the end of a minute I was taking that ninety-degree turn past the Wash-Hand Basin when the order came again, 'Stop!'

I froze. Fast as the order had come, it was too late for whatever purpose he had in mind. Again he studied me intently.

'Go back again.' This time, when I say stop, stay exactly in whatever position you are. Don't move your head, shoulder, anything. If one foot is before the other, remain exactly like that. Do you understand?'

'Yes sir.'

'I don't even want you to turn and face me. Walk as you normally walk to the pantry. Don't change your pace or anything. I may not even stop you this time, if I do, it may not be at the same place. I may shout STOP any time at all along the way. Now, is that clear?'

*Front room, house frontage.

Clear, but highly mysterious. I could not understand what this was about and tried hard to recollect how I walked. It seemed to me that nothing had changed in my way of walking, but who could tell? Only Essay.

I expected the order to be given in a different place this time but no. It came at precisely the same spot and I obeyed his instructions, I hoped, to the letter. Now what?

On his face was a glint of satisfaction. He leant back and contemplated my existence for a long moment. He nodded slowly.

'What is your hand doing on your mouth?'

My hand? Mouth? I thought backwards rapidly.

It was true. My hand was resting lightly on my mouth, somewhat to the left of the face. And the strange thing was that it was wet. I held it away from my face. There was no doubt about it; my fingers were wet.

'Don't you know what you do every time you pass that wash-hand basin?'

'No sir.' Although now, glimmerings of a peculiar cleansing rite had begun to surface in my mind. There was the recollection of an arm snaking out of its own volition, dipping in the basin . . . yes, I thought I now knew what Essay had patiently observed. The fresh, moist feel of my lips confirmed the rest of the motion. Passing by the **Wash-Hand Basin**, my hand flew to the basin, dipped, flashed over my lips, left to right. Catching myself at it several times after this, I wondered if it could be a form of madness.

It had been going on for a long time; the cure took just as long. Every member of the house was ordered to watch me, shout on me just before, or report me if it was too late. Then I would be made to walk past the basin several times over. Joseph took delight in tiptoeing after me, making me leap out of my skin as he imitated Essay's voice and shouted on me to stop. If neither parent was in, Lawanle or Nubi or indeed any of the 'cousins' tried to assume their role of drill-master. Even Tinu, older by a mere year and some months, got into the act. I felt a fervent need to lock them all up, beginning with her, in the dark interior of the Wash-Hand Basin and pour the slop from the basin over their heads.

The rains set in again. Harmattan, when the skin chapped and the vaseline, metholatun and pomade jars rapidly emptied, vanished from memory until the following year. A habit which had began with the Harmattan, when I would linger by the wash-basin and

61

moist the cracked skin of my lips also disappeared with that season, never to return. How it had grown into such an unthinking, stream-lined motion did not puzzle me for long; there were other habits to be picked up, then abandoned forcibly or be replaced by others before they came to the attention of the ever-watchful Essay or The Wild Christian.

I never did discover how Adesina had lost his position with the Synod, and if he ever got it back. He left the house, like so many others before him, dejected, tearful. His eyes cast a last appealing look at Wild Christian who had stayed on the periphery of the discussion; normally she would not even remain there, but the Synod somehow involved her as well since it was a church affair. To the man who could not be trusted with funds, I heard her play the same dutiful role I had now learnt to expect:

'Well you know, it's the Headmaster's decision. I couldn't ask him to act against his conscience.'

V

Even the baobab has shrunk with time, yet I had imagined that this bulwark would be eternal, beyond the growing perspectives of a vanished childhood. Its girth has dwindled with time and the branches now give only a little shade. There was a name for the school bell-house, a description at least, a place in the family of physical things—it came back without effort—the Only Child of the Distant Church-Tower. Only now, even the distance between the bell-house and the church tower has shrunk. White as a pillar of salt, the church-tower still dominates mango trees, the *orombeje* tree in' the churchyard, the cenotaph also which, although placed outside the church walls, seemed to belong to the same extended family of St Peter's church. The church tower is sometimes framed against the steep road towards Iberekodo, nudging dwarf rusted roofs along its sides. Aké, Ibarapa, Itoko, then over the hill into Mokola, the Hausa quarter, before Iberekodo itself. The hive of brown shacks, pink and orange bordered houses, stops abruptly before the crest and gives way to the ordered wall and broad gates of the chief's stable. Hidden within the hillside on either side of the road are the twin-markets of Ibarapa, night and day markets, the night to the right, the day, left. None of this has changed.

But the more intimate things have. Baobab, bell-houses, playing-fields and paths. Even Jonah. At Sunday School the teacher looked through the window for inspiration, waved at a nearby clump of rocks but rejected them. On the other side of the school building, hidden from us was a rock that was smoothed by our feet. It appeared to cover the earth—at least from where the junior schoolroom ended, to the cemetery outside the parsonage at the higher end, the furthest point from the main gates.

'You know where the school does its clay modelling? The whale that swallowed Jonah was bigger than that rock.'

The eager ones nodded assent. 'Yes, whales are enormous.'

'Bigger than houses.'

'Even ships.'

'Bigger than aeroplanes.'

We had heard the occasional drone of an aeroplane, even seen its moving speck in the sky. A hand pushed a piece of paper towards me. I read,

'My father's house is bigger than a whale.'

I was really indifferent but replied, 'Liar!'

I would not read his response, feeling sufficiently crushed. That was my rock. My own very private rock. And now the Sunday School teacher had turned it the common property of these lying, boastful, querulous others. She had intruded into a private abode, one of many. Different from that sleeping, eating, living place which belonged equally to Essay, Wild Christian, siblings, vague relations or 'ọmọ ọdọ'—a vague expression for something between servant and family appendage—Jonah was my own very secret habitat. And now the Sunday School teacher had turned Jonah into something from the Bible.

For after that, the patient, placid presence, hitherto unnamed, became Jonah. Permanently. Its mystery became complicated in a world of biblical tall tales whereas before, it had remained unaffected even by the weekday activity of mixing clay on its vast body, using rain water that had gathered in numerous oval holes. Who made those, we did ask, not that we were really curious. But the modelling classes never touched the intimate lives Jonah and I lived at weekends, for the school went home while I remained in the parsonage and could walk over to climb up its steep sides and sink through its broad back into deep immobility. There were other rocks in the compound, rocks with clumps of bamboos, smooth inclines down which we all slid and yelled. Jonah was bare, solitary and private. Until the school teacher turned it into a fairy tale. Swallowed and sealed up in a whale's belly! It did not sound wholly improbable but it did belong in a world of fables, of the imagination, of Aladdin's lamp and Open Sesame. Whereas before . . . I experienced the passing of a unique confidant, the loss of a replete, subsuming presence.

The guava tree was another, not the luxuriant, generous tree beside the communal water-tap, overlooked by the pastor's square, squat residence. This other was some distance away, near the infant school building. It was protected from stones and sticks because its fruits were usually closer to the ground and, in any case, it did not give off much fruit. But it had large, dark-green and fleshy leaves

64

and one of its branches was weighted almost to the ground. This guava tree had an affinity with the rainy season, nothing really tangible, except that it did not seem to be itself except in the rainy season. Under brooding clouds it performed the double feat of existing yet retreating into an inner world of benevolent foliage spirits, moist yet filled with a crisp vitality, silent yet wisely communicative. It was also without time. So was Jonah in a way, but the guava had this indefinable assurance of swallowing time, making it cease to exist. I sneaked out of our house in the morning and suddenly it was dusk, yet I had no recollection of any action beyond being among the branches. I watched Joseph, or Nubi walking up the stone-lined path. Nubi was of course later baptized like all non-Christians who came into the household. After that, we had to call her by her Christian name, Mary. She would come up the broad path and turn first towards the pond where she knew we often played, flicking flat pebbles to skim off the slime-covered surface or simply watching the ducks. She walked up wiping her brow with the loose tip of her wrapper, calling out my name. She belonged to another world, one which however became real enough when she yanked me expertly from my perch.

'You are going to eat the cane tonight, you wait.'

I stumbled all the way, keeping up with her speed. She looked at me at last with some concern.

'Can't you start shivering?'

'I am not cold.'

'Who asked you if you were cold?'

'You said, couldn't I start shivering?'

'Idiot. Ọ̀dẹ̀. It rained this afternoon. Anyone could have caught a cold.'

'But I haven't.' It had rained too. I now remembered taking refuge in the deserted schoolroom. She felt my clothes.

'You haven't got wet anyway. That would have made things worse for you. Still I don't understand why you didn't come home after it stopped raining, instead of going to sit up in that tree.'

I understood at last. 'I could say I was trapped by the rain, couldn't I?'

'What an idiot! It stopped raining over two hours ago. That's why Mama sent me for you. We all thought you were in the house all that time.'

'But I told Joseph I was going to the school compound.'

'He told her. But you've stayed so late. Pity you haven't got a fever. It's standing in the corner for you at least.'

Nubi was wily, that much was becoming clear. Had she played that game before? Timidly, I inquired.

She chuckled. 'You forget, Mama's medicines are not very pleasant.'

'But you have faked a fever before, not so?'

'Listen you silly. You ask too many questions.'

'No, tell me.' I really wanted to know.

'I don't have to fake shivering when I see I'm going to receive Mama's flogging. I start shivering from the moment I know she is just waiting to let loose. You'd be surprised, but it is actually she who says, have you got a fever? She's never realized that one can start shivering from the thought of that *pasan*.'*

'So you say yes?'

'Of course you idiot. Wouldn't you?'

'But you always have a temperature,' I insisted. Temperature was again one of those magic words. If the Wild Christian said you had Temperature you had Temperature. Since we cooked on an open hearth I always wondered how, if you put a palm against the forehead of any of us in that unventilated kitchen, you would not discover Temperature. Essay, I sometimes observed, was not that impressed by Temperature.

Nubi conceded that she had never fully understood Temperature. But it helped to have it, and she always had it at the right time.

'Do you think I have Temperature?' Vaguely I felt that it might be possible, since I had been running to keep up with her. She felt my forehead.

'Not a chance. I think you are going to feel that stick.'

But the walls have retained their voices. Familiar voices break on the air, voices from the other side of the rafters. Isara was second home—Essay's natal home. All the grandparents were Father and Mother—and somehow we said these as if with capital letters. There the rafters were smoky, bare of the usual ceiling mat. There were objects in corners of the roof, wrapped in leaves, in leather. Some were not so mysterious, since Father would often reach up into such a bundle, one that seemed caked with the accumulation of a hundred

*Whip.

66

years' drought. Yet out of it would come nothing more puzzling than kolanuts, or snuff. Isara was another kind of home, several steps into the past. Age hung from every corner, the patina of ancestry glossed all objects, all human faces. Our older relations were differently aged from those in Abeokuta, relations on our mother's side. Laterite, mud houses, floors of dung plaster, indigo dye on old women's hands—I did not like that, I hated the touch of hands transformed by the indigo gloss. And it was in Isara also that we saw so much indigo-green tattoo on the arms and bodies of women.

New Year meant Isara. Smoked pork, the flavour of wood smoke, red dust of a dry season, dry thatch. New Year was palm wine, *ebiripo*, *ikokore* . . . a firmer, earth-aged kind of love and protection. Isara was filled with unsuspected treats, as when Father pulled down yet another ominous bundle from the rafters and it turned out to be smoked game, ageless in its preservation. Our women were darker in Isara, much darker. Buba, wrapper and shawls were also of those varied shades of indigo, though occasionally one would encounter the white shawl, or a bright yellow headgear which further receded the wearer's face into an ancient shadow.

I could not understand why Father's rafters in Isara should be so bare, yet so full of surprises, while the ceiling at the parsonage, though sealed up was, beyond the scuttling of mice, devoid of mystery. Occasionally the termites took a hand. Suddenly the ceiling mat fell on our heads—the termites had long been silently busy and no one suspected they were everywhere. A long-forgotten box of papers was pulled out from under the bed and we found its contents ruined by termites. They travelled into the roof from along a hidden crack in the wall and went to work. Suddenly the iron sheets were exposed; between the zinc roof and the mat—nothing. In fact, the ceiling often bred tantalizing thoughts of a nocturnal visit by Father, impatient for our New Year visit, secreting his mystery parcels in the ceiling to last the long wait. It was a teasing, unsettling thought. So finally, I had to make a hole in it.

I had not planned to, though I often intently pierced the matting with my expectations. A loud, truly deafening noise was the first awareness I had that anything was wrong. It brought the world to an end. Something smacked against the mat, an instant later another sound, dull yet crisp announced that something had passed through and hit the metal sheeting of the roof.

But the definition of those sounds came much later, for I was at this point on the floor, the explosion having startled me off my chair. I believed also that I was paralysed and refused to move: I had been shot to death, there was no other explanation for the suddenness of my descent to earth, none other for the lack of pain or the full clarity of my senses. Obviously, I had attained a heavenly dimension. Moreover, HM was in his bedroom at the time; I was waiting for him to emerge when it happened. There was no motion, so it could not be his bedroom whose door still seemed so plain to the eye.

The preceding moments regained focus. Yes, I had been sitting in the front room, under the porcelain clock. I occupied the chair where visitors sat who had business with my father. His air-gun leant against the wall and I sat in the chair by the door, waiting for him to come out so as to accompany him, as usual. Like Jonah, like the Guava Tree and the bell-house, Essay-on-the-hunt was another private existence. He never spoke. I followed him, sometimes carrying his gun, picking up the birds he shot, mostly wood pigeons. Sometimes a hawk or kestrel, a squirrel—once, even a small *emo*.* I recalled the excitement that followed the shooting of a rare bird, hitherto unseen, perhaps a migrant. We went through the deserted school compound and into the surrounding bush. Rocks loomed before us and he climbed carefully, first handing me the gun. When he reached a firm ledge he reached out for his gun and I climbed after him. We sat and waited. Or we climbed down the other side, then we might make the return by a wholly different route, walking down the path that ran along the school wall on the outside and entering by the main gate. Perhaps the bookseller or the catechist would stop him then while I went ahead with the day's bag.

Huddled close against the floor, scenes of past excursions flashed through my mind, so certain was I that I was dead. I had drifted off perhaps into a frequent reverie while caressing the stock of the rifle. My hand must have found the trigger. Then it became clear to me that I was not dead, so, naturally, a different terror took its place. Indeed only then did any fear intrude. Acceptance of my death had come easily: very different was the thought of my father's reaction to my carelessness.

I scrambled up, but slowly. Still no movement from the bedroom. Was it mere imagination? I was certain I heard the door creak. It

* A wild rodent, rat family.

68

would be like him, I thought, to peer through and watch my reactions. The gun still leant against the wall, in pulling the trigger I had not even knocked it down. A whiff of something burning stung my nostrils and I forced back a sneeze, scraping against a chair. This time there was no doubt in my mind—something moved behind the door. I fixed my gaze on the porcelain clock, marvelling that it had not been hit. The muzzle of the gun still pointed directly at its base. Its face was decorated by a windmill and two women with hooped skirts and strange, tight-fitting caps. On the other side of the diamond-shaped face, a flock of birds flew over some fields. For the first time, and for a very brief moment, I wondered if my father had bought that clock because of the birds. All the design was blue. The porcelain looked fragile. Would I escape a beating?

He is watching, I thought. Perhaps he thinks I am wounded. So that also became a possibility and I began to look for traces of blood. None. Still no movement from his bedroom. But I knew him. He was the opposite of Wild Christian who would by now have rushed out. First consideration: is he wounded? Finding him intact, a barrage of blows ten times more lethal than I could imagine a bullet through the flesh. Certainly more disorientating. By contrast HM might pursue his original plans as if nothing had happened. The hunting excursion, home, supper, small talk, visitors, disputation on predestination or the War. Evening prayers, then . . . .

'Wole!'

No, I was not going on any hunt with him, let him formulate his punishment as he wished but I was not going to be kept in suspense, trotting by his side, carrying his gun and picking up fallen game as if nothing was going to happen. Whatever he was planning behind that door . . . I leapt up and was out through the door before he could even gather up his voice. A few moments later I lay panting on the back of Jonah, keeping a watchful eye on the path through which he must pass if he still meant to hunt.

At different times, something was always going to be the death of 'that son of yours'—this appeared to be my mother's fervent belief. And the most persistent threat to my existence at Aké appeared to be day-dreaming or brooding. How she described it depended, I found, on the seriousness of whatever lapse had been caused by the ailment. She lost no chance to remind Essay of the need to cure me of it before it was too late, so now I conjured up her presence and watched her react to the news that her prophecy had nearly been fulfilled. I told

69

you before, I heard her say, so I won't say anything more. Only to expand, a few moments later, on the dangerous effects of so much brooding in a child. She was not alone. We knew of parents who took their children to 'native doctors' for a cure for the same complaint.

I was now truly worried; it seemed as if Wild Christian might after all be right. Only one other event had succeeded in my paying any attention to her complaint—this was the incident of the rose-bush. We were all in the backyard, she was cooking, which meant that the entire household was occupied with running trivial errands for her, holding a spoon or a cup, receiving a slap if the fire had burnt down or the pot had over-boiled. Unless I was especially picked upon, I would manage to escape being a part of the disorder, usually by going to read in the front room, or even simply from being seen just completing my lessons in the front room. It was recognized that I had special chores in the house. I took some share in the cooking but it was really a token share, much less than that of Tinu for instance, or of any of the 'cousins' who lived with us. One of these special chores, one which I chose for myself and enjoyed doing, was looking after Essay's garden. I watered the plants, pruned dead stalks and discouraged the spiders from spinning their webs across the crotons. The roses came for the most careful tending. I was murderous with the goats which sometimes succeeded in penetrating our defences to nibble at the flowers. Nothing would do but to lock the gate on them, then drub them thoroughly with stones and cudgels. Once we nearly beat a goat to death. He lay panting and bleeding in the narrow path leading to the gate. The aim of one of our cousins had been a little too true and the stone had been much larger than the ones which, by unspoken agreement, we normally used.

When we opened the gate at last, the goat was too weak to climb out. Terrified now, we doused it with cold water, then heaved the wretched animal over the step. We locked the door and watched it through a gap while we prayed that it would recover and go away before Essay returned. He approved of us chasing out goats, not locking them up and murdering them. It was with immense relief that the tortured animal staggered up at last and wobbled off unsteadily. The following day it was back again, in the parsonage. If it had come into our garden again, I would have killed it.

Only my father himself surpassed the jealousy with which I guarded the flowers, as one of HM's staff discovered, painfully. He acquired a name from his harsh encounter with this jealous regard—

'Lẹ̀-mọ́'—Stick it back on!—an episode which also made our neighbours, and Essay's colleagues, marvel at the nature of that strange being the Headmaster, who would pursue an impossible demand with such single-mindedness.

Odejimi, the teacher, thought at first that it was a typical HM joke, a mistake which many people committed because of the Headmaster's fussless way of meaning what he said. The teacher had arrived in school, a pink rose stuck in the button-hole of his jacket. My father admired the rose, then asked him, very ordinarily, where he had obtained it.

'Oh, in your garden of course, Headmaster.'

Essay did not change his tone when he said, 'Ah, I thought I recognized it. You like roses I see.'

'Oh yes indeed sir. And I must congratulate you. Really, you have a wonderful garden. I never knew it or I would have visited it more often.'

'Oh? So how did you discover I had a garden?'

'I was passing by sir, and your back gate was open. I saw the blooms through the opening and I could not believe my eyes. You hide your light under a bushel, Headmaster.'

'Thank you' said Essay. And there the matter was left.

School over, he sent for Odejimi. 'Ah yes, your rose. I can't quite remember who you said gave you permission to pluck a rose from the garden.'

Odejimi looked puzzled, then corrected the mistake. 'Oh no, I never said that anyone gave me permission.'

My father looked surprised. 'Really? You mean you just went into the garden and helped yourself.'

'Precisely sir. I mean, I hope you don't mind.' Very belatedly, Mr Odejimi was beginning to get a message.

'Not at all' my father assured him. 'But I would like you to return it now. You know, to the place where you found it.'

There was a long silence. Odejimi briefly lost his syntax and appeared to stammer. 'Er . . . to returning it sir? You mean return it to the er . . . to your garden.'

'Yes please, that is, if you do not mind.'

'Of course Headmaster. I am er . . . really sorry that you took offence. I should have asked your permission.'

'That's all right. Just return it where it belongs and we will forget the matter.'

Odejimi smiled broadly, relieved that no direr consequences were to follow. He picked up his books and marched briskly towards our house. Essay watched him cover half the distance, then followed him. His uncanny sense of timing ensured that both he and Odejimi met exactly at the back gate, Odejimi already on his way out, beaming.

'Oh I see you've finished' Essay remarked.

'Yes indeed, sir, I've left it in the flower-pot.'

'Good. Let's just go and see how it's doing, shall we?'

A baffled Odejimi followed his boss to the scene of crime. There, slumped over the rim of the pot was the wilting rose. Essay took a long look at the object, then craned his neck a little to the side to discover the stalk from which it had been cut.

'But it came from that stalk originally, didn't it?'

'Oh yes' confirmed Odejimi, his voice most sprightly in his eagerness not to contradict. 'That was the precise stalk from which I er . . . removed it.'

'Good. Lẹ mọọ!'

'Beg your pardon sir?'

'I said, Lẹ mọọ.' And with that final instruction, Essay turned and walked into the house. He calmly set about the tasks he would normally perform at that hour, paying no further attention to the teacher.

I had raced ahead from school to brief Tinu and Dipo. Together we now watched the hapless man open and shut his mouth as the fishes did when they were brought to the house for sale, still alive. His rechristening was instant—he was now Mr Lẹ-mọọ.

Lẹ-mọọ made a move at last. Holding the rose in his hand with great tenderness he entered the house. My father was in his bedroom. Lẹ-mọọ stood in the front room, faced the door which led to the bedroom. For one moment we thought he would commit the ultimate folly of following my father into the room, he looked sufficiently confused to have done anything in that moment. However, he merely coughed to attract attention.

'Excuse me sir. Er, sir. . . . Headmaster sir.'

Essay made no attempt to conceal his movements in the room. For almost an hour Lẹ-mọọ remained on the spot, the dead flower in his hand. From time to time he punctuated his wait with, 'Sir, if I may just explain sir . . .', 'if I could just have a word with you sir;' 'Please Headmaster, I wonder if . . . I mean, if I could only. . . .'

An hour passed before Essay emerged from the room. The space

72

between his table in the front-room and the chairs arranged against the wall next to the parlour was not wide enough to take two people at a time, and his eyes opened in measured exasperation of finding a total stranger blocking a passage in his own home. Lè-móọ flattened himself against the edge of the table, but Essay did not attempt to pass. Instead, he waited. It took another full second before the teacher realized that he was about to add to his catalogue of sins and he leapt backwards, apologizing profusely, stumbling over his words and feet. Essay ignored him and went to the backyard. He took one look at the flower-pot, looked at Odejimi who had followed him there, and gave a thin pitying smile that sent the teacher licking his lips in fright. It was a smile we all knew, it was accompanied by a movement of his head from side to side. We turned cartwheels in the pantry in a fever of excitement, for we had recognized the commencement of a long, difficult lesson for the erring teacher. We settled deeper into our ringside seats, speculating on the possible lines of development.

Lè-móọ underwent a mental transformation at some point during the next hour, because his next specific act was to try and hold the dismembered rose to the stalk. He began by freezing a long time, staring into vacancy. Then he turned towards the flower-pot, his movement like a sleep-walker's, and again he held the rose to its parent stalk, pressing the two severed points together. When he let go, the rose fell into the bed. It was a big disappointment. Seeing his fixed stare into nowhere, watching his lips working in some strange fashion, we had come to the conclusion that he was working a spell, either on Essay or on the rose. It became clear that it was the latter when he held the flower against the stalk and we were set to cheer, thinking that it would work. It failed, and Lè-móọ stared into the pot, then raised his head up with his hands, clutching both sides, and bellowed in anguish:

'Ye e! Mo k'ẹ́ran!*

I suddenly felt pity for him.

The next moment, he was standing stiff-backed, animated. His eyes had lit up with a GREAT IDEA and he bolted from the house as if from hell. We felt profoundly disappointed. Surely Odejimi, a teacher under the HM should know better than that. Could this be the great idea that had occurred to him? Running away? No one

*Ah, I'm in trouble!

73

escaped Essay, certainly not someone who had tampered with his roses.

It was not until the return of Wild Christian from the shop, with Odejimi in tow, that we learnt the true nature of his inspiration. He had gone to solicit the aid of mother in appeasing the wrath of the Headmaster. The journey from the shop to the house, a mere ten minutes walk must have taken an hour, since Lẹ̀-mọ́ọ insisted on prostrating himself to her at every step, wringing his hands and repeating that he was a doomed man unless my mother could do something for him. The slow procession continued right into the backyard where Wild Christian commenced her preparations for the evening meal. She promised a hundred times that she would do her best but, nothing would satisfy Odejimi unless she somehow produced Essay on the spot and got him to say that all was forgiven. Wild Christian sent off at least four of the children in all directions to spy out Essay's movements; only then did the poor man relax, getting in the way of mother's cooking by offering to do every chore including stirring the soup. He had to be prised from the grinding stone and was finally expelled to the furthest corner of the top of the yard with a bottle of lemonade and a saucerful of chin-chin. I took them to him and, assessing full well his state of mind, spoke kindly to him.

'You don't feel like eating at all, I'm sure.'

'Oh yes, no, I mean yes, I don't. Please, thank Mama but yes, I mean tell her no thank you. Very kind of her. Kind woman. Is HM in yet!'

Tinu was waiting round the corner. We shared the chin-chin and drank the lemonade. For me, he had now paid his dues and I had no further interest in his agony. We could not after all chase him round the yard like a goat.

It was close to midnight when Odejimi left the house that day, an exhausted, chastened teacher. Wild Christian did not broach the subject immediately; she merely served Essay his dinner, pretending not to understand the purpose of the quick survey which he made of the backyard when he returned, and the tight pursing of his lips on failing to see Lẹ̀-mọ́ọ anywhere. Afterwards, she remained closeted with him for about an hour. When she came out, she sent some food to Lẹ̀-mọ́ọ who had not moved from his hide-out in the yard. She had to go out herself and force him to eat, to our intense disappointment.

74

The bell rang for evening prayers. I had no doubt whatsoever that Lè-mọ́ọ was on his knees, praying hard with the family but on his own behalf. After prayers, Essay sat in the front-room, reading. Of his knowledge of Lè-mọ́ọ's presence in his backyard, he betrayed no sign. I did not sleep. When the house had fallen completely silent, Essay went through the parlour to the yard. I heard him shout,

'Is Odejimi there?'

Startled from his doze, the ill-starred man snapped out a 'Present, sir' and stumbled over objects towards Essay. He repeated, 'Present sir, I'm right here sir, very sorry sir.'

Then followed the cool, measured voice of Essay,

'Don't you have a bed to sleep in?' There was silence, then. 'Well, good-night. Secure the gate after you.'

When I heard *my* name forced through a choked pipe, the sound of it near-identical with the first escape attempts of piped water after the long drought of Harmattan, I knew that an unbelievable disaster had befallen the house. I came back to earth thoroughly frightened, for Essay had appeared at the outer door and his face was going through unaccustomed changes of horror, incredulity, intense agitation. Essay, the cool, deliberate HM pointed a shaking finger in my direction and I had to acknowledge that, unbelievable though it was, the voice that had called out my name was indeed his.

In my hand was a stalk of *ewedu*.* I leant against the half-barrel filled with earth, the bed of the new rose-bushes on which I had lavished much time and care. The buds were appearing for the first time, two or three had actually begun to open. The strange aspect was that they now lay in shreds, flogged to death by my own hands. If Wild Christian had not had her helpers constantly passing or awaiting orders in front of her, she would have seen the action long before and called me to my senses. But she was seated on a low stool, fussing with her pots and pans, while the children mostly had their backs to me. When Essay stepped on the threshold of the outer dining-room door, the sight that confronted him over the cooking group was this: his Number One Gardening Assistant, leaning against the barrel, the *ewedu* stalk in his left hand going gently up and down into the rose plant, a hypnotized stare into nowhere on his face. The fresh young petals lay wounded on the bed, caught among

*A vegetable.

75

the thorns and branches. Even the leaves were broken, stamens were cut in half at the filaments, the crop lay piteously on the leaves of the calyx, the younger stalks had been slightly bruised by the gentle but persistent strokes of an ewedu baton which had been conducting some music in my head. The disaster was total. In broad daylight, in the presence of a large number of people who, as if through the wiles of the devil—nothing else could account for it—had been so positioned that they could not even see or suspect and warn, I had physically assaulted Essay's roses and inflicted mortal wounds on them.

At least Lè-móọ had something to attempt to glue back on the plant; where did one begin in all this?

I had never loved Wild Christian as I did at that moment. Responding to her husband's bellow of pain, she looked up and took in the situation. She breathed a soft 'A-ah' and her eyes filled with pity. The next moment Essay charged across the intervening space and his fingers affixed themselves to his favourite spot, the lobe of my ear, only this time, he was not merely pinching it to hurt but was trying to lift me up with it. Wild Christian moved very swiftly. It was one of the few times in her life that she interfered with Essay's punitive decisions, going as far as detaching my ear from his fingers and pleading with him.

'Dear, you must *know*. He must have been dreaming. Ah-ah, isn't he the one who spends all his time looking after the garden. His mind wasn't here. He didn't know what he was doing.'

Essay's snorts diminished to heavy breathing, then became regular. He appeared to calm down. He took one more look at the battered plant, shook his head in self-pity, and strolled away from the scene.

Wild Christian sighed. 'Something just has to be done before you kill yourself or set fire to the house.'

VI

I lay on the mat pretending to be still asleep. It had become a morning pastime, watching him exercise by the window. A chart was pinned to the wall, next to the mirror. Essay did his best to imitate the white gymnast who was photographed in a variety of postures and contortions on that chart. There was a precise fusslessness even in the most strenuous movements. In . . . Out . . . In . . . Out . . . breathing deeply. He bent over, touched his toes, slewed from one side to the other, rotated his body on its axis. He opened his hands and clenched them, raising one arm after the other as if invisible weights were suspended from them. Sweat prickles emerged in agreed order, joined together in disciplined rivulets. Finally, he picked up the towel—the session was over.

From the window-sill he next picked up his chewing-stick and a cup, the stick moved over an impeccable set of teeth, scrubbed deep into the corners, up and down the front teeth. He spat neatly into the cup. From time to time he grunted a response to the greeting of a passer-by. Once or twice he would actually consent to return a half phrase to a passing neighbour, a phrase with discernible words, but I felt that this caused him an effort.

After a while he picked up his towel, rolled the ends of his wrapper in a lump about his waist or tied them around the back of his neck and went out of the bedroom. I followed the sound of his slippers through the house and into the backyard where he would stroll, pausing to examine his roses and pick off some withered petals. Occasionally his voice would ring out, summoning someone to perform an errand, probably calling for his clippers to snip off a withered branch. Often, simply standing still among his plants, gazing through the flowers into his distances.

The room gave off an ordered mustiness, in contrast to Wild Christian's bedroom. Hers was a riot of smells, a permanent redolence of births, illnesses, cakes, biscuits and petty merchandise. This varied from the rich earth-smell of *ɑ̀ṣọ òkè*,* to camphor balls

*A hand-woven cloth, much valued.

77

and hundreds of unguents. Some of the household, including a grown-up maid still wetted their mats at night, so there was a permanent tang of urine in the air. In any case a sick child was instantly transferred from the mat on the floor to her enormous, four-poster bed where the mattress further absorbed the effects of a bladder whose training had become temporarily slackened by strange fevers. Afterwards the mattress would be turned over to the sun for a whole day, but it never completely lost that acrid tang which suffused the room even with both windows fully open.

Wild Christian's bed was twice the size of Essay's, at least it always appeared so. It had huge brass knobs on all four posts and the railings at the head and feet of the bed had little brass spheres which could be unscrewed. For some reason, the railing at the foot was removed altogether, which saved us quite a lot of punishment. Now when we unscrewed the tiny spheres at the surviving end, played with them and lost them, we could obtain spares from the discarded railing which lay hidden in the big store-room.

The four-poster with those shiny knobs, and the enormous dresser were the only items in the room which aspired to any definable form or shape. Everything else in the bedroom was resolutely, even fanatically set against order or permanence in any form. Bundles were piled underneath the bed, baskets of soap, trayloads of tinned sardines, pilchards, packets of sugar, bolts of cloth, round camphors and square, leaf-wrapped parcels of shea-butter or black, local soap. Jars of sweets, home-made and imported, such as Trebor mints, rested on the window-sills side by side with odd pamphlets, bibles, hymn-books and tattered books. Tightly sealed tins of kerosene, palm-oil, groundnut oil, enamel bowls of *gari*, beans and dried corn were stacked in a corner . . . my father would come into the room in search of something, look around, give up and go out shaking his head in patient despair.

The top of the chest of drawers was marked by the same profusion of disorder, only, its inhabitants were of a different species from the insatiable cavern beneath the bed, the wall corners or the window-sills. Jewellery boxes, isolated beads, bracelets, ear-rings and other ornaments, a leather-bound bible, hymn and prayer books all with silk ribbon markers were the approved residents. There were also china pieces decorated in high relief like the cicatrix on the face of an *ara-oke*,* and other ornate curios which multiplied at festivals, or

*Someone from the hinterland, considered 'bush'.

78

with the arrival of visitors from outlandish places. Yet, at night, sufficient space was created on the floor where a mat was spread to sleep a constantly varying assortment of children—sometimes as many as twelve—there being no more avid a collector of strays than Wild Christian, tacitly aided by her husband. We never knew her to say No to any of those parents, guardians or relations who brought their ward for 'training', or simply to be cared for. Some ran away, only to be brought back again. Some arrived with their heads full of ringworms, their stomachs distended from poor diet, their feet eaten by yaws and with lice in their hair. Others came well trimmed and groomed, their boxes full of new clothes, their pockets full of spending money.

'What are all those portmanteaux for?' Wild Christian would ask, her face deceptive in its innocence, but fooling no one.

'Oh, just a few changes of clothing.'

'I see. Well, leave him two shirts and a couple of shorts, leave him a *dansiki* for church, and take the rest back. As for money, make sure you leave him with none of his own. If he needs pocket money, let him come to me.'

Wild Christian's bedroom manifested the very nature of the children whom she took under her wing; it waged war against itself yet created a sense of belonging. The bedroom, not their parents, appeared to have given birth to this family, spewed them out only to resorb them and make them children of the house. In the calm and privacy of my father's bedroom I would wonder about these parents who willingly abandoned them to the home of 'headmaster' and his wife. I wondered what my sister felt about it all, unable to enjoy the intimacy which I derived from my privileged position in father's bedroom. Dipo was still a baby. Since he was a boy, I expected that he would later join me in *our* room; that seemed only right.

It was a room whose mustiness came from accumulated papers—frayed journals, notebooks, files, seasoned leather cases and metallic trunks, leather shoes carefully laid out. Twice a year Essay reduced the volume of papers by holding a bonfire from which we snatched glossy catalogues and intriguing journals, over which we pored. They belonged to a different, unreal world. By lifting the hanging bedspread, my eyes could rove at ground-level round the cardboard cases and trunks, all awaiting the next disgorgement, wondering if they knew of their fated end in a bonfire.

The room was full of dust-motes, caught in the beam of sunlight

79

that came through the window. Through it I reviewed the bookcase with its neatly stacked shelves. I had already sampled several of their hoard, leaving even Essay astonished at my appetite for books, yet even he did not know how deeply I had burrowed into his bookcase. I had casually drifted into dusting his bedroom, finally easing out Joseph whose duty it was. Half of my working hour was spent devouring his shelves. Wild Christian lost no opportunity to show me off to her visitors and, at the beginning, I needed no prompting to begin showing off. But then she had to bring Tinu into the act, disparaging her comparative lack of attainment. In place of my delight at being invited to read came discomfort, then resentment. Tinu was the closest playmate I knew and a protective bond had grown between us which only showed when she was hurt or threatened. Helping her with her homework I regarded the same as doing my own; I could not see the difference nor understand that Essay found it necessary to ask questions which were so obviously designed to catch her out. Reducing her before strangers was, however, the ultimate crime.

Wild Christian's sense of the ultimate crime was different; it consisted very simply of manifesting 'èmí èṣù', the spirit of the devil, at any time, but most unpardonably in front of visitors. The catalogue of 'èmí èṣù' was quite sweeping, and it included showing even the slightest evidence of 'unwilling' in the face of a parental order. No child of HM and his wife, no ward, no 'ọmọ ọdọ' was about to commit such a crime; alas, a few had faces which betrayed them even before the thought was formed. Wild Christian constantly impressed upon me that I was principal of these. Thus I resorted to failing to find the books through which I was to demonstrate my cleverness to visitors, I developed sudden fevers, which unfortunately were not believed, since they were not accompanied by 'Temperature'. Bukola was the only child I knew who could effortlessly manipulate 'Temperature', and hers was always in the opposite direction—her body would simply go cold. Lacking her talent, I took to vanishing when ordered to find a book and perform to visitors.

I had an ally. It was no more than a fleeting expression, and Essay never permitted himself more than that once to show disapproval. It was also likely that he did not really mind when the exhibition took place among his 'own people'—like his debating circle—but once at least I caught him wince in discomfort, then turn away to hide his distaste. My disappearances took on a bolder turn, books vanished,

Essay's bedroom door somehow got mysteriously locked and the key was missing. I grew reckless, and it seemed the normal order of things.

Now I sought ways to let the household know that father and I belonged in a separate world. Wild Christian watched the progressive abandonment of participation in the general household ordering and let it go. 'Papa gave me some homework' was final, it brooked no argument. But the seeming triumph did not come without its rooted fears. I sensed, not battle, but demarcation lines being drawn, yet even these required a measure of defiance which escalated every day. I would deny it to myself, yet I knew that it was taking place; the treatment of my own sister was merely the first event to bring it to my uneasy notice.

Deep down, I felt I was headed towards a terrible punishment. I could not define how I had deserved it, nor how to avert it. The song in the story which my father had told me the previous night came back to mind like a special warning,

> Igba o l'ọwọ
> Tere gungun maja gungun
> tere
> Igba o lẹsẹ
> Tere gungun maja gungun
> tere
> Igba mi l'awun o
> Tere gungun maja gungun
> tere*

The Tortoise was lying of course. Claiming he knew neither hand nor foot of the cause of his terror was quite typical of his deceitful nature. But the sight of gourds which broke off their moorings on the farm and began to chase him over rocks and rivers must have been most unnerving. The song appeared far more suitably applied to me: every time Wild Christian accused me of being possessed of 'ẹmi èsù', I was simply puzzled that no one else appeared to share my deep sense of injustice. I had not after all, provoked the situation. I roved through the woods on the next expedition with one fearful eye on

*The gourd has no arms.
Tere gungun etc.
The gourd has no legs
Yet the gourd is pursuing the tortoise.

anything bulbous. There were no gourds on the farms or in the woods of the parsonage but there were the baobab trees with their velvet-cased oval fruits, the shape and size of grinding stones. I saw them raining down on me, then pursuing me through the woods. If Wild Christian prayed hard enough, perhaps it could happen.

My eyes fell on the exercise chart; that offered some escape from disturbing thoughts. I stood up and began to strike some of the postures of the callisthenist.

'What do you think you are up to?'

Lawanle had just come in. The intrusion was unpardonable. 'Don't you know you are supposed to knock before entering Papa's room?'

'Since when did you become Papa?' And she came further into the room.

'It is still *our* room' I insisted.

'It won't be much longer' She said. 'You are getting older you know.'

'What difference does that make?'

'You'll find out when it's time' she shrugged. 'Now come on. Mama is asking what you are still doing in the room. Why haven't you had your bath?'

'What am I going to find out?'

'Oh god, come on. Must you always follow one question with another question? That is what is wrong with you, you like arguments too much, you fancy yourself another Papa don't you?'

'What am I going to find out?'

She half-sung, 'That there will be some CHANGES in this house.'

'What changes?'

Lawanle let loose her derisive laughter. 'Someone is going to find out very soon.'

'All right, I am no longer interested. Keep your secrets.'

Pulling me into a corner of the parlour, she asked, 'Didn't Papa tell you he was travelling?'

'Where to?'

'You see. It is always a mistake to answer even one question of yours. All one gets in return is another question.'

I lied. 'I knew he was travelling because he told me an extra story last night. He does that when he is going to be away for some time. In fact he told me two more but I fell asleep in the middle of the last.'

'Then he should have told you where he was travelling to.'

By now we were crossing the parlour and approaching the back-yard, so further conversation was impossible.

As I scrubbed myself in the bathroom I felt ill with apprehension. Lawanle's words had merely increased the unease which was lately surreptitiously transmitted to me—those sentences that began on mother's tongue, but were never completed. The fleeting dis-approval of some privilege extended to me by Essay, the pursing of the mouth as I made off with my mat to his room while Tinu, cousins and all retired to the common mat. I hated the communal mat, I realized quite suddenly; it went beyond merely feeling special in Essay's room. I hated it with a vehemence that went beyond the fact that some of the others, much older than I, still continued to wet the mat. I simply preferred to be on my own.

My father travelled; I moved into Wild Christian's bedroom. I awaited his return with a different kind of anxiety—his return would be testing time. On the first night of his return I made to resume my normal sleeping-place but was prevented by mother's casual voice saying,

'Wole, why don't you sleep with the others tonight? You shouldn't abandon them just because your father is back. And your baby brother is getting used to climbing down to sleep with you.'

In the dark, I dissected the tone. Was this to be just a token ex-pression of me caring about being with others? I did not for one moment believe in Wild Christian's concern for Ladipo's feelings; even so, I permitted myself to hope that my reinstatement was only deferred a night. Normal relations would resume the following night.

That following night, I lay on my mat in the dark and cried. My transfer was permanent. And there could be no mistaking the rather guilty half-smile of confirmation on my father's face.

Ladipo was growing fast in his cot. He was born with a noisy, excessive energy which constituted another reason for keeping clear of that maternal dormitory. He had long begun his efforts to climb over the cot and had succeeded once or twice, chiefly by falling down from the top of the cot, so desperate was he to get on the mat with us. It occurred to me then that this child was born with no sense at all, if he actually wanted to leave the sheltered peace of his cot to join that medley of bodies on the mat. Sleeping there brought on the wildest dreams. A tree would fall over my body and I would struggle

83

awake; it was an arm or a leg flung over me. Some of the other sleepers were veteran warriors of sleep—they went to sleep only to *ja'run'pa*, to fight tremendous wars which took them from one corner of the mat to its extreme opposite, rolling and mowing down bodies on the way, ending up in the morning upside down in the wrong place or miraculously back in their original position. I would wake up in the night after a violent struggle with pythons that had tied up all my limbs, suffocating under slimy monsters from a mythical past, unable to utter the scream for help which rose in my throat.

Nothing disturbed the blissful repose of these warriors and other victims of their campaigns. They slept and snored soundly through it all, led from the bed by the stentorian basoon of Wild Christian. On waking up in the middle of night, the sounds in the room approached the sounds in the Blaize Memorial Canning factory where we were once taken to watch the grapefruits, oranges, guavas and pears being cleaned, sliced, pulped, canned by a series of monstrous guillotines, motors and flapping belts, pistons and steaming boilers which spluttered, belched, spat, thundered and emitted measured jets of liquids that went into the cans and bottles.

In the mornings there would often be the argument about who had actually left the wet patch or two on the mat. Wild Christian was a specialist in unravelling that short-lived puzzle. She pronounced on the matter with such detective ease that she verged on the mystical, considering the unpredictable positions in which the suspects found themselves in the morning, far from the scene of crime. Gradually it dawned on me that there was a characteristic shape and smell formed by the puddle of every human being, the secret of which could only be known to parents, including surrogate parents. Of the latter, my only doubts were whether the secret was mystically transmitted or formed part of the character-notes brought by the actual parents of the 'cousin' when he or she was handed over.

'You have to watch him Ma'am. He doesn't steal, no, I have never caught him with that terrible habit. But he is lazy, ah, he is lazy That pawpaw hanging from your tree over there, which doesn't even have enough energy to move out of the way of a bird's beak, is not half as lazy as this wretch you see before you.' And with her finger jabbing in the head of the totally bewildered youth, 'You see that half-eaten pawpaw, that is what children's brains become when they don't use them. We say Study, but you won't study. You want to become an *alaaru* carrying loads for half-pennies at Iddo station. Look, you won't even have a head to put the load on if you don't exert your brain now, because it will just collapse. Your brain would have turned to pulp, pecked by birds in your sleep like that pawpaw mash you see over there. . . .'

It was the mother's last public duty before washing her hands of the reluctant student. But then, as she departed, she would invariably remember one final detail which always had to be whispered. No amount of eavesdropping by Tinu or I ever caught what this strictly-between-parents secret was. The truant mother would, almost guiltily, certainly with much furtiveness, draw Wild Christian aside and a brief, intense, one-sided conversation would follow, with direct glances at the changeling. After giving much thought to the problem of the communal mat, I was left with only the one conclusion that it was at this secret session that characteristics of the new entrant's urine puddle were passed from one mother to the other.

The diversions of the public streets frequently spilled into the parsonage. The sounds carried well before; we followed its course and could tell within minutes if the event would pass us by, in which case we rushed to the ladder and other improvised stands which provided us with a panorama of Aké, over the churchside wall that had nearly proved my undoing. I could now race up the ladder with the rest. If the spectacle poured over the crest of Itoko's sky-grazing road towards Aké, it would turn the corner of the church compound towards the palace; retain a straight course past the cenotaph of the warrior Okenla and round the bookshop towards Igbein and Kuti's Grammar School; or best of all, pass right under our noses along the untarred road between the church compound and our wall, to turn either left towards the Aafin or right in the direction of the General Hospital. Depending on what occasion it was, the parsonage would also receive the noisy guests; funeral processions however did not pay courtesy calls on us, though they were often just like weddings, or outings of dance societies.

The hearse led the way, drawn by pall-bearers; sometimes a horse took their place but this was not very often. The coffin was smothered in wreaths made of plaited palm branches into which flowers had been woven. If it was headed for St Peter's, the church-bell began tolling some minutes before the cortege came within sight, solemn, single strokes at intervals of between thirty and sixty seconds. We could almost feel the slow tramp of feet through the ground, accompanied by creaky turns of the hearse wheels. Often they appeared silently, each face set with grief, compassion, or the sense of occasion—these last we easily detected. They were the ones who fussed over a card which had become displaced from the wreath, their lips were pursed in an unchanging manner and they turned to whisper something or the other to the actual mourners at exact intervals. At the church, the hearse was relieved of its burden which was then taken by a group of men into the church. It always seemed strange that, in spite of all the funerals at St Peter's, no one had ever worked out a comfortable way of taking the coffin from the hearse, carrying it up the few steps, through the aisle between the pews and on to the two cross-benches in front of the altar. The coffin appeared inordinately heavy no matter who had died, the bearers staggered under the load and we always waited for one of them to stumble and bring the coffin down with a crash. It never did happen.

Some processions however arrived for the church service already hymning or chanting refrains to prayers or other mutterings by a robed cleric who led the procession or brought up the rear. Such singing was soft, appropriately restrained. It was nothing beside the scene that followed after the actual internment which followed directly after the church service. The file of solemn, weeping women and their stiff companions broke formation and spilled over the street in ecstatic dances. Hands which had been clasped so formally in front of the mourners waved cheerful goodbyes to anyone along the road as if each person stood for the relation they had just buried. Trumpets appeared from nowhere, clarinets, drums, tambourines and trombones—it all depended on how elderly or important the deceased had been. Even the empty hearse appeared to be affected by the mad gyrating, not surprisingly, as the two men who were still attached to its handle had also thrown themselves with energy into the dance. They appeared to have their own special motions: a few steps to the right, then the left, back again into a straightforward course, then up went the handle and before it came down they had turned to face the rest of the procession and thus continued to dance backwards, pulling the hearse along. The women's lungs were the more powerful, pumping energy into the singing without diminishing the manipulations of their buttocks:

Ile o, ile o
Ile o, ile o
Baba (Iya) re'le re
Ile lo lo tarara
Baba re'le re
Ile lo lo, ko s'ina*

One spectacle we did not relish. Indeed, except for the urchins who followed them, this kind of spectacle had nothing of the festive about it. Whatever form it took, its principal feature was this: a youthful culprit with evidence of his or her transgression tied to the neck or carried on the head. Next came the guardian or parent, wielding the corrective whip from time to time. As they went through the streets, layabouts and urchins were encouraged to swell the numbers, jeering and singing at the top of their voice. They picked up tins and boxes along the way and added an assortment of rhythm to which the culprit was expected to dance; often it was the offender who supplied the lead while the mob provided the refrain. Most of the time, the tired, humiliated wretch was a young woman, a fact which made some impression on me.

It was perhaps the only time that the kindly Mrs B. earned my silent rebuke. Her maid was suffering from the same incontinence as afflicted the majority of the cousins and house helps in our house. One morning we looked out, attracted by the sounds of the familiar stick-on-can beat within the parsonage itself. The sound came from the bookseller's compound and we soon made out the words:

Tòólé, Tòólé, a f'òkò ìtò borí
Suúlé suúlé fóko nùdi* *

And then she came in sight. The offending mat was rolled and borne on her head, the procession went from house to house where a stop was made and the girl had to dance her dance of shame. At each house, Mrs B gestured and the music stopped briefly:

'Look at her. Sixteen and she still wets the mat like a newly-born. I

*Home, Home
  The elder has gone home
  Directly
  The elder has gone home
  Home is he bound, he will not miss his way.
* *Bed-wetter, bed-wetter,
    With a piss-pot for a head-cover
    Excretes on the mat and cleans her anus with fibre.

87

don't know what to do with her Auntie, I just don't know what to do with her. She is old enough to be preparing for the matrimonial home, but is she to go there with wet mat and coverlet? Look at the ungainly, gormless, unprepossessing object. In any case, who is going to look at it and want to put it in the house? She doesn't even seem to know that the market for husbands is not open to such as it . . . Shut up!' Down came the whip on the blubbering mess, about her shoulders, back, then legs making her skip, so that without any further prompting, the orchestral jangle was resumed to the skipping of her feet.

'Did I ask you to blubber? Dance, atoo'le! You really think anyone is impressed with all that crying? Come on, sing out! Those fit to be your children are drumming for you, they stopped pissing in their beds ages ago. But you have no shame, so dance when they beat for you.'

How long it lasted depended on the stamina of the guardian, or on a chance meeting with a capable pleader, at home or on the street. When they came to our house, Wild Christian stood and watched until she judged that Mrs B was ready for appeasement. Then she stopped the drumming and singing beckoned to the maid to come nearer.

'Is this a good thing for you?' she demanded.

The maid appeared to be confused, or maybe she did not even hear the question. Mrs B raised the whip. 'I think she has gone deaf and dumb. Let me open up her ears a little.'

Wild Christian gestured restraint. Mrs B let fall her arm and the admonition was resumed:

'Is this a good thing for you? At your age, to be paraded through the streets like this. A grown woman, still wetting her mat, is this good? That is what I asked you.'

'No, ma, it is not good.'

'SPEAK UP!'

The maid skipped in anticipation and found her long-distance voice. 'No ma, it is not good. It is not a good thing.'

'Good. But do you know that this is all for your own good? That you are being helped so that you will not go and disgrace yourself elsewhere?'

'Yes ma, I know it is for my own good.'

'Are you going to make an effort to change?'

'I will change ma. By God's power I promise to change.'

The exchange lasted a while, ending with a short sermon. Wild Christian then turned to Mrs B, 'took the rest of the punishment on herself.' Mrs B. curtsied, the maid knelt fully on the ground and said her thanks, the urchins had begun to drift away, knowing that the fun had ended. I watched Mrs B and maid, the former leading, walk back in the silence that had descended once more on the parsonage and wondered if the maid was still going to wet her mat that night. Lawanle said the treatment always worked, but only if in addition, she roasted the egg-nest of the praying mantis and ate it. Lawanle claimed to have made a particular cousin eat at least a dozen egg-nests of the praying mantis plus a special potion prepared according to the recipe of an old woman at Ibarapa. She had used it successfully for her own cure several years before. All of them were agreed that at home Wild Christian was doing it all wrong. Sending the offenders supperless to bed was not going to solve anything; they only ate more during their last meal, which was not permitted later than five in the evening. And anyway who could keep an eye on them throughout to make sure they didn't drink water to shore up their bedtime hunger? It was a matter for the *babalawo** and he, Lawanle insisted, would probably prescribe the very method employed by Mrs B.

Mrs B, when she brought her road-show to our house, had actually succeeded in redeeming herself in my eyes. One did not have to look closely to see that she actually pulled her blows with the whip. If I was in any doubt about it, one look at Wild Christian confirmed it; she was plainly amused by what Mrs B considered corrective lashes. In any case, she *knew* Mrs B. If Wild Christian had been wielding the whip, that maid would not have skipped, she would have leapt out of her skin and continued dancing even when asked to stop.

In a similar spectacle where the offence was more serious, such as stealing, the urchins were encouraged to participate in whipping the culprit. Stealing meat from a soup-pot was considered particularly heinous, though why, I could not understand. If the thief, when caught, had already swallowed the evidence of his crime, he was made to carry the soup-pot on his head, and his mouth was smeared with oil from the pot. The outing could go on day after day after day. The complainants never seemed to have enough, such was the outrage of these soup-pot guardians. I thought, after all he has eaten the meat, no amount of dancing and flogging would bring it back.

*Oracle-priest; diviner.

And a piece of meat always seemed too small and insignificant to conjure up the number of people who turned out on parade. As Wild Christian prepared dinner that evening while we hung around fetching and holding for her, conversation turned to the morning's exhibition. Wild Christian threatened similar cures for our own mat-wetters and other types of miscreants. Because she expected it, she read disapproval on my face.

'Wole is planning to dip his hand in the pot, that's why he disapproves.'

I denied that I disapproved.

'Or maybe he has been doing it already, only we haven't caught him.'

'If you caught him he would lawyer his way out,' Joseph warned.

'Not with me,' Wild Christian promised. 'It's his father who has all that patience. When I clobber him as he opens his mouth he would soon discover I don't stand for any nonsense.'

'Anyway,' contributed a cousin, 'Wole is more likely to steal toffee or sugar or powdered milk, ovaltine and things like that.'

I glared a challenge at that cousin. His face betrayed nothing but I wondered what he knew. Obviously nothing. By now he would have blackmailed me if he had known that I had been dipping regularly into the tin of Lactogen. After Dipo was weaned and had begun to eat solids, the big tin of Lactogen lay in a corner of the pantry, forgotten. I had developed a passion for the powdered delicacy, it seemed the most exquisite taste in the world, soft, melty, light on the tongue. It was not merely a question of stealing a handful at a time; I had appropriated the entire tin which nobody remembered, secreted it among other bric-a-brac in the pantry, from where it emerged from time to time to satisfy my craving.

It was at least a month later before the tin was discovered, but by then nobody knew how much had remained in it in the one year or more since it was last opened. If I had not been so desperately hooked, I would have known that Wild Christian would be suspicious of its long disappearance and would keep watch on the level of powder it contained. Her suspicions were soon confirmed, so she summoned everyone, asked questions and issued a general warning. That should have been sufficient. It was not only that she was on the war-path, she was clearly planning something exemplary for the foolhardy thief whenever he was caught. Perhaps she already knew the milk-thief and knew that it was now a habit. Inspired guesses came mysteriously to Wild Christian. But I was hooked. Still, a week passed before I abandoned all further resistance, watched the physical disposition of everybody else and homed on the tin. Wild Christian whom I had last seen preparing vegetables further up the yard, opened the pantry-door a little and nodded:

'Good. So it's you. I thought so. I've always known it.'

I believed her. Normally she would by then have drowned out the external world with a barrage of blows. This time she was unusually calm. And she visibly gloated as if a long-awaited moment had been reached. Her self-satisfaction bothered me, it appeared to go beyond the crime. Again I had the uneasy feeling that I had foolishly walked into a trap.

'We will wait until your father comes. When he has finished with you, you will then come and eat my own punishment.'

Alone in the pantry, I began to plan to run away. It was not just a question of getting caught, there was something much too pat about the whole act, as if everyone had been waiting for just this moment and had in some way, played a small role in bringing it about. One thing was not going to happen: I was not providing a spectacle for anyone, neither within the parsonage nor on the streets of Aké. Once again I was struck with the disproportionate attention paid to a tin of powdered milk whose existence had long been forgotten. I had placed it under my personal protection for nearly two months and had grown to regard it as my private booty. My mind was made up; I would run away, first emptying the Lactogen on the floor as a final protest.

I moved furtively from the pantry to the bedroom, to the front-room where most of my books were, packed them into a small bag and awaited the right moment to escape. Essay returned from school and, as I expected, Wild Christian immediately ensconced herself with him in his room to report the terrible discovery. It was the right moment, and I tip-toed through the parlour and into the front-room. A moment later and I would have gone, but the voices were coming out loud and clear from the bedroom and I hesitated, then settled down to listen. My mother was evidently displeased that Essay would not personally deal with the offence. I heard him grumble,

'You should have flogged him. Why bother me?'

I heard her reply, 'But he must have finished half that tin. I remember very well what level it was when I last used it for Dipo. It

91

was very nearly full. I had just opened it before he lost all interest in milk or anything like that.'

Unperturbed, Essay insisted, 'Then punish him for the whole tin. I still don't understand why you didn't just beat him on the spot.'

Wild Christian knew when she was getting nowhere. She whirled out of the room so fast that I had just enough time to fling the bag over the lower-door on to the pavement outside. As she hauled me into the backyard with her, all I could think of was the tell-tale bundle lying on the front pavement, containing my favourite books and clothing. She shouted for her stick and even before its arrival I found myself leaping about the backyard, dodging wild blows from fist and feet, felled by some and rolling with others. Till the last moment, I kept fearing, and hoping that she would attempt to transfer the event outside our own backyard; in my mind I rehearsed the swift movement down, the bundle of my possessions snatched up and then—a continuous run through the parsonage, through the streets, heading nowhere but everywhere, away from a household whose subtle hostilities had begun to prickle my skin. I now blamed the entire household for my banishment from Essay's room. Of the many strange thoughts which crowded my mind under the beating was one which claimed with complete assurance that I was being proved right, I had for long suspected that my place was no longer in that house. The certainty simply came and stayed with a host of others. They crowded my head without any particular order, without any attempt to resolve themselves, probably simply to help me forget the actual pain of the beating. Only, they proved far more painful than the blows. By the time it was over I had decided that it would be best to pursue my original plans, pick up my bundle and seek my fortune away from the parsonage.

When I sneaked out later, not much later, the bundle was gone. Joseph had found it, had picked it up and restored its contents where they belonged. I did not know what to make of his action after he admitted to it, but it seemed a natural thing for him to have done.

That same night, when the whole house was asleep and Wild Christian was shaking the roof with her snores, I tip-toed into the pantry, filled my mouth with powdered milk. In another second I was back on the mat. In the dark, I let the powder melt, dissolve slowly and slide down the back of my throat in small doses. In the morning I felt no pain whatsoever from the pounding of the previous evening.

VII

Change was impossible to predict. A tempo, a mood would have set-led over the house, over guests, relations, casual visitors poor relations, 'cousins', strays—all recognized within a tangible pattern of feeling—and then it would happen! A small event or, more frequently, nothing happened at all, nothing that I could notice much less grasp and—suddenly it all changed! The familiar faces looked and acted differently. Features appeared where they had not been, vanished where before they had become inseparable from our existence. Every human being with whom we came in contact, Tinu and I, would CHANGE! Even Tinu changed, and I began to wonder if I also changed, without knowing it, the same as everybody else.

'If I begin to change, you will tell me won't you?'

She said, 'What are you talking about?'

'Haven't you noticed? Joseph, Lawanle, Nubi, everybody is changing. Papa and Mama have changed. Even Mr Adelu has changed.'

Mr Adelu was one of our most frequent visitors. Compared with some others, there was nothing remarkable about him. This made it all the worse that Mr Adelu should change. From the bookseller now, I expected no better.

But occasionally, I did detect the cause. The birth of Dipo brought about such a CHANGE, indeed, it began long before his arrival. There was nothing whatever to remark about Wild Christian, who was then anything but wild, except that she had begun to bulge. I could not then tell whether she ate a lot or not, but it appeared normal that grown-ups should grow in whichever direction suited them. I hoped myself to grow some day towards my father's height, but I was in no hurry about it. What was curious was that Essay appeared to change far more—in his habits—than Wild Christian who simply bulged and bulged. Still, a howling brother, endowed with superabundant energy appeared at the end of that change, and somehow that explained all that had gone before. Essay's worried looks disappeared, to be replaced by endless smiles and chuckles. The house appeared to loosen up in every way. Visitors streamed into the house and I sought the refuge of Jonah more and more to escape the noisy changes.

The changes sometimes were mundane, domestic. The parlour furniture would suddenly affect Wild Christian in some way and then it would vanish, only to re-appear in a new arrangement. The intervening hours would be spent hunting bed-bugs which had made a home in the parlour cushions. Seams of the cushion-covers were carefully explored, a needle was heated over a candle and then—a sizzling sound, the end of a bed-bug. Next, to find their eggs, brush the flame lightly over them and hear them give off brief crackles, dull explosions, ending in a charred spot. When the arm-chairs and the drink stools went back, a CHANGE had taken place. Some never went back, demoted to the store-house in the upper backyard or to the front-room where visitors first rested, while Essay was summoned. Even the immutable homilies, embroidered, framed and glazed would be transposed around the walls. I looked up expecting to see REMEMBER NOW THY CREATOR IN THE DAYS OF THY YOUTH only to find EBENEZER: HITHERTO HATH THE LORD HELPED US.

Sometimes, the nail from which the homily was hung had merely been moved a foot or two towards or away from the front-room. The consequences were serious. It meant that Essay could no longer be seen reflected long in advance of his arrival home, from the moment when he stepped through the door of the primary school on to the broad path that led almost straight down to the gate of the parsonage. He was visible until two-thirds way down the path, when he was picked up by HONOUR THY FATHER AND THY MOTHER—this was the moment to abandon all mischief. Within the house itself, REMEMBER NOW THY CREATOR picked up his reflection as he emerged from the bedroom, the ageless curtains flapping. This put an end to whatever we were doing wrong at meal-time in the dining-room. We often studied in the front-room, where the material that really held our interest was quickly hidden in the desk the moment Essay, having finished his gardening in the backyard appeared within THE LORD IS MY SHEPHERD, suitably surrounded by the crotons that grew in profusion just outside the dining-room window. The framed homilies were a lifesaver and we worked hard to restore them to their spying functions. Unable to tamper with the nail itself, we resorted to tilting the frame, shortening the cord on one side or placing clumps of the nest of a home-wasp behind the frame. The piece of dried mud, if discovered, would evoke no surprise, as wasps built their nests in the ceilings where they remained until someone felt an inclination to prise them off.

There was the CHANGE in sleeping arrangements. Not mine alone. Suddenly everyone was banished from Wild Christian's bedroom. The parlour became the new bedroom; chairs were moved aside, the centre-table was placed in the corner, mats were spread out and pillows placed in position for those who used them. At night Essay had to pick his way through the sprawling bodies to get a drink of water. That was a pleasant change. There was a lot more room in the parlour and one no longer woke up with his nose pressed against a sack of black-eyed beans.

The CHANGES sometimes came from reports. Even without meaning to eavesdrop, it was nearly impossible not to listen to conversations going on in any part of the house. Visitors came, spoke, argued or cajoled, sought something from or offered something to Essay, usually Essay, but sometimes also Wild Christian. Some were total strangers; they came within HM's orbit once and disappeared for ever. Yet they took away with them a part of those motions of reliance, accustomed gestures, codes and confidences which secured us within the walls of HM's home. Imperceptible at first, we found that attention had been withdrawn from or was now being trained on some of us. There was a new language to be learnt, a new physical relationship in things and people. Once or twice, I felt that the entire household was about to prepare for a journey, to be uprooted from Aké in its entirety. Yet no one could tell me where to, how or why, and we never moved.

Yet, even CHANGE often acted inconsistently. Until the birth of Folasade, I had believed that Change was something that one or more of the household caught, then discarded—like Temperature. Folasade's was permanent. She came after Dipo; unlike him, she was a quiet child. And then, from morning till night, she cried, rolled about in her cot, and kept the whole house awake. She did not reject food outright but ate with great difficulty. We could see the effort in her eyes, barely ten months old. When we reached for her hand through the railings of the cot, she clutched the offered finger with all her strength, holding on. Then suddenly she would twitch, her eyes changed as the pain washed over them, she began to cry all over again.

95

Our parents spent hours in Essay's bedroom; we could hear them talking but could make out no words. They spoke very softly. The maid was sent for, questioned. Her voice was clear enough, whatever she was being asked, she denied. She was vehement, called on God to witness. She repeated over and over again 'Nothing happened, nothing happened at all sir.' She came out of the bedroom, her face set, aggrieved by false suspicion or accusation.

Folasade was taken to hospital. She went in the morning and did not return until late afternoon. Her little trunk was encased in plaster from beneath the arm-pits to her buttocks. Wild Christian carried her, not on her back, but in her arms, wrapped up in a shawl.

She still cried from time to time. But many nights she merely lay awake. I got up from the mat, knelt by the cot and looked into the silent pools of her eyes. She did not appear to acknowledge me. Day after day Folasade lay on her back, was brought out to be fed, changed, then returned to her cot or increasingly on to our mother's bed, propped with pillows on both sides. She was so still that the pillows seemed superfluous. Folasade simply lay still and stared at the ceiling.

One day, I came on the maid sitting by herself, crying. I had noticed for some time that she was to be found more and more by herself. The others would not talk to her. I saw a plate of food beside her, untouched. When I asked her what was the matter she frightened me by a sudden intensification of her weeping so that it took a long time before I made out that she was actually saying between sobs:

'I swear I did not drop her. I swear by God I did not drop her any time. I looked after her, at no time did she drop from my hands, I swear.'

She was seated on the steps which led to the store-room of the Upper Backyard, overlooked by one of the windows of mother's bedroom. I now heard that window being opened. When I looked up there was the face of Wild Christian; never before or since then would I see such a concentration of grief and rage all at once as she stared straight at the weeping maid. The window had been flung open, there was nothing furtive about it. I saw then that she must have heard the maid, had been keeping her eye on the girl. What made her decide to confront her, even silently, just then, could have been the sound of my voice. The maid looked up and saw her. Her tears dried instantly.

96

Later that evening, the maid was summoned again. This time the questioning took hours. Before it was over, I had fallen asleep. By the morning the maid was gone, she and her luggage.

So were Essay and Wild Christian. So was Folasade. Whatever they finally extracted from the girl had sent them straight back to the Catholic hospital at Ita Padi. There was little gaiety in the home during their absence, only anxiety. The maid's departure, the disappearance of both parents with the baby foretold some momentous development but we did not know what it was. It was Joseph who revealed that the maid had packed her things that night and been escorted out of the house by him, on Essay's instructions. Where they had gone with the baby he did not know, but he had looked over the wall under which they passed and, the direction suggested the hospital at Ita Padi.

There was no change in Folasade's appearance when they returned, no change whatever in her motions when she was placed in her cot. Wild Christian spent more and more time in Essay's room even when he was at school. She simply lay in bed or was on her knees, praying. She prayed a lot.

One morning, her motions appeared somewhat more purposeful than before. A man whom we knew simply as Carpenter—he had his workshop at the corner of the road along our churchside wall—came into the house with a small wooden box, square-shaped. My father took it into Wild Christian's bedroom.

Through the door, I heard her say, 'I think the children should see her first, don't you?'

There was a brief, mumbled discussion, and then we were summoned.

Folasade was laid out in a long white dress which covered her plaster and stretched over her feet. Her eyes were closed and she was just as still as she had been for several weeks past. I looked at Tinu who stood there impassively. Wild Christian stood by, a sad sweet smile on her face, saying things which I could not understand, only that we were not to feel sad about anything, because Folasade was now out of pain. 'You see, she does not suffer any more.'

Again I looked at Tinu. I expected her to do or say something, mostly do something, after all she was the elder. But Tinu kept her eyes on the body, looked once slowly at both parents, then turned to continue her mute, expressionless study of our sister.

Suddenly, it all broke up within me. A force from nowhere pressed

97

me against the bed and I howled. As I was picked up I struggled against my father's soothing voice, tears all over me. I was sucked into a place of loss whose cause or definition remained elusive. I did not comprehend it yet, and even through those tears I saw the astonished face of Wild Christian, and heard her voice saying,

'But what does he understand of it? What does he understand?'

There was no CHANGE after Folasade's departure, none whatever. I daily expected a cataclysm of unthinkable proportions but it never happened. If the house had picked itself up by the roots and floated skywards, I would have shown no surprise, but nothing happened. The normality was almost overbearing and I began to suspect a conspiracy between our parents to ensure that this time when CHANGE would be so reasonable, even necessary, it did not happen.

As if it did not matter, as if it signified nothing at all that Folasade had not only died, but had chosen to go on her very first birthday.

The flimsier structures of Aké, built of unbaked mud could not stand up to the rains of July and August. The corrugated iron sheets were penetrated by the wind which ripped them off, flung them over other roofs, leaving the rain to find the weakest point in the walls, dissolve the mud and flush out the household. But sometimes the rain acted first; it found the crack in the thin cement coating, soaked it to its foundations, then the house collapsed on its inmates. A wet, shivering survivor, a growing pool about his feet, stood in the front-room and told the tale of disaster. He was escorted to the backroom, stripped while Essay rummaged in his trunks for some old clothing and Wild Christian prepared a steaming mug of tea, almost treacly with sugar and milk, and a chunk of white bread liberally spread with butter.

Although the house had crashed in Aké itself, far from the parsonage, the *agbara* which flowed past our raised pavement now brought with it all the debris of that house, and the faces of its victims one after the other. Smoke-caked rafters jostled with medicine bottles, a chamber pot followed, astride it was a child's doll, white, blue-eyed and flaxen-haired. She sat with one leg slightly raised and one arm pointed to the sky.

Mrs Adetunmbi came all the way from Ikereku, disconsolate. Even in the front-room she ran from spot to spot, wringing her shawl, indeed her motion was closer to attempting to wash her hands in the

98

shawl. 'E gba mi, e gba mi'* . . . she said that she was going to
fetch firewood, she hasn't been back. The rains stopped over four
hours ago but still she is not yet back . . . e gba mi o, Headmaster,
e gba mi . . .'

*But what do you want Headmaster to do? The rains may have
stopped but the* agbara *is still rushing and swelling. Mama, I have
just seen the face of your daughter floating past our doorstep; I did
nothing to stop her.*

'Where are you going?' Wild Christian opened the window as I
sneaked past.

'Only to the school compound.'

'To do what?'

'To pick some guavas. They'll be plenty on the ground after this
rain.'

'Tell Bunmi to go. You will only catch a cold.'

'She can't. It's my guava tree.'

'Are you mad?' Wild Christian nearly exploded. 'I said you are
going nowhere. Come back here!'

I returned, stood with my legs apart. She continued to stare, so I
put my hands behind my back.

'Did you hear what I said.'

'I heard, Ma. I was returning to read my book.'

'And what do you say when you are talked to?'

'Yes, Ma.'

A long baleful glare. 'Take yourself out of my sight.'

'Yes, Ma.'

I caught Bunmi as she came out of the back gate. 'If you touch my
guava tree, their *iwin* will visit you at night.'

'Go away, you see you don't even know anything about spirits. It
is *òrò* which lives in trees, not *iwin*.'

'Just touch the tree and see who is right. I've warned you.'

'You are only jealous because Mama wouldn't let you go and pick
the guava.'

'Even the ones on the ground, I warn you. Touch them and you'll
see.'

When she returned, she reported my threats to Wild Christian.
Later that evening at dinner, I saw her glance at me from time to
time. When Essay had finished his meal, she announced quite
loudly, looking at me all the while,

*Save me, save me . . .

'I'll come with you now to discuss . . .'

Essay grunted, 'Oh, all right.'

Bunmi jabbed her finger in the direction of my nose. 'Now we shall see who is going to chop that stick tonight.'

'For what? What offence did I commit?'

'Stubborn. When I told her what you said she said you were getting too stubborn. She said she was going to tell Papa.'

'For telling her, both the *iwin* and *òrò* will get you tonight.'

I went to the front-room to read, expected the summons to come any time. I found I did not much worry about it.

'What are you staring at?'

'Your nose.'

'I shall tell Mama you have been rude again.'

'One can only be rude to one's elders. Who do you think you are?'

'Rudeness is rudeness. Mama says we are to report you if you are ever rude again.'

'Did I abuse you?' I demanded.

Bunmi stared at me, the same look of puzzlement came into her eyes. 'What is the matter with you Wole? Why do you want to quarrel with everybody?'

'Leave me alone.'

But they would not. Acting on instructions it seemed, but they simply would not. Alone, Bukola suited my mood. I escaped to the bookseller's as often as I could. Bukola knew how to be silent. Even when she spoke, she transmitted a world of silence into which I fitted. She picked up pebbles and weighed them in her hands, thoughtfully. She ate as if she ate with *other* people. I watched her intently, seeking something that would answer barely formed questions. She glided over the earth like a being who barely deigned to accommodate the presence of others. With her, I found some peace.

I always knew when Wild Christian was going to discuss me with Essay, it very simply transmitted itself to me on a wave of hostility. I would not hestitate, I went and eavesdropped. Sometimes it was Tinu who came to call me. At other times Nubi or Joseph would inform me, gleefully, as if to terrify me. I strolled casually past them, then went and pinned my ear to the curtain.

'It is not new,' Wild Christian was saying, 'he has always tended to brood.'

100

'Then there is nothing to worry about.'

'But it is not healthy. It is not natural in a child. When he had only Tinu for a playmate it wasn't too bad. But for some years now he has tended to wander off by himself. And now this . . .'

'If it has to do with Folasade,' counselled Essay, 'It will wear off.'

'And then spending so much time alone with you. That really cut him off the rest of the family.'

'So I am now to blame . . .'

'I wasn't blaming you dear. I am just trying to see that we mustn't encourage him any more. Especially as it is making him headstrong.'

'I hadn't noticed he was headstrong.'

'You are away most of the time, you don't notice. And of course these children won't come to you and tell you.'

It would end with Essay promising to watch me more closely.

'We must take him out of himself,' my mother persisted.

'All right, all right.'

The Odufuwa came to visit, but it only lifted my spirits a little. Mrs Odufuwa was quite simply and without dispute from any but the blindest man with the coarsest sensibilities, the most beautiful woman in the world. I bore her husband no grudge, after all, he was my godfather, so he should prove no obstacle to my marrying this goddess once I had grown to manhood. I followed her about as she strolled in the garden with her husband.

She had nicknames for everyone for she could not, as a 'wife' of the house, call us children by name, at least not those who were born into the house before she became a wife of the family. And so Tinu was 'Obinrin Jeje', the gentle woman—which I considered a most observant choice, and it only confirmed Mrs Odufuwa's cleverness. I came next, and I was Lagilagi, the Log-Splitter. Before I could even wield a vegetable knife, I had insisted on helping Joseph with the splitting of firewood, employing an axe. The goddess had observed me at my exertions, and the name stuck. Hitler's world power thrust had just begun to percolate to us. The German race had acquired a fearsome, bellicose reputation—it was inevitable, Dipo could only acquire one name—Jamani!

The goddess and her husband were moving leisurely through the flowers; I followed them. Joseph was in the vicinity, preparing logs for chopping. Wild Christian was somewhere on the periphery. I simply followed, stopped when Odufuwa stopped, touched the roses at the stalk where she had briefly sniffed them, brushed the croton

101

with my hand where her sleeve had brushed. Then from nowhere came Jamani to ruin it all, not so much walking as preening and turning cartwheels, leaping out in front, falling behind only to re-emerge far ahead of the evening strollers. I watched his antics with an older brother's indulgent amusement.

Mrs Odufuwa turned round, looked at me and said, 'Lagilagi, I understand you work as hard on these flowers as your father.'

I savoured the moment, rolling the sound of her voice all over again through my head. Then came Joseph's jarring voice saying,

'Which Lagilagi? You shouldn't call him that name again Madam. He cannot *la* anything. He is so lazy he can't move a fly off his nose until it has begun to produce maggots.'

First, I wondered how Joseph, a Benin, had suddenly picked up such earthy Yoruba argot. He was *kobokobo*,* still spoke Yoruba with his individual quaintness even after several years with us. Yet there he was tongue-bashing me in true Yoruba market style without any strain. And for no reason. I stared at him, open-mouthed.

'Is that true, my Lagilagi?'

Dipo came bounding in view and Joseph pointed at him. 'Look at his brother, almost three years his junior. He is far tougher than the one you've named Lagilagi. I bet Dipo can already lift that axe and split wood with it.'

I moved forward without one moment's hesitation, lifted the axe and stuck it in a nearby log.

Then Wild Christian joined in. 'All he does is sneak off into corners by himself—reading, always reading. He pretends to be busy with books because he cannot tackle anything else.'

I was hurt. What had I done? Why did they try to reduce me in the eye of my future wife? I looked from one to the other and they were grinning, laughing at me.

Nubi emerged from nowhere. Something was building up, something prepared outside of me, yet I was at the centre of it. Nubi now said,

'If he sees a fight he will run. He cries when he is touched as if everyone wants to beat him.' She sniggered. 'Hm, who wants to commit murder? If you touch him he will faint, then die altogether of fright. Me? No thank you, let him run under the skirts of his books.'

*Rude expression for those who do not speak the local language.

102

Who were they talking about, I wondered. Everything said around me sounded like the findings of a serious study, so they could only be talking about someone and of specific deeds, or non-deeds. That someone appeared to be me yet I could not recognize myself in what they said. Joseph suddenly stopped Dipo mid-somersault and held him, turned his head to face me:

'I bet Dipo can give him a thorough beating.'

'Of course he can,' said Wild Christian. 'He'll beat him until he begs for mercy.'

My only concern was to see what Mrs Odufuwa was making of this. Did she believe any of it? She stood with her husband beside the dwarf guava tree with a puzzled smile on her face, and I only thought how unfair it was to subject her to such an unbecoming spectacle.

Nubi suggested, 'Why don't we see for ourselves? Dipo will beat him soundly.'

Dipo, never one to resist any invitation to action, began to square his little fists. He struck a fighting pose and leapt from side to side in a war-dance all his own creation. I had never seen such excitement on his face! Cheers rang out from all sides while I stood limply, patronizingly amused by his antics. He was like a gnome, so frisky and so full of joy at being alive and among attentive grown-ups. But then, with no warning at all, only the sound of Joseph's 'Come on Dipo, show him,' this compact little creature launched himself at me, fists flying. I was borne backwards by the sheer weight of the charge and could no longer separate the different causes of the ringing in my ears.

From far distances I heard voices, protests, admonitions. Time had passed, how much time I did not know. There was a period of total emptiness in which I remembered nothing, only a storm of rage in my veins. But now I felt hands under my arms, strong hands, desperate, even trembling hands under my arms against which I struggled with equal desperation. Then I recognized Joseph's voice:

'Wole, o to, o to?* Do you want to kill him?' spoken with his quaint Benin accent.

And Wild Christian's voice, more soothing and disturbed than I had ever heard it, 'Wole, we were only teasing you. You should have remembered that he is only your junior brother. Ah ah, whatever it was, you should not have got violent with him.'

*Enough, that will do.

The skies fell on me. I shivered so violently that Wild Christian put her hand on my forehead and looked anxious. In the background were Dipo's howls. He had been carried into the dining-room where he was now being consoled with sweets and fruit juice. Wild Christian turned her head towards the sound and once again, a strange look came into her eyes. There was such deep pain and confusion, there was fright also, I thought. Anyway it was a different mother from whatever it was I last saw in her.

'But why?' she repeated, more to herself. 'It was all a joke. Did you want to kill him? He's only a baby you know, you shouldn't have taken him so seriously.'

Dipo's howls had gone down, and Joseph came out. It could have been my imagination, but I felt that he deliberately gave me a wide berth. His words however left him in no doubt about how he felt. To ensure that he was at his most cutting, he did not even design to address me directly; indeed I now understood why he had cut such a wide curve around me. 'I suppose,' he said to no one in particular, 'the big brother is feeling pleased with himself. I don't even know why we bothered. We should have let him kill his own brother, which was what he wanted.' He let out a deliberately prolonged hiss, 'Shee-aaw? Some people don't even know how to conduct themselves as elders.'

Wild Christian shushed him, but I saw no difference in both their attitudes. I was overwhelmed by only one fact—there was neither justice nor logic in the world of grown-ups. I had imagined that I was the aggrieved one. What did occur I still was not sure of, beyond the fact that I had come to being violently prised off a squawking bundle that was my brother. But I also recollected clearly enough that I had not provoked the situation. I had joined the others in enjoying the clowning of Dipo—until he launched himself at me like a rocket. Where was I at fault? Still, I was faced with the fact—the entire world was united in finding me guilty of attempted fratricide, and there was nowhere I could seek redress.

Whatever it was all about, it was enough for Wild Christian to exert herself to make me understand something in connection with the episode. After the normal evening prayers she called me into the bedroom and, as she usually did over any trivial to critical problem with a child, made me kneel and pray especially with her. Then she spoke to me. There were warnings on the dangers of allowing the devil to come between one and his natural love and care for the rest

104

of the family. It was so easy to be possessed by the devil, she said. The phrase, *emi esu* occurred repeatedly and I really began to wonder if I had not truly become possessed by the soul of the devil. There was that 'black-out' period of which I remembered little.

Dipo was a favourite of both Tinu and me. His energy and humour left us constantly entertained. Moreover, he was considered not yet old enough for punishment, so we foisted on him many of our own mischiefs. He was always ready to own up to breaking a vase which Tinu or I had knocked down in a fight or admit to leaving a door ajar which let in the goats. Later, as he became wiser, he demanded payment for his services—a piece of meat, a toffee or an extra piece of yam. He became so adept at extracting payment—preferably in advance—that we decided that he would end up in charge of Wild Christian's shop and be gaoled for profiteering. Could that Dipo have angered me so much that I no longer knew what I was doing? The thought was deeply alarming.

From Joseph and the others I eventually gathered that I continued hitting him long after he was down, crying, and beyond defending himself. I denied this heatedly. But then, there was that *emi esu* which Wild Christian tried to exorcise with her constant prayers; could this really take a child over without his knowing? If only there was a way of sensing when one was being taken over, one could take necessary precautions. I had long lost faith in the efficacy of Wild Christian's prayers. There were several of her wards over whom she prayed night and day. She took them into the church and prayed over them, found any excuse, any opportunity at all to drag them before the altar and pray over them. They continued to steal, lie, fight or do whatever it was she prayed against. The scale of such perversity, it seemed, must be beyond the remedy of prayers since the two had the entire church to themselves and God was not being distracted by other voices from that same direction. I had no doubt that prayers worked for Wild Christian herself, she seemed to thrive on it and she claimed her prayers were always answered. It was different for the rest of us who had allowed entry to *emi esu*, and there was little even she could do about it.

I resolved to guard against it in the future, at least, to guard against what seemed a kind of blacked-out violence. And indeed, a less distressing explanation surfaced in my mind: that I had merely lashed out against the whole world of tormentors and that Dipo had been unlucky to time his war-dance for that moment. There was another solace. I waited with some anxiety for the moment when Essay would be given a report of the event, but he never was. On the contrary I obtained a distinct feeling that every care was taken to ensure that he was kept in ignorance of what had occurred.

VIII

Workmen came into the house. They knocked lines of thin nails with narrow clasps into walls. The lines turned with corners and doorways and joined up with outside wires which were strung across poles. The presence of these workmen reminded me of another invasion. At the end of those earlier activities we no longer needed the oil-lamps, kerosene lanterns and candles, at least not within the house. We pressed down a switch and the room was flooded with light. Essay's instructions were strict—only he, or Wild Christian could give the order for the pressing of those switches. I recalled that it took a while to connect the phenomenon of the glowing bulb with the switch, so thoroughly did Essay keep up the deception. He pretended it was magic, he easily directed our gaze at the glass bulb while he muttered his magic spell. Then he solemnly intoned:

'Let there be light.'

Afterwards he blew in the direction of the bulb and the light went out.

But finally, we caught him out. It was not too difficult to notice that he always stood at the same spot, that that spot was conveniently near a small white-and-black object which had sprouted on the wall after the workmen had gone. Still, the stricture continued. The magic light was expensive and must be wisely used.

Now the workmen were threading the walls again, we wondered what the new magic would produce. This time there was no bulb, no extra switches on the wall. Instead, a large wooden box was brought into the house and installed at the very top of the tallboy, displacing the old gramophone which now had to be content with one of the lower shelves on the same furniture. The face of the box appeared to be made of thick plaited silk.

But the functions continued to be the same. True, there was no need to put on a black disc, no need to crank a handle or change a needle, it only required that the knob be turned for sounds to come on. Unlike the gramophone however, the box could not be made to speak or sing at any time of the day. It began its monologue early in

107

the morning, first playing 'God save The King' The box went silent some time in the afternoon, resumed late afternoon, then, around ten or eleven in the evening, sang 'God Save the King' once more and went to sleep.

Because the box spoke incessantly and appeared to have no interest in a response, it soon earned the name *As'oromagb'esi.** An additional line was added to a jingle which had been formed at the time of the arrival of electricity. Belatedly, that jingle had also done honour to Lagos where the sacred monopoly of the umbrella by royalty had first been broken;

Elektiriki ina oba
Umbrella el'eko
As'oromagb'esi, iro oyinbo* *

At certain set hours, the box delivered THE NEWS. The News soon became an object of worship to Essay and a number of his friends. When the hour approached, something happened to this club. It did not matter what they were doing, they rushed to our house to hear the Oracle. It was enough to watch Essay's face to know that the skin would be peeled off the back of any child who spoke when he was listening to The News. When his friends were present, the parlour with its normal gloom resembled a shrine, rapt faces listened intently, hardly breathing. When The Voice fell silent all faces turned instinctively to the priest himself. Essay reflected for a moment, made a brief or long comment and a babble of excited voices followed.

The gramophone fell into disuse. The voices of Denge, Ayinde Bakare, Ambrose Campbell; a voice which was so deep that I believed it could only have been produced by a special trick of His Master's Voice, but which father assured me belonged to a black man called Paul Robeson—they all were relegated to the cocoon of dust which gathered in the gramophone section. Christmas carols, the songs of Marian Anderson; oddities, such as a record in which a man did nothing but laugh throughout, and the one concession to a massed choir of European voices—the Hallelujah Chorus—all were permanently interned in the same cupboard. Now voices sang, unasked, from the new box. Once that old friend the Hallelujah

*One who speaks without expecting a reply.
* *Electricity, government light
  Umbrella, for the Lagos elite
  Rediffusion, white man's lies.

Chorus burst through the webbed face of the box and we had to concede that it sounded richer and fuller than the old gramophone had ever succeeded in rendering it. Most curious of all the fare provided by the radio however were the wranglings of a family group which were relayed every morning, to the amusement of a crowd, whose laughter shook the box. We tried to imagine where this took place. Did this family go into the streets to carry on their interminable bickering or did the idle crowd simply hang around their home, peeping through the windows and cheering them on? We tried to imagine any of the Aké families we knew exposing themselves this way—the idea was unthinkable. It was some time, and only by listening intently before I began to wonder if this daily affair was that dissimilar from the short plays which we sometimes acted in school on prize-giving day. And I began also to respond to the outlandish idiom of their humour.

Hitler monopolized the box. He had his own special programme and somehow, far off as this war of his whim appeared to be, we were drawn more and more into the expanding arena of menace. Hitler came nearer home every day. Before long the greeting, Win-The-War replaced some of the boisterous exchanges which took place between Essay and his friends. The local barbers invented a new style which joined the repertory of Bentigo, Girls-Follow-Me, Oju-Aba, Missionary Cut and others. The women also added Win-de-woh to their hair-plaits, and those of them who presided over the local food-stalls used it as a standard response to complaints of a shortage in the quantity they served. Essay and his correspondents vied with one another to see how many times the same envelope could be used between them. Windows were blacked over, leaving just tiny spots to peep through, perhaps in order to obtain an early warning when Hitler came marching up the path. Household heads were dragged to court and fined for showing a naked light to the night. To reinforce the charged atmosphere of expectations, the first aeroplane flew over Abeokuta; it had a heavy drone which spoke of Armageddon and sent Christians fleeing into churches to pray and stay the wrath of God. Others simply locked their doors and windows and waited for the end of the world. Only those who had heard about these things, and flocks of children watched in fascination, ran about the fields and the streets, following the flying miracle as far as they could, shouting greetings, waving to it long after it had gone and returning home to await its next advent.

One morning The News reported that a ship had blown up in Lagos harbour taking some of its crew with it. The explosion had rocked the island, blown out windows and shaken off roofs. The lagoon was in flames and Lagosians lined the edges of the lagoon, marvelling at the strange omen—tall fires leaping frenziedly on the surface of water. Hitler was really coming close. No one however appeared to be very certain what to do when he finally appeared.

There was one exception: Paa Adatan. Every morning, Paa Adatan appeared in front of Wild Christian's shop opposite the Aafin, before whose walls he passed the entire day. Strapped to his waist was a long cutlass in its scabbard, and belts of amulets. A small Hausa knife, also in its sheath, was secured to his left arm above the elbow ,and on his fingers were blackened twisted wire and copper rings—we knew they were of different kinds—*onde*, *akaraba* and others. If Paa Adatan slapped an opponent with one of his hands, that man would fall at his feet and foam at the mouth. The other hand was reserved for situations where he was outnumbered. It only required that Paa Adatan slap one or more of his attackers and they would fall to fighting among themselves. The belt of amulets ensured of course that any bullet would be deflected from him, returning to hit the marksman at the very spot on his body where he had thought to hit the immortal warrior of Adatan.

Paa Adatan patrolled the Aafin area, furious that no one would take him into the Army and send him to confront Hitler, personally, and end the war once and for all.

'Ah, Mama Wole, this English people just wan' the glory for den self. Den no wan' blackman to win dis war and finish off dat non-sense-yeye Hitler one time! Now look them. Hitler dey bombing us for Lagos already and they no fit defend we.' He spat his red kola-nut juice on the ground, raging,

'When dey come Mama, dem go know say there be black man medicine. I go pile dem corpse alongside the wall of dis palace, dem go know say we done dey fight war here, long time before dey know wetin be war for den foolish land. Oh er . . . Mama,' he rummaged deep in the pouches of his clothing, 'Mama Wole, I forget bring my purse enh, look, big man like myself, I forget my purse for house. And I no chop at all at all since morning time . . .'

A penny changed hands, Paa Adatan saluted, drew out his sword and drew a line on the ground around the shop frontage. 'Dat na in case they come while I dey chop my eba for buka. If they try cross this

110

line, guns go turn to broom for dem hand. Dem go begin dey sweeping dis very ground till I come back. Make dem try am make I see.'

I followed Paa Adatan once to watch him at breakfast. The foodseller already knew what he wanted and set before him four leaf-wrapped mounds of eba, lots of stew and one solitary piece of meat which sat like a half-submerged island in the middle of the stew. Paa Adatan left the meat untouched until he had demolished this prodigious amount of eba, each morsel larger than anything I could eat for an entire meal. Halfway through, the stew had dried up. Paa Adatan hemmed and hawed, but the woman took no notice. Finally,

'Hm. Iyawo.'

Silence.

'Iyawo.'

The food-seller spun round angrily. 'You want to ruin me. Everyday the same thing. If everybody swallowed the stew the way you do, how do you think a food-seller can make a living from selling eba?'

'Ah, no vex for me Iyawo. But na Win-de-war amount of stew you give me today.'

She spun round on her stool, ladle ready filled, and slopped its contents into his dish. 'Only na you dey complain. Same thing every day.'

'Good bless you, god bless you. Na dis bastard Hitler. When war finish you go see. You go see me as I am, a man of myself.'

The woman sniffed, accustomed to the promise. Paa Adatan set to, finished the remaining mounds, then held up the piece of meat and suddenly threw it into his mouth, snatching at it with his teeth like a dog at whom a lump of raw meat had been thrown. His jaw and neck muscles tensed as he chewed on the meat, banged on the low table and issued his challenge:

'Let him come! Make him step anywhere near this palace of Alake and that is how I go take in head for my mouth and bite am off.'

He rose, adjusted the rope which strung his trousers and turned to leave.

'By the way Iyawo, make you no worry for dem if den come, I don taking your buka for my protection—Aafin, de shop of Headmaster in wife, Centenary Hall, my friend the barber in shop and that cigarette shop of Iya Aniwura. If any of Hitler man come near any of you, he will smell pepper. Tell them na dis me Papa Adatan talk am!'

Head erect, chest defiant, he resumed his patrol.

One day, a convoy of army trucks stopped by the road, just in front of the row of shops which included ours. Instantly children and women fled in all directions, mothers snatching up their and others' toddlers who happened to be by. The men retreated into shops and doorways and peeped out, prepared for the worst, ready to run or beg for their lives. These were not the regular soldiers who were stationed at Lafenwa barracks. They were the notorious 'Bote', recognizable by their caps. They were said to come from the Congo, and were reputed wild and lawless. People claimed that they descended on shops, took what they needed and left without paying, abducted women and children—raping the former and eating the latter. To call a man Bote became an unpardonable insult; to await their approach was the height of folly.

I was in the shop with Wild Christian who of course had no interest in the Botes' reputation. As every other shop in the vicinity had either shut its doors or been abandoned, they made for ours and asked to purchase the items they required—biscuits, cigarettes, tinned foods, bottled drinks and sweets. I climbed up to take down jars from the shelves, handed them down to Wild Christian. Suddenly I heard a sound which could only be defined as the roar of a dozen outraged lions. Through the space between the soldiers' heads and the top of the wide door I saw the figure of Paa Adatan, his face transfigured by a set, do-or-die expression. He was naked to the waist, his usual bulbous trousers had been pulled up from the calves and tucked into his trouser-band. In one hand I beheld the drawn sword, in the other, a *serę** into which he muttered, then waved it round in a slow circle before him.

The soldiers turned, stared, and looked at one another.

Wild Christian had heard and recognized the cause of the commotion but was paying it no heed.

Paa Adatan cursed them. 'Bastards! Beasts of no nation! Bote Banza. You no better pass Hitler. Commot for that shop make you fight like men!'

The soldiers did not appear to understand a word, but the gestures could not be mistaken. They whispered among themselves in their

* A mini-gourd with magical powers.

112

strange language, raised their eyebrows and shrugged their shoulders. Then they turned back into the shop and continued with their purchases. Three or four sat on the pavement before the shop and watched.

Wild Christian, her view blocked by the soldiers, could not see Paa Adatan at all. At the intensification of Paa Adatan's curses, she grew worried, asked me what was happening.

'He is dancing now,' I reported.

Paa Adatan had indeed begun a war-dance. He sang at the top of his voice,

> Ogun Hitila d' Aké
> Eni la o pa Bote*

Some of the soldiers stayed on to watch him while others continued to buy up every eatable item in the shop. Wild Christian inflated the prices by at least twice what she normally charged, but they did not mind at all. On the contrary, they even gave me a packet of their own biscuits which were thick, sweet and crunchy. We spoke in sign language throughout, with plenty of smiling, shrugging and hand-waving.

The trouble began when they attempted to leave. Paa Adatan stopped singing, drew a line across the ground and dared them to step over it. He himself retreated some way back from the line, leapt up and made a wild rush at the line, sword outstretched, came to an abrupt stop at the line—on one leg—rocked his body for some moments on the leg, spun round and returned to starting-point from where he repeated the process over and over again.

The soldiers were now bewildered. Wild Christian finally pushed her way out, remonstrated with Paa Adatan.

'Enough Paa, enough! They are our friends. You are stopping them from going to fight Hitler.'

'Dey be Bote,' Paa Adatan replied. 'They and Hitler na the same. Look them. Cowards!' He shook his serę at them. 'Put down those goods wey you tief or I go give you message take go Hitler.'

It was all over a short while later. Two of the soldiers left in the trucks had crept up behind Paa Adatan. They seized his arms from behind and disarmed him both of sword and serę, pinioned his arms to his sides. Paa Adatan fought back like the true warrior he was. He

---

*Hitler's war arrives in Aké.
Today we shall kill these Bote.

threw them off, fought through the wave of bodies that engulfed him, bore them to the ground with him and continued to struggle. No blows appeared to be struck, it was all wrestling, and a titanic struggle it proved. Paa Adatan fought like one who knew that the entire safety of Aké resided in his arms, legs and torso. He was a rugged terrain which had to be captured, then secured tree by tree, hill by hill, boulder by boulder. They sat on each limb, breathing and perspiring heavily, shouting orders and curses in their strange language. Then they brought some rope and bound him. Even then, he did not give in.

The soldiers then stood in a circle, wiping off perspiration and watching him. They marvelled, shook their heads, looked for some explanation from all the faces that had emerged one by one from shops, windows, nooks and corners after Paa Adatan had begun his act. No one however could speak to them, though some nodded affirmation when a soldier turned to the watchers, touched a finger to his head and raised his eyebrows.

Paa Adatan, in his bonds, struggled to a sitting position, looked at his captors and shook his head.

'O ma se o.* The glory of Egbaland is lay low inside dust.'

Some *ogboni* were now seen rushing from the palace, having heard of the incident. Their appearance seemed to convey to the soldiers some semblance of authority so, with signs and gestures, they transferred all responsibility for Paa Adatan to them, handed over his sword and *sere* and climbed back into their lorries and drove off.

A debate then began. Should the police be called? Was it safe to untie Paa Adatan? Should he be transferred to the Mental Hospital at Aro? They argued at the top of their voices while Paa Adatan sat in his bonds, impassive.

Finally, Wild Christian had had enough. She left her shop and calling on me to help her we began to untie Paa Adatan's bonds. There were immediate cries of fear and protest but we ignored them. One of the men made to restrain her physically. She rose, drew up her body to its fullest height and dared him to touch her just once more. I bristled to her side and called the man names which would have earned me an immediate slap from Wild Christian in other circumstances. An ogboni chief intervened however, told the man off

*How pitiful!

114

and himself completed the task of loosening the remaining knots in the ropes.

Paa Adatan, freed, rose slowly. The crowd retreated several steps. He stretched out his hand for his sword and replaced it in his scabbard. Next he took his *sẹrẹ*, dropped it on the ground and crushed it with his heel. The explosion was loud; it startled the watchers who moved even further back, frightened. He walked slowly away. He moved with a sad, quiet dignity. He walked in the direction of Iporo, vanished bit by bit as the road dipped downwards before it turned sharply away, round the Centenary Hall. I never saw him again.

About this time also, another feature of our lives disappeared for ever. Essay and Wild Christian collected strays. It seemed a permanent aspect of our life at Aké; with very few lapses, there was always an adult who appeared without warning seemingly from nowhere, became part of our lives and then disappeared with no explanation from anyone. Sometimes it would happen that mother had something to do with the sudden evaporation of Essay's strays.

Wild Christian stayed at her shop most of the day and, for some of Essay's strays, this was the sensible period to descend on their protector and friend. Before she left she ensured that her husband's breakfast was on the table—*akara* balls and *ogi*; *moin-moin* and *agidi*; bread, omelette and tea; or boiled yams and omelette or fish stew—one or more of these combinations served for breakfast. But the real treat was that rarest of delicacies—*leki*—made of crushed and skinned black-eyed beans and melon-seed oil, a teaspoonful of which, in the sharing, could cause week-long hostilities in the household. I had a place of observation between the legs of the tallboy. It was understood in the household that when I occupied that position, I took care of his plate and whatever was left in it. The dish itself was, however, sacrosanct. That is, until You-Mean-Mayself entered the household.

We all became practised in his unique accent and would entertain ourselves and Wild Christian with mimicries that sent her friends falling over with laughter. Strangely enough, I considered Mayself's incursion into our lives sufficient compensation for the diminution of those choice morsels which father left on his plate, whenever he observed me with my eyes fastened on his jaw movements from between the legs of the tallboy. There was an emotional wrench when

115

the dish was *leki* but generally, Mayself's constant replenishment of our repertoire of his vocal nuances and eyelid flutter more than made up for it. Tinu and I, the cousins, and later even Dipo vied for honours in reproducing his variations on the reaction of startled surprise to a normal hospitable question:

'Have you had your breakfast?'

'Mayself? Nyou.'

He was short, rather light-complexioned and had a small, box-like head. HM's regimen was to go to the school to conduct the opening, then return home for a leisurely breakfast. By then, Wild Christian would be in her shop. Mayself was at the house either before my father went off to school or was home awaiting his return. He sat in the chair below the porcelain clock in the front room, picked up a magazine or a book and browsed. When mother was out of town, he would arrive even earlier, perhaps while my father was doing his exercises in the room. We hid our giggles from HM, knowing very well what would be the consequences of making fun of a guest. Later of course, we mimicked him openly.

Eventually, from his bedroom, the bathroom, his stroll in the garden or from school, father would return, greet his guest courteously and go about his business. There were times, especially during the holidays when he breakfasted late, sat a long time at his front-room desk to finish some work, then proceeded to a breakfast already turned cold. He chatted sometimes with his guest, engaged in some mild-to-passionate debate on the politics of the day, the news and rumours of war or some local agitation. We waited. Sometimes, tired of waiting for Mayself's act we sent someone to remind Essay that his breakfast was ready. Or to ask if his *ogi* or bean pottage should be re-heated. We never doubted that he knew the reasons for our solicitude, nevertheless he reacted normally, inquired what there was for breakfast, then, before issuing instructions for extra *moin-moin* or *akara* to be placed on the table, he turned to his guest and enquired:

'Have you had your breakfast?'

Mayself's face then rose from the journal in which he had buried it during Essay's planning of breakfast. He looked up, startled, stared at first in any direction except the one from which the question had so clearly emanated. Suddenly he realized his mistake, turned to the questioner, registered visibly that the question had, surprisingly, been directed at him. There followed a quick intake of breath as the novelty of the question, one which could never before have been pronounced in his hearing, etched a huge surprise on his face. Only then came the predictable, ritual answer:

'Oh, you-mean-mayself? Ny-ou.'

The first section emerged clipped in spite of a full exaggeration of the vowels. The second, the "Ny-ou" by contrast, which faded into an upper register, was like the mewing of our cat and it was this I think which sent us into paroxysms of laughter, burying our faces in cushions of armchairs behind which we were hidden. You-mean-mayself resumed his browsing, father his work until the supplemented breakfast was announced. Essay then rose, paused for him, and they proceeded solemnly into the dining-room where, displaying every sign of being as fastidious an eater as his host, Mayself nevertheless proceeded to eradicate any ideas in our minds that elegance of table manners was necessarily inimical to a hearty appetite—a fallacy into which we had fallen from Essay's own eating patterns. Then again I would wonder if it was worth it, this ephemeral entertainment, especially on days when the price was a loss of left-overs in the shape of bean-paste in melon-seed oil!

Wild Christian habitually served out both man and wife portions in the same dish even when she would eat separately. She had an aesthetic feel for food; certain dishes went with certain foods and, for *leki* she always used a coracle-shaped, flowery porcelain of a near-luminous whiteness. She piled it about three-quarters high, carefully wiped the edges of any smear before sending it to the table. Since she had to be at the shop early she had her breakfast sent on to her, her *real* breakfast, that is. For Wild Christian took no chances with her stomach. She began the day with a kind of tasting-breakfast, a pre-breakfast which matched, in quantity, what my father would eat for the entire morning. The maid then prepared her real breakfast according to her instructions. About two hours later came what could be called her elevenses, a sort of Consolidation Snack. This consisted of whatever was left in the dishes from father's breakfast, plus anything that caught her fancy from nearby foodsellers. On *leki* days she looked heartily forward to the Consolidation Snack.

Alas, one day there was no Consolidation Snack. Mayself had seen to it.

Until now You-mean-mayself had been a joke. Wild Christian had still to meet him, being kept from home by her shop, debt-collecting, purchasing trips both within and out of town. Our portrayal of him became so much part of household life that Wild Christian would even call Essay to come and watch his children perform. Now it was different. Wild Christian was patient. She raised the matter in her usual innocent manner; a wife whose domestic routine had been disturbed, merely wanted to enquire what might have caused such a thing. Half-way through supper she said,

'I hope the *leki* was all right this morning?''

That morning, father had returned from school only to be summoned back before he could begin his breakfast. He left his guest at the table who then proceeded to finish the *leki* to the last lick. An outraged Nubi reported this gluttonous limit to Wild Christian.

HM had not even known what was served for breakfast. ''Oh, was it *leki*? I had the children prepare me something. I had to rush back to school . . .'

She pretended surprise. 'But how stupid of them. The *leki* was there all the time. Joseph!'

Joseph ran in. 'Joseph, where is the breakfast I prepared for your father? Why wasn't it placed on the table?'

Against father's 'Em-em-em-em-em' Nubi's voice rang out, 'We put it on the table, Ma. Papa's guest ate it all.'

Her eyes rounded. 'Oh? You didn't tell me you had a guest dear. I would have prepared some more.'

'Oh it's all right. I was no longer hungry when I returned anyway.'

They continued with supper. Some moments later she asked, 'Who was he dear? Is it someone I know?'

'Oh er . . . an old friend. I doubt if you've met.'

She shook her head good-humouredly. 'He must be a very strange friend. Do you mean a friend ate all your breakfast and left you nothing.'

'Oh it didn't matter.' Essay tried to shrug it off. 'The children prepared something for me.'

Wild Christian was too shrewd to pursue the matter further. But she had given notice. When she was ready, she would deal with that inconsiderate friend.

He became a fixture during the mid-year holiday. The rains provided sufficient excuse—not that he needed any—sometimes it would rain without once stopping for weeks. No one would dream of turning out a guest in such weather, anyway Mayself was not very anxious to leave. He began to stay for lunch, then dinner whenever mother travelled anywhere or was not back in time for Essay's dinner.

But matters came to a head, finally.

Wild Christian had served lunch both for Essay, herself, and allowed for the unexpected guest or two. Mayself was no longer regarded by us as a guest so that when she was confronted by empty dishes and she asked what guests had called on Essay, we replied truthfully, None. Essay was not yet home.

'Are you children trying to tell me that your father ate all the food in these dishes by himself?' she threatened.

Eyebrows raised in the Mayself surprise curve, we chorused, 'Papa himself? Ny-ou.'

'I see.' sighed Wild Christian. 'So it's him again.

And we went into a performance of the latest variations.

'Are you ready for some lunch?'

'Mayself? Oh, net reilly. But perhaps you are . . .'

'In that case let's have some lunch.'

'Oh er . . . yes Headmaster.'

'Would you like some supper?'

'Mayself . . . oh er . . . net unless . . .'

'I'll just see what the children have set up . . .'

But Wild Christian was no longer amused. We saw the battle-light in her eyes and felt a twinge of pity for Mayself who had permitted a touch of greed to ruin the real pleasure we derived from his presence in the house. It was now a little more than the fact that this guest deprived her even of her own specialities. Essay, she knew, was a spare eater and an exceedingly polite host; it followed therefore that he was not getting enough to eat. At their next meal-time together she glanced at father and asked,

'But dear, are you sure you are getting enough to eat?'

'Of course. Do I look underfed?'

'No but . . . Well, I want to make you that kind of yam pottage you like so much tomorrow. What do you think?'

'Which one is that?'

'Made with *ororo* and a bit runny. And of course I'll use some of that smoked pork Father has just sent us from Isara . . .'

'Oh yes, yes.'

'Dear are you listening? I want to be sure you get enough of it to eat.'

'Of course. Why not? I'm not going anywhere tomorrow. Yes, a good idea.'

A short silence. She moved closer to the bone. 'Are you expecting visitors tomorrow at lunch?'

119

Our whisper was deliberately audible: 'Mayself? Ny-ou.' HM pretended he had heard nothing.

'No-o-o. No. Mr Adelu might call of course but . . . No, I'm not expecting anyone.'

'Well, if you do have anyone at lunchtime could you send for me at the shop? I mean you could always have something else in the afternoon and reserve the pottage for the evening. I am making it specially, and it is, after all, Father's smoked pork from Isara.'

'Yes, yes, by all means. As you like.'

She plotted it all with Nubi. As soon as Mayself arrived Nubi ran to inform her and took mother's place in the shop. That day, we waited in the front room assiduously engaged in studies. Not a page was turned over. Wild Christian arrived. Mayself leapt up from his chair, the model of old-world courtesy. He bowed low over her hand:

'Gyud meerning Madam.'

Thin-smiling, Madam exchanged courtesies. Essay, on the other side of the table, smothered a very fractional smile; he was intuitive about plots. We guessed he would simply let matters take their course.

'I thought I would come and see to your pottage myself,' she explained. 'These children might spoil it and Father did send that delicacy specially for you.'

'But the shop . . .?'

'Oh, Nubi can handle most things now. In any case today is a slack day, with all this rain. I'll just go and get it ready.'

Not a flicker of anticipation betrayed Mayself's interest in the conversation, his face remained buried in the book in deep concentration. Under the desk we pinched one another. What strategy had she decided on?

The bustle and smell of preparations reached us in the front room but it was doubtful if any mouth among ours watered that day Heads bent resolutely down, our eyes were nevertheless fixed on the little man before us. At long last the voice from the kitchen rang in summons:

'Woleee.'

'Ma.'

I received nudges as I squeezed past others, each saying, this is it. When I reached the dining-room I saw that the table was already laid—for two. There was also a small tray containing a small saucer of biscuits, and a glass.

'Go and ask the gentleman whether he prefers ginger-ale or orange squash.'

I did as I was told. This time his surprise was genuine.

'Mayself? Eouh, derzn matter. Tell madam anything thank you.'

So Wild Christian chose for him. As she handed me the tray she herself prepared to follow. That puzzled me. Mayself again sprung to attention. I lay the tray down on the table beside him.'

'Oh Medm is so kind, so kind. And you must help me thank Headmaster too. Mr Soyinka is really most hospitable, a real gentleman if I may say so.'

She smiled sweetly. 'Please don't mention it.'

'Oh but I must, I must. A very kind soul, his qualities are very rare.'

Mother indulged him with some further five minutes of pleasantries, then interrupted: 'I hope you will excuse him just for a short while . . .'

'Of course madam of course . . .'

'Some rather important family matters have come up . . .'

'Oooh, ooh . . .'

'Family problems.' She smiled, then looked at father. 'Dear, I know you are busy today so perhaps we can discuss things over your lunch.'

I had regained my seat by then. A cousin wrote in his notebook—10/10—grading her performance as superlative, a verdict which we all endorsed. Essay rose, acknowledging defeat and murmured an Excuse me. Mayself sprang to his feet—Quite, quite—and did not resume his seat until they had both passed from the room.

She kept Essay in the dining room for nearly two hours, bringing up every possible subject under the earth. Mayself munched his biscuits with his habitual daintiness, yet they disappeared with that contradicting speed whose mechanics remained a mystery we tried to solve long after Mayself had disappeared from our lives. He did not of course give up so readily. He turned up again the following day and the day after, but his adversary had left instructions and she would be summoned. She entered the house from then on through the backdoor so that the first intimation that Mayself had of her presence was her voice summoning one of us. That presaged the arrival of a tray of biscuits and orange juice. She no longer turned up in the front room at all but simply sent word to father to 'spare her a moment'. Mayself's conduct was correct to the last, profuse in his

121

thanks, yet partaking of what hospitality he received as a pleasant incident in his life. He disappeared finally, and the house became the poorer for his absence.

The first we knew of the existence of our Uncle Dipo was when a smart-looking bespectacled man in army officer's uniform came upon us unannounced in the yard. We fled. Nothing like it had ever happened and, with all the war alarms, there was little doubt in anyone's minds that Hitler had indeed arrived and was about to ship us off into slavery. Essay had travelled out of town. Wild Christian was at her shop; neither had warned us of an impending visitor. We did not hear him come through the front door, the front room and the parlour, so we scattered to Upper Backyard, barricaded ourselves in the storeroom, others in the latrine. Two cousins and I raced up the ladder and threw ourselves flat on the roof, ready to dive over into the street on the other side if Hitler pursued up there. We did nothing of the sort for the moment however. Instead we dragged on our bellies until we could look over the other edge of the roof into the yard.

The stranger did not give chase. Instead he remained on the spot and seemed to sway a little. His eyes appeared to be fused with his spectacles so that what struck me most was that his face glowed centrally through a pair of head lamps, like a motor-car. His gentle, swaying motion added to his air of the unreal, and I began to change my opinion about his real identity; I now thought that he was perhaps a ghost. And then he raised his head, rocked forwards and backwards with a more distinct motion and exploded:

'Bastards! Where are they?'

The stranger moved forward and there was no longer any room for error; we had seen a few drunks before. Hitler, ghost or the devil himself, the stranger was clearly drunk. He moved forward, coming up the yard in the same direction we had fled. His eyes fell then on one of our huge water-pots, buried deep in the ground and partly opened. This was the favourite pot of the house. It was sheltered both by a wall and two luxuriant crotons on either side; at all times of the day, its water was cool and refreshing. The stranger went towards the pot, swayed, unbuttoned his fly and began to urinate in it.

Cries of outrage were torn from me and the two cousins who, from our vantage point had witnessed this unspeakable act of desecration. It was wholly outside the range of our imagination. We had seen the

122

occasional guest staggering in the yard from rose-bush to rose-bush, trying to rejoin his companions in the front room through the kitchen-door, even keeling over as he tried to unbutton his flaps in the bathroom. But to urinate in a water-pot!

The next moment we were scaling down the ladder as fast as we had climbed up it. Shouting abuses on him we tugged at him, pummelling him with all our strength. With the one hand which was not busy guiding his member he swiped us off easily,

'Get away from me you Burmese imps!'

It was the first time I had ever heard such an expression, but I did not wait to puzzle out what Burmese imps were. I sprang for his back, landing with such force that it catapulted him forward. The lid of the waterpot was knocked backward and his face went into the pot which was half-empty, the same motion however bounced me over his head so that I landed in a heap and was wedged between the pot and the wall. The cousins had seized hold of one of his legs and were dragging him backwards, screaming for help.

Neighbours arrived almost at the same time as the other children who had hidden in Upper Yard. They saw the uniformed man sprawled over the water-pot and fell back. I had scrambled up from my brief imprisonment and was screaming at the top of my voice:

'It's this Hitler! He is urinating in our pot!'

But Hitler was motionless. When the neighbours finally approached and lifted up his head he had passed clean out. They kept him there and stood guard.

Mother arrived from the shop soon after—someone had sent for her. She recognized the stranger at once and exclaimed,

'But I thought he was still in Burma!'

The neighbours helped to get him to bed, having first chased us off so that he could be made to look decent. Wild Christian shook her head all through supper, refusing to answer our questions beyond saying,

'He is your Uncle. He enlisted over the objections of his entire family——he has always been a wild one.' But she would not tell us his name.

The following morning, by the time we woke up, our Uncle Dipo was already awake. Cleaned, he looked spruce and commanding even in civilian clothes, and was eating breakfast, seated in Essay's chair. When we returned from school, he was gone. To all our questions Wild Christian would only reply that he had returned on leave unexpectedly and had now gone back to his new station. The water-pot was emptied, scrubbed, an entire bottle of Dettol was then scrubbed into it, and the pot neglected for some days. Then it was scrubbed with soap all over again, rinsed out, then left to dry. Only then did it resume its place as the water-cooler of the household, but I never again drank water from it without inwardly grimacing.

Our own Dipo continued to grow in energy and mischief, nothing could daunt him. One day, he vanished. For several hours his absence remained unnoticed. At home, it was mostly thought that he was in the shop with Wild Christian; she of course had no idea that he was anywhere but home. He vanished shortly after breakfast, soon after he had received a few mild strokes for some offence. It was a new world for our brother, this world of beatings, facing the corner, 'stooping down' which required that the culprit stand on one leg and raise the other and stoop over forwards, resting one finger on the ground. The other arm was placed penitently on the curved back. Another favourite punishment was standing up with arms outstretched, parallel to the ground. The cane descended sharply on the knuckles of the miscreant if either arm flagged, just as, in stooping, an attempt to change the leg earned the offender severe strokes on the back. We had a 'cousin' whose offences somehow constantly earned him the stoop. He became so inured to the posture that he sometimes fell asleep under punishment.

Dipo had witnessed every member of the household undergo one form of punishment or another as a matter of course. The beleaguered population of children had trained his innocence to own up to offences which he never committed because he was still too young to be punished. When the induction came, Dipo did not at first realize that it was the end of his immunity; to him, it must have seemed a mistake. Then it happened a few more times and he sensed that the period of charmed existence was gone for ever. Dipo vanished. The household was thrown into turmoil for a few hours before he was brought home by a would-be traveller. Dipo, after roaming through Abeokuta for the greater part of the day had found his way to a motor park. When he tried to board the lorry however, both the driver and the passengers could not help observing that he appeared too young to be travelling by himself. Inquiries began, a policeman was fetched—in the meantime, the child had been tricked out of the park into a nearby shop—finally, Dipo was returned home accompanied by the sympathetic traveller.

124

What either parent made of the adventure we did not know or care; to the rest of the household, Dipo was an instant hero. He looked so vulnerable when he returned in tow of these two adults that my first feeling was one of fright for him. No one looking so defenceless should have been driven to the dangers of such an adventure. Then I took to wondering if our parents would let this affect their over-ready recourse to the cane for every infraction; they did not. As for Dipo, by the following day he was bouncing irrepressibly around as if nothing had ever occurred. No trace of the adventure or its after-effects showed in his demeanour. We began to look on him then as a species of being apart, obviously indestructible. Perhaps a year later, long after the visit of the mystery Uncle, Wild Christian anounced that Dipo's name was to be changed to Femi. She explained that it had been on her mind for some time because children named Dipo always turned out wild and ungovernable. The change of name left us mostly indifferent, but I hid my own astonishment. Once again I felt a helpless confusion—did these grown-ups ever know what they wanted? It did not seem possible that this was the same Wild Christian who had egged on Dipo not so long before, who, with the conniving of Joseph and Nubi had set him on me. Now she was changing his name because he had responded only too well to their own proddings? I mused on the problem for weeks afterwards; each time his new name was called, I was mystified anew.

But the soldier-of-fortune had a name at last. In spite of Wild Christian's careful silence on that theme, I decided that his name could be none other than Dipo. As the new entity, Femi, joined the household, Uncle Dipo joined the procession of strangers who marked our lives with their vivid presence, then departed, never to be seen again. His duration was the briefest, but like a true Dipo, the most sudden and tempestuous.

IX

It was understood in Isara that the children of the Headmaster did not prostrate themselves in greeting; our chaperon always saw to that. The children of Headmaster on arrival for Christmas and New Year had to be taken round to every house whose inmates would be mortally offended otherwise. On the streets we met relations, family friends, gnarled and ancient figures of Isara, chiefs, king-makers, cult priests and priestesses, the elders of *osugbo* who pierced one through and through with their eyes, then stood back to await the accustomed homage. We were introduced—the children of Ayo—at long last we were in one place where Essay's name was called as a matter of course—the children of Ayo, just arrived to celebrate *ọdun*. The elder waited, our chaperon smiled and explained.

'They don't know how to prostrate, please don't take offence.'

Reactions varied. Some were so overawed by these aliens who actually had been heard to converse with their parents in the whiteman's tongue that they quickly denied that they had ever expected such a provincial form of greeting. A smaller number, especially the ancient ones whose skins had acquired the gloss of those dark beaten *ẹtù* *merely drew themselves up higher, snorted and walked away. Later, they would be mollified by the Ọdẹmọ, the titled head of Isara, to whose ears their complaints might come. Perhaps the fact that we were related to this royal house eased their sense of being slighted, we only observed that when we met the same ancients again, they smiled more indulgently, their frowns eased to amused wrinkles at the strange objects whom their own son of the soil had spawned in some far-off land. And perhaps news of an embarrassing encounter at the palace had spread to them.

After church service one Sunday, our first, I accompanied Essay to the Ọdẹmọ's palace. When we came into the parlour, a number of the chiefs were already seated, so were some faces I had never seen before, including a heavily-beaded and coralled stranger, in a

*Locally woven cloth, much valued.

126

wrapper of *aso-oke*, who was very clearly not of Isara. He spoke and acted more like a brother-chief to the most senior of the chiefs, even carried himself as if he was the Odẹmọ's equal.

We entered, the Odẹmọ hoisted me on his knees and asked me a number of questions about school. The usual cries went up 'A-ah ọmọ Soyinka, wa nube wa gbowo'* and they stretched out their hands.

Kabiyesi put me down, I went and shook hands round the assembly. The tall, self-consciously regal man was standing by a cupboard, lazily waving a fan across his face. When I came to him, he looked down on me from his great height and boomed out in so loud a voice that I was rocked backwards on my feet.

'What is this? Ọmọ tani?'**

A chorus of voices replied, 'Ọmọ Soyinka' pointing to my father who was already in close conversation with Odẹmọ. The stranger's lip turned up in a sneer; in the same disorientating boom as before he ordered,

'Dòbalẹ̀!'***

The response from the parlour was good-humoured, bantering . . . of course you don't know, they are these 'ara Egba', the children of Teacher, they don't even know how to prostrate.

The stranger's eyes flashed fire. He looked from me to Essay, to the chiefs, back to me and then to Odẹmọ. 'Why NOT?'

I had recovered from the onslaught of his voice and his truly intimidating presence. In place of it, I felt only a cold resentment of his presence in that place and finally, his choice of Essay as his enemy. I had never given the question of prostration much thought except that, on the red dusty roads of Isara and its frequent dollops of dog and children's faeces, prostration did not seem a very clean form of salutation. I would not, I knew, have minded in the least prostrating to Father, or to the Odẹmọ, or indeed to some of the elders seated in Odẹmọ's reception room or those others who flocked to Father's house to drink their thanks to the gods for our safe arrival. But I would have tried every dodge in the world to avoid prostrating on those streets whose dust stuck to one's clothes, hair, skin, even without dragging oneself on the ground or placing one's nose to a patch of urine, human or canine. To this arrogant stranger however,

* Ah, Son of Soyinka, come over and shake hands.
** Whose child is this?
*** Prostrate youself!

127

not even Essay and his Wild Christian could make me prostrate, even if they had a change of mind!

Coming directly from the Sunday service probably brought the response to my head, certainly it was no justification which I had ever thought out before, or heard used in any argument. I heard myself saying, with a sense of simply pointing out the obvious,

'If I don't prostrate myself to God, why should I prostrate to you? You are just a man like my father aren't you?'

There followed the longest silence I had ever heard in an assembly of grown-ups. Odẹmọ broke the silence with a long-drawn whistle ending by swearing: 'O-o-o-o-o-oro baba o!' And turning to Essay, 'E mi ṣu' wọ re kọ?'*

My father shook his head, gestured with open hands that he had nothing to do with it. Odẹmọ's voice had made me turn to look at him, then round the room at a surprising identity of expressions on the faces of all the guests. Suddenly confused, I fled from the room and ran all the way back home.

At the end of that vacation, Essay decreed that full prostration should commence, not only in Isara, but in our Aké home.

The Odẹmọ visited us frequently at Aké, his visits were one prolonged excitement. Essay was so wrapped up with him that we took the utmost liberties, knowing that he had little time for us. Daodu was one other visitor—except that he never stayed over-night—who earned Essay's undivided attention. To us however, the Odẹmọ was simply Essay's close friend, he meant little else. It was the women traders who brought the flavour, the smell and touch of Isara to Aké. They frequently arrived late at night like a weather-beaten caravan, heavy-laden baskets and fibre sacks on their heads. They were filled with smoked meats, woven cloths and local oint-ments, *gari*, yam flour, even tins of palm oil. They arrived close to midnight, lit their fires in the backyard, cooked and kept to themselves. Wild Christian would take them extra food and Essay would visit them in turn to receive messages and news from home. Their self-containment made a deep impression on us for they made no attempt to become part of the household. Only two of them ever came into the front-room to talk with Essay, and we found out later that they were his aunts. It was incredible that Essay should have aunts, it did not seem possible that he could be encumbered by such

*By my Oro ancestors! Did you teach him that?

128

extra relationships. Anyway, he never called them Auntie.

A new sound would enter the house, the deep dialect of Ijebu, which we did our best to imitate. When Essay conversed with the visitors, we were lucky to understand a sentence or two. They appeared to speak a new language, not the Yoruba we spoke so thoughtlessly. Around their fires in the yard, this sound filled the night like a weird cultic dirge not dissimilar from the chanting of the *ogboni* which sometimes reached our house from their meeting-house at the Aafin. The storehouse in Upper Backyard was cleared out and given over to them for their stay but, unless the weather was bad, they spread their mats out in the open air, and slept.

In the morning they were gone before we woke. They returned with depleted sacks and baskets, all their produce sold in the market for whose day they had timed their arrival. The following day they would visit the shops, buying other forms of goods which they would take back and sell in Isara. They departed at dawn the day after, leaving behind a tang of smoke and indigo.

I had expected to walk to Isara; instead we went to the motor-park with our loads and entered a lorry. The lorry was not bound for Isara however, it stopped at Iperu, leaving the journey uncompleted by some seven miles. After waiting nearly half the day for further transport, Essay decided that we should walk. The luggage was divided up among us and we set off. Only then did I remember why I had imagined that it was a mere casual walk all the way from Abeokuta to Isara—it was what the traders did every market-day! They set out at dawn with their heavy loads and walked the whole day, arriving at our house at night. It did not seem possible! I asked my father if the women had been telling me the truth and he said Yes, they did walk. Occasionally, he said, they would take two days, especially if they had too much merchandise to carry. They stopped at a village on the way and rested the night. I tried to think how long the journey had taken us by lorry but had no idea. I no longer felt tired. Dipo was strapped to the back of a maid. My excitement rose as we drew near our other home, the home of those dark women who trudged all day to dispose of smoked meats and woven cloth and spoke in a language of dirges. We were almost at the entrance of Isara when a lorry appeared but we still piled in gratefully and entered Isara in a cloud of the reddest dust that could possibly exist on the surface of the earth.

It was these itinerant traders, our shadowy guests at Aké who now

129

rushed to become our guides, explaining us to their world. They basked in their contact with us on our own grounds, proudly explaining us to the bewildered and soothing our passage with the resentful. They fought over us, became fiercely possessive. They would have fed us morning till night but here, Wild Christian was at her most unbending about our accepting food outside the walls of our grandfather. This went beyond the mere censure on GREED. She was morbidly afraid that we would be poisoned.

Our Ijebu relations, it seemed, had a reputation for poisoning, or for a hundred and one forms of injuring an enemy through magical means. We were drilled in ways and means of avoiding a handshake, for various forms of injury could be operated through the hands. One would return home and simply wither away. Thus we perfected the technique of bowing with our hands at the back; the more persistently a chance acquaintance proffered his hands, the more resolutely we kept our hands behind, bowing respectfully and looking permanently on the ground. It became a game, Tinu and I would compare notes afterwards on evasion tactics.

No amount of strictures could keep us from the caravanserai when they came to Aké. Wild Christian did not know of the many nocturnal visits we paid to them in the yard, the questions with which we plied them, and our relishing of both smoked meat and the smoky stories they told us, far different in tone from even the most exciting of Essay's stories. Now visiting them in their own homes, I sadly watched much of their mystery dissipate. Father's mud-huts were very sparsely furnished, his wardrobe consisted of no more than two or three agbada, a few buba and trousers for casual wear, caps and his chieftaincy robes, but none except his farming or hunting gear was patched or threadbare. The homes of these traders depressed us, their shabbiness could not be disguised. Beneath their joy at our presence we now sensed the strain of sheer survival, a life made up of forty-mile treks laden with merchandise. Their one 'dress of pride' was worn in our honour whenever they came to take us out, and the same dress would appear again at the most important festival of the year, the New Year itself, then disappear, we knew, until the next festival.

Isara was not the most sanitary of places. There were communal *salanga*, deep latrine-pits, usually well-kept. But it seemed to be accepted that children's excrement could be passed anywhere, after which the mongrel dogs which roamed about in abundance were summoned to eat it up. If they were not available, flies swarmed them until they finally dried up, were scattered by unwary feet at night, churned through by bicycles and the occasional motor lorry. And there were uncultivated patches in between dwellings into which faeces were flung or expelled directly by squatting adults. For us it was a constant source of astonishment that these grown-ups did not mind that they were perceived, in broad daylight, with buttocks bared to the bush. Coming from an afternoon spent watching the gold and silver smiths, the paths and streets became a contamination of the visual feast I had partaken in the workshops of Isara's crafts-men. I displaced their apprentices at the bellows and held crucibles for their molten metals. Back in the streets, the noise and stench were a startling descent from the silence and the purity of their motions. Often, the thought of the obstacles to be avoided kept me at home or at Father's. His simple mud-house was clean, which for us meant normal. Once I asked Essay why we could not bring to Isara those Sanitary Inspectors who descended unannounced on Aké households, if only for the duration of our stay. Essay appeared to look round nervously, as if to ensure that no one had heard me. Then he made me promise only to remind him of it after we were back in the parsonage.

Father had promised often to take me to his farm but he had several duties in connection with the festive season, so he suggested that I ask Broda Pupa to take me to his. It was an outing I was not to be denied and life became a torment for Broda Pupa until he agreed to tackle Wild Christian for permission. He was our neighbour, owned a barber's shop a few doors from where we stayed. Harmful medicines could also be passed through the head, so it was a measure of his closeness to the family that Wild Christian sent us to Broda Pupa for our Christmas-and-New Year hair-cut special. Getting her to agree that I go with him to his farm for a whole day was not so easy however, but Broda Pupa had a flexible sense of humour that soon adjusted itself to Wild Christian's vulnerable sides. And of course there was Father's own authority which counted for much, as long as he was around at the right moment. So finally, with the additional security of a genuine cousin, who was as close to manhood as any of my Isara companions, we set off one early dawn for Broda Pupa's farm.

'Come on, ara Aké,' he shouted as he waited outside the door. 'I am taking you to school.' He handed me a cutlass to carry saying, 'Here is your pencil. Your exercise book is waiting for you at the end of an hour's walk. Are you ready?'

131

I was never more ready. I jumped down and fell in between him and Yemi, drawing the morning dew into my lungs. The dust was not yet stirred, the Harmattan dew disguised the smell of the streets which would grow rank by noon.

Broda Pupa's timing was accurate, the walk lasted just about an hour. There was a hut on the farm and its contents provided us with a quick breakfast before we set out to work clearing a fresh patch of land, shoring up ridges with the hoe and gathering fruits into a large basket. Harmattan was a period of drought and I could not understand why everything here should be so green, the ground soft and rich. Broda Pupa explained that the area was drained by a large stream, one of whose tributaries we had crossed on the way. From time to time he would fake a mock alarm: 'Watch that scorpion!', making me leap out of my skin. When that no longer worked, he vanished silently into the bush, reappeared behind me and drew a slithery branch along the back of my neck.

'All right,' I said, 'Don't blame me if I think you are a snake and lash at you with my cutlass.'

It was Yemi who went up to meet the only snake we encountered that day. He had climbed up a kola-nut tree to crop down some pods. He had hardly begun, was still shinning towards the branch where the heaviest pods were clustered when we heard him call out, so softly that we just managed to catch it.

'Broda!'

'Did you call? Yemi!'

There was silence for some moments, then we heard Yemi moving among the branches, with obvious stealthiness, and in a different direction. Brother Pupa was puzzled and shouted angrily.

'What are you doing? The kola-nuts are not in that direction.'

A few more moments passed and then we heard Yemi, by now totally hidden by the luxuriant branches,

'There is a snake, a monstrosity coiled round the branch where those kola-nuts are. I think it's an *agbadu*.'

I glanced panic-stricken at Broda Pupa. He was by no means ruffled. He called out to Yemi, 'Is it moving?'

'No, but it's watching me.'

Broda Pupa laughed. 'What else do you expect him to do. See you climbing towards him and then take a nap? Now listen, you've moved away from the trunk now haven't you?'

'Of course', and I thought Yemi sounded testy. 'He is in that direction on the other side of the trunk.'

'All right. Listen to me. Don't move back towards the trunk. Just look down and tell me if there is a branch below you which can take your weight.'

There was a pause, we heard the rustle of leaves as Yemi parted the branches. 'Yes, there is.'

'Good. Then you don't have to jump all the way down and break your neck. Lower yourself on to that branch, and don't make any sudden move. Just climb down as you would if there were no snake watching you.'

Yemi made the required manœuvre. I couldn't help feeling scared for Yemi and resentful towards Brother Pupa. He could afford to make light of the whole thing, he wasn't up in the tree.

The next moment a body came crashing through the leaves. Yemi had missed his footing or the branch had proved not as strong as he thought. Fortunately he landed on a soft piece of ground and he soon picked himself up, babbling:

'Broda, it is huge. It is monstrous! That isn't a snake at all, it's a sorcerer up there I swear. It's a sorcerer.'

Broda Pupa snorted. 'Is it? Just gather me a pile of stones will you? But first show me where it is exactly so I can keep my eye on it.'

We followed Yemi to a point below the cluster of kola-nuts. Yemi was right. It didn't take long for me to identify it because it was just like another thick branch of the tree, except that it was black, jet glistening black and its body pulsed a little, but that could have been my imagination.

Broda Pupa nodded with satisfaction. 'Good. I was just wondering what we would eat with our yam for lunch.'

I thought he was joking. 'Nobody eats snakes' I said.

He looked at me, a slow dawning in his eyes. 'Ah, I forgot, omo teacher. The teacher's children don't eat things like that. They eat bread and butter.'

'No, that is not what we eat. But nobody eats snakes.'

'Well, we'll soon see. Yemi, get me that cutlass and you, omo Teacher, keep an eye on the snake. I think I'll cut the kind of sticks we need myself. Yemi, you gather the stones.'

'Suppose it jumps down?' I asked.

'Speak English to it', Broda Pupa said, and left me alone.

I spent the ten minutes they were gone contemplating the snake. It was fat and unruffled. It did not look as if it was going to come down

133

in a hurry, but I did not really know the habits of snakes. Those we had encountered at Aké were usually killed by grown-ups, long before I came on the scene. I had seen some live ones slither past and had simply fled, reporting their presence to grown-ups. In any case, none of them had ever approached anything this size.

They returned at last. I watched Broda Pupa's methodical preparations. I could not help reflecting that he had applied the same approach to obtaining Wild Christian's consent for my day's excursion to his farm. Essay was already preoccupied with so many civic matters, people were always calling on him or he was attending meetings somewhere, so it was largely left to Wild Christian to veto even the most innocuous proposals. But Broda Pupa was determined, in any case I gave him no peace of mind. He applied the same deliberation now to plucking that snake off its perch, first grading the stones by size, rejecting some, setting some aside—as it turned out—for me. He performed the same service for the sticks, weighing them in his hand, cutting some down to shorter lengths, then putting aside one long, heavy ended sapling.

Satisfied, he selected the throwing point, explaining, 'We don't want Wole's stones bouncing back on that branch and hitting us on the head do we?'

I turned to him but he quickly snapped, 'Keep your eye on the animal.'

Satisfied at last, he directed me to the pile of small-size stones and gave final instructions:

'I'll throw first. Yemi follows with his stones, and Wole finishes off the snake with his pebble. We repeat the process until that snake falls down to the reception committee. Is everybody clear on that?'

I nodded, already infected with the excitement.

Broda Pupa launched the first cudgel. It flew through the few intervening leaves and thudded against the mid-section of the snake, shaking it out of its complacency and nearly taking it off its perch. As the snake propelled itself forward in fright, it was stopped short by the smack of Yemi's stone against a branch just in front of it. Almost at once Brode Pupa's stick whistled through the air, without awaiting my own turn.

'Come on Teacher, you are too slow.'

I launched my pebble at the same time as Yemi threw his, saw mine rise barely up to the level of the lowest branch before commencing its journey back to earth.

'Very good, very good. With our big English hunter around no farmer need ever lack for meat.'

The pair kept up the incessant barrage. The snake was disorientated, moved backwards and forwards, climbed to the very highest perch but the stones and sticks found him there. I had long given up trying to contribute my pebbles, convinced that Broda Pupa never intended more than that I should not feel left out. I occupied myself with watching the futile efforts of the snake to escape. Finally, it plunged downwards. I noticed then that Brother Pupa had already picked up the heavy sapling with his left hand. As the snake fell downwards he transferred it to his right and was on top of the snake before it could recover its reflexes. A blow landed on its body and the next thunked squarely on its head. It writhed with incredible energy, lashed out in all directions. Broda Pupa banged it once more on the head, then stood a few feet away.

'Give me the cutlass,' he ordered.

Yemi moved to give it to him but he said, 'No, no, give it to Wole to bring to me.'

He stood too close for my liking to where the snake was writhing. I took the cutlass and hesitated. Then I saw that he stood between me and the snake anyway. Before the snake could lash at me—which it seemed to want to do very much—it would have to go through Broda Pupa. Nonetheless I stretched out the cutlass to him at arms-length.

He shook his head. 'No no, omo teacher. When you hand over a cutlass or a knife to someone, always hold it by the blade. I mean hold it so that you don't cut yourself with it, but make sure that you present the handle to him, not the blade. That is how we do it on the farm.'

I obeyed him. 'That's it. We'll make a farmer of you yet.'

'I am going to be a doctor' I said.

'Nothing wrong with that,' he said, cutting off the snake's head with one blow. 'But you can still keep a farm. I am a barber after all, and I keep a farm.'

I had never thought of that. And then I thought of Essay, 'Papa is a Headmaster, but he is also a gardener.'

'You see. He was raised here.' He tossed the cutlass to Yemi who knew what to do without being told. He scooped up the head with the flat of the cutlass, went to one side and began to dig a hole.

'Why are you planting it?' I demanded.

'Always remember this. A snake's head is still dangerous even after

135

you've cut it off. Someone may step on it and the poison will go into his body the same as if a living snake had bitten him. Always bury it deep in the ground, and preferably away from used paths.'

Yemi's choice was the base of a large tree, between its roots. Brother Pupa next selected a yam from his barn and gave it to me.

'Can you peel yams?'

'I cook at home sometimes. For the whole family.'

'Good. Yemi will build a fire while I skin the snake. Since you don't eat snake meat you'll have to eat your yam with palm oil.'

We busied ourselves with preparations for the meal. Peppers were plucked from the farm, a few vegetables were prepared, a bottle of palm oil and other condiments emerged from the well-stocked barn and, within an hour, a sizzling fragrance of snake meat ragout had overcome the smell of green leaves on the farm. When the stew was nearly ready, Yemi looked up.

'Broda, why don't we use the mortar?'

'You mean, pounded yam?' Brother Pupa put on a look of innocence.

Yemi nodded. 'I know some people who can fight their best friends for pounded yam.'

'Oh, I don't know anyone like that. But, yes, let's go the whole way. It's some people's first day on a farm.'

I protested. 'We have a farm on the way to Osiele, just outside the town.' That was true. I had accompanied Essay there once or twice but it was mostly cared for by a farmer whom he employed.

'Well, as I said, your father was raised here. He is a farmer's son. But I know his work doesn't give him much time to have a farm like this one. I mean, have you ever spent weeks on your farm?'

I shook my head.

'You see. What about a night?'

'Never,' I admitted.

'Or cooked a pot of stew like this or eaten pounded yam on the farm?'

'We don't have an *abule** on it like you do.'

'Ah-ha that is what I am talking about. If Teacher's wife had agreed, we would have spent the night here.'

I clutched eagerly at the idea. 'We can. You can say tomorrow that it grew too dark and we decided to pass the night here.'

*Hut (or village, farmstead).

136

Brother Pupa shook his head. 'She will have a search party after us if we are not back by nightfall. Come on, help Yemi with the hot water and let's pound this yam. I am hungry.'

So indeed was I. When we began eating, I had been certain that I would not touch the snake meat. When the stew was poured into a dish however, I was astonished to find that the meat was not slimy and mottled but an attractive white, firm yet tender-looking, with the consistency of either chicken or rabbit. I decided to taste a little and was again astonished that it tasted in between rabbit and chicken meat. I gave silent thanks for narrowly failing to deprive myself of such an unexpected treat. It was also something to boast about when I returned to Aké, feeling certain that it was a rare pupil indeed who would claim that he had ever feasted on a snake. Broda Pupa nodded approval at the appetite with which I now attacked the meat, pushed more pieces to my side of the dish.

A short rest after lunch, to give the sun some time to 'burn itself down,' and we completed the weeding of the plot, baring the young cassava to light. Then we set off home with bundles of yams, a basket of oranges, some vegetables and peppers.

'School' was not over for the day however. We were half-way home and close to a crossing of paths when we heard a human cry. Broda Pupa stopped, signalled to us for silence and listened. It was a continuous cry of someone in pain. It drifted out nervelessly and the distance between the sound and us lessened gradually. I could hear that it drifted closer and closer along the path which was about to cross ours, that it was a man's voice and that it sounded like the cry of a child long after it had been beaten, a long continuous moan of a suffering whose acuteness had passed.

The wailer finally came in view and we gasped. His face, arms and neck were swollen to twice their normal size. It was not an even swell, but a series of close lumps, the size of *awuje*.* The man shuffled rather than walked along the path. He stared ahead of him and did not even seem to notice us. From his half-open lips drooled the incessant moan as if his mouth, his vocal chords had themselves become debilitated.

Brother Pupa shook his head in pity. 'He is from the village over there. He has only a short distance to go.'

'What on earth did that to his face?' I asked.

* A broad bean.

137

'Bees,' they both replied. 'He must have run.' Yemi added.

'Well, what should he have done?' I asked, 'Wouldn't you have run?'

'Oh no. You must never do that. Just fling yourself on the ground fast and roll away from the spot.'

'Suppose it's thick bush and you can't roll.'

'Get down as low as you can to the ground,' Broda Pupa advised. 'Get right down to the earth as close as you can, and roll away. Don't stand up and don't run. Get yourself flat on the ground and roll. Even if you land on thorns, stay on the ground, and roll.'

Towards the end of our stay, by pretending to be with our new kinswomen, the trading chaperons, I succeeded in joining a hunting party of my own age-group. They were as usual all much older than I. Our weapons were catapults, stones, sticks, whatever else was handy. Jimọ was the leader. He divided the group into beaters and marksmen, I being naturally among the beaters. I had brought down a lizard or two, even a small bird with a catapult at Aké, but I could not pretend to be in the class of Jimọ and his mates who frequently knocked down a running squirrel with a shot from the catapult. I was nevertheless determined to excel myself as a beater. As we moved through the bush in a line, I poked in every hole with a stick, thrashed every suspicious looking clump of bush and shook down saplings. My lungs expanded to match the rousing cry of the others;

'*Gbo, gbo, gbo, gbo; gba, gba, gba, gba.*'

Jimo and the sharpshooters, catapults, stone and cudgels at the ready, waited at the other end of the demarcated grounds. I moved towards yet another shrub, shook it and was instantly rewarded with a sharp pain on my forehead. Another followed almost at once, and then I saw them. An angry nest of hornets, swooping down to punish the intruder. Even as I hit the earth, I felt that Broda Pupa would have been proud of me. His instructions resounded clearly in my head and I obeyed them as if in a practice drill, thinking how provident it was that, barely two weeks before, we had met the victim with the puffed-up face, I again experienced the elation of feeling that I was under some special protection; in Isara, this was a constant, unquestioned state of mind, nothing could even threaten to unsettle it.

Jimo cancelled the rest of the hunt. I had received none other than the first two stings and I protested, but he was not to be deterred. It could lead to a fever, he said, and then he would get blamed. Everyone, it seemed, was eager not to be responsible for any mishap to the children of Teacher. I was however too full of having saved myself, by a lesson whose timing bordered on omens, on the supernatural, to mind this irritating attitude which·befell us from the singular misfortune of being 'Teacher's children'. I bore my wounds proudly home and displayed them—not to Teacher and Wife—but to that other parent who had become a fellow conspirator, who truly embodied the male Isara for me in its rugged, mysterious strength, the female complement of which I had earlier obtained from the trading women.

Except that his was smaller, Father's head was almost identical with the Canon's, but he made up for its size by the energy it radiated. It looked hard, truly impregnable, I really did believe that not even a gunshot could penetrate that head, that any bullet would simply bounce off its round, hermetic casting. In spite of the quantity of hair on it, Father's head nevertheless gave an impression of being smooth, the smoothness of iron-plating. He was also a much smaller person than his son, but every inch of him gave off such power that he effortlessly dominated all who came near him. The fact was barely discussed but I knew that he belonged in that same province of beliefs as the *ogboni* of Aké, as the priests and priestesses of various cults and mysteries against whom Wild Christian and her co-religionists sometimes marched on some special week-end of the year, preaching the word of God to them in market-places, on the streets, in their homes. The occasion chosen for such a forage was the anniversary of the missionaries' arrival in Egbaland; their mission was to perpetuate the spirit of those missionaries and bring a few more pagans into the christian fold.

In my secret heart, I feared for Father. I did not see how he would escape the religious onslaught of Aké once the forces began to close on him—from Essay simply by example and the occasional quiet discussion, from Wild Christian by pointed silences, ostentatious preparations for those celebrations of Christmas which belonged only to Christians. New Year embraced everyone, but Christmas had its own hundred-and-one gatherings, worships, communions, prayer-meetings both at home and in closed and open spaces from which outsiders were excluded. Wild Christian had a way of 'leaving out' the unbeliever, especially one in whose household she belonged.

For the moment however, Father appeared indifferent to the word of God. When I narrated the incident of the bees, and the coincidence of the earlier warning, he did not say, as Wild Christian would have done, 'God moves in mysterious ways'; he remarked instead:

'Ogun protects his own.'

I had heard that name before. I said to him, 'Ogun is the pagans' devil who kills people and fights everybody.'

'Is that what they teach you?' he asked.

'Yes. Isn't it true?'

Father scratched his chin, pierced me with his eyes. Then he asked me the most unexpected question,

'Do your playmates ever beat you up?'

I told him, 'Sometimes. But mostly they are afraid to touch me because I am the Headmaster's son.'

'So that's what you tell them when they want to fight you? You mustn't touch me because I am Teacher's son.'

'No, I don't say it, they say it themselves.'

'What do you mean? How do they say it?'

'They snap their fingers at me and say, 'You're lucky. If you weren't the Headmaster's son, you would have smelt pepper today'' I think they are afraid they would be dismissed from school if they touch me.'

'And you. Do you think Ayo would do that?'

'No. What some of them don't know is that if we fight, we get punished. Any time we return home with torn clothes or somebody reports that we have been in a fight we get punished.' And then I wondered what he must think of this situation which had always struck me as manifestly unfair. 'What do you think of it, Father? We get beaten outside, and then we return home only to get beaten. It's not right, is it?'

Father's eyes twinkled with inward merriment. Except that his eyes were much larger and brighter, he had the same trick with his eyes as the Canon, they wrinkled at the corners almost half-way to his ears when he was amused. He got up now and headed towards the cool corner where he pulled out a keg of palm wine. I did not wait to be asked to fetch the calabashes from the cupboard. I continued to explain,

'They say only children who lack training fight, that it is Satan's work. And to make matters worse, the whole of Aké knows that we get flogged if we get in a fight, so, the ones who do not attend our school, they don't care. They are not afraid of being punished in school. They provoke us saying, fight back if you dare. They land a quick blow and run away. Or else we run away.'

He looked at me intently. 'Are you sure you don't run away because they are bigger?'

'Oh, they are all bigger anyway. I don't think I have ever quarrelled with anyone my size.' Then I remembered, and added, 'Except once with Dipo.' I was overcome with embarrassment. 'But they provoked me, Mama included.' The whole scene was replayed through my mind and I recounted it to him. I asked, 'Father, they are not very consistent are they? Punishing us when we fight outside, then provoking my brother against me!'

Father scratched the stubble of his chin. 'You will understand that later. They were trying hard to do the right thing, but the wrong way.'

He filled my calabash halfway and filled his to the brim. He blew the froth away and drank it all down. I sipped from mine, watched his face for comments. It grimaced.

'That man is lazy. I've told him, if he doesn't go further up the stream for my wine, I shall stop him bringing any more wine to this house. The tree from which he got this is over-tired, in fact all the trees at the bottom of Larelu's farm are over-tired, but he is too lazy to go half a mile further upstream. He shook his head in emphasis, 'All right, I'll see to him. *Alakori!*'*

Just the same, he refilled his calabash, took out an *orogbo*,** crumbled its thin skin between his fingers and bit into it, 'That should hide the taste a little. Now, let's continue. Your father wants you to go to that white man's school in Ibadan. Did you know that?'

'Government College? Yes, he has said so. But I'm just finishing Standard Three. So that is still a long time away.'

'Not so long in your father's planning. Ayo doesn't believe in letting children ripen in the body before he begins to force their brains.' He frowned suddenly. 'Wait. Did you say you were in Standard Three?'

'Well, I have just passed into Standard Four.'

His armoured head went up and down slowly, like a male lizard's. 'Yes. That is what your father was talking about. At the end of next year you will have finished Four. After that, he wants you to go to the

---

*Hopeless character.
**A hard nut with stimulant properties.

secondary school. He says it is in this New Year, this one we are entering now that you must take the test for your new school.'

'Yes. I will take both the tests for Abeokuta Grammar School and Government College.'

He nodded again. 'And unless my memory is playing me tricks, you are now exactly eight and a half. Is that right?'

'Yes, Father.'

'So, if you pass into this Government College, you will leave home and enter a boarding school. You will be on your own for the first time, away from your parents, at the age of nine and a half—am I right? Is my counting correct so far?'

I assured him that it was, beginning to sense where all this was leading. I got ready to disagree with him, to assure him that I was not afraid to leave home, indeed, that I was anxious, even desperate to leave home. I did not want him protesting to Essay that I was far too young.

'You think that is far too young to leave home, don't you Father?'

'No. Children leave home for other things too, not just for books. No, I was just thinking that you might find the others too old. Look, even in Ayo's school, in Abeokuta where the people have had their eyes opened much longer than here by the white man, haven't you noticed how much older your classmates are?'

I agreed that I had. 'But I kept beating them all in class,' I assured him. 'I have no trouble at all.'

'Yes, your father tells me that. But you have not got my point yet. Here, people don't go to secondary school straight from primary. They can't afford to. Very often they go on to Standard VI Primary where they get this certificate they call Asamende.'

'As Amended' had entered the folklore of education as the ultimate goal in book striving for would-be pupil teachers, sanitary inspectors, railway conductors and so on. I smiled, but Father misunderstood.

'It's no laughing matter. With Asamende they go to work, save up enough, then go to secondary school where they try, try, try to reach Standard Eight. That is where most of them stop. Few manage to reach the ultimate Ten Books. Now, do you see what I am getting at? If you think your mates in primary school are now much older than you, think what they will be like in the secondary schools. They will be men—*garapa-garapa*! A few would have got married already and will even be hiding a child or two round the corner. You will be

142

sharing desks with MEN, not boys!' He rubbed the stubble on his chin and chuckled. 'They will arrive with their shaving-soap and razor.'

When his chuckles had subsided, he grew solemn again. 'Now, here is Ayo, very ambitious for you. He wants to send his son into battle and believe me, the world of books is a battlefield, it is an even tougher battlefield than the ones we used to know. So how does he prepare him? By stuffing his head with books. But book-learning, and especially success in book-learning only creates other battles. Do you know that? You think those men are going to be pleased when you, whom they are nearly old enough to spawn, start defeating them? Hm? Tell me that. Has Ayo ever discussed that with you?'

I was now thoroughly alarmed. A straightforward occupation like sticking one's head in books and passing examinations was taking on ominous proportions. Father saw that he had made an impression on me and re-filled my calabash. 'Drink your wine, it's quite weak. Even if you drink the whole gourd Eniola can't complain that I am turning you into a drunkard.'

That was the other thing. Father was one of the few people who called Wild Christian by that name. The two Ransome-Kuti, Daodu and Bere and the Odemo also called her that, or Moroun, so did one or two relations who popped up from nowhere from time to time and vanished just as abruptly. To others she was Mama Tinu or Mama Wole, or Iyawo Headmaster. Father continued watching me intently.

'Human beings are what they are. Some are good, some evil. Others turn to evil simply because they are desperate. Envy, hm, you mustn't make the mistake of thinking that envy is not a powerful force for the action of many men. It is a disease you'll find everywhere, yes everywhere. Your mother knows that too. I have seen that much. The only trouble with her is that she thinks she knows what to do about it. What does she think I am alive for?'

I was puzzled at this, I did not understand him and I said so.

He tucked his chin into his neck and shook it about like a battling cockerel, 'O-ho, you think I simply bring you all here for the New Year without looking out for you? O-oh, if that is how you do things at Aké, that is not how we take life here. There is more to the world than the world of Christians, or books. So, enough for today. You and I have business tomorrow.'

I felt a thrill of expectations. Perhaps another outing to the farm, this time Father's own farm. As usual I could not help asking, 'What business, Father?'

He stood up. 'Oh yes, I forgot. They say you never stop asking questions. Go on and play with your friends. I've arranged it all with your father, only I had not decided on the day. Now I think we'll get it over with tomorrow.'

He saw on my face that I was too intrigued now to leave without some further explanation but, he shook his head. 'Tomorrow. But you will come back and sleep here tonight. Go on.'

In Isara we occupied a house by ourselves. Wild Christian that is, and the children. Essay slept in Father's house. From the moment of our arrival in Isara he ceased, in effect, to be part of the Aké family, the Mr & Mrs ended and he moved back into the Isara fold, and the obligations of his hometown. There were constant consultations, town meetings, family meetings, church council sessions, Obaship affairs . . . a hundred duties that a whole year, sometimes less, had kept waiting for him. He spent much of his time with the Odemo but it was not merely duties that kept him there. The Odemo, with one or two others such as my godfather who was the husband of my wife-to-be, obviously relieved the narrowness of discourse which Essay now experienced in Isara. I often wondered if the Odemo was not equally desperate for his kind of company.

It was not a rigid arrangement; often one or more of us would simply camp down at Father's and sleep there. There were always mats and space on the dung-plastered floor of what served as the living-room. In spite of Wild Christian's emissaries, I spent half the nights of Isara in Father's house; this was however the first time that I received a direct order to sleep there. My curiosity was intense as I went to sleep—which did not come until well into the night.

I woke up early to find Father bent over me, an oil-lamp in his hand. It was not yet daylight but there were already two other figures in the house. I saw their forms in a corner of the room, one was clearly an elderly man, the other a young boy, only slightly taller than I was. Instinctively I looked round to see if my father was around but he wasn't. I assumed that he was still fast asleep in the inner room.

My mind still on a planned excursion I asked, 'Where are we going?'

'Are you fully awake?'

144

I nodded. 'Go and have a wash, I've left a pail of water in the yard.'

I obeyed. As I walked past the two figures I noticed, on the floor between them, a clay dish, a bottle of palm oil, several small tin containers filled with powders, mostly dark colours. A flat plate contained some metal implements and what looked like the fragment of a shell. Puzzled, I had my bath, shivering from the coolness of the morning air and a sense of foreboding.

When I returned, I noticed that the stools and chairs had been re-arranged. The palm-stalk upright had been moved from its position against the wall to near centre of the room. A low stool, an *ipeku* was placed before it and on this, the elderly stranger was just positioning himself. The boy knelt by his side, re-arranging bottles, jars, trays and the strange assortment of implements.

'Come and sit here,' Father commanded, pointing to the palm-stalk chair. I obeyed.

He moved from the door to face me. 'You remember what we talked about yesterday?'

I replied 'Yes.'

'Good. Now listen very carefully. What you are about to undergo will give you pain but . . . LOOK AT ME!'

I snatched my eyes back from the sinister tray and looked into his burning eyes. 'That's better. Keep your mind away always from a source of pain. Now, this boy here, he is your own age. It is up to you to decide if you want to shame yourself by crying before him. He paused, boring into me with his eyes. Since he appeared to expect a reply, I said,

'No, I won't cry.'

'I know you won't. I just wanted to remind you, in case you forget. It will pain you of course, you are not wood, so it must pain you. But you are not to cry.'

I was now wholly paralysed by fear, but that did not stop my heart racing. I waited for the worst. I still had no idea what was in store, only that I was expected not to cry, however painful it was. And then I remembered something.

'When Folasade died, I cried.'

Father stopped in his tracks. The stranger paused also, looked at Father in some puzzled way. I saw that Father was taken aback, not knowing what to make of this. Finally,

'Folasade? Ah, yes. Hm.' And he went off in a private reverie.

'That child was *abami*. I told Ayo at the time—*abami gidi*!* Going off like that, on her very day of birth, hm. Anyway, that was different. A man cannot argue with his soul. Ibanuję, ko m'omode, ko m'agba'**

He nodded abruptly to the stranger. I felt my right ankle suddenly in the grip of a vice, the heel pressed against the ground. Just as swiftly, the hand moved to the ball of my foot, pressing downward and maintaining the pressure of the heel against the ground. The little boy swabbed the ankle with a wad soaked in something, the next moment the elderly man had seized the most scalpel-like of the metal objects, dipped it in the clay dish and a sharp pain began at my ankle and shot up my body to the brain. I yelped! The left hand kept my foot firmly fixed to the ground. As I cried out I would have twisted my body, only there were now two strong hands, Father's, keeping my shoulders pressed against the backrest of the chair.

As if in a dream, I looked down and saw the same blade flash into the dish and out again, until the pain in my flesh was no longer defined by moments. The bites of the blade merged into one another and I stared down at the arc of incisions in fascination, at the anklet of blood oozes which progressed round my ankle. After that first sharp cry, my body bound itself to silence, but the tears that were forced out in that moment continued unchecked as I gritted my teeth together and forced back every sound. Father's fingers dug into my shoulders as my body contracted with every incision. I could no longer look down. I shut my eyes, glued my teeth together and waited for the end of the ordeal. The tears ran, unchecked.

A soothing band encased my ankle. When I looked down I noticed a wide swathe in the mixture of the dish. Binding my ankle now was the strip of cloth which had been soaked in that mixture. The boy was quite gentle. Even as I sank into the luxury of the cessation of pain, the blade had bitten into my other ankle. But the shock had passed, and taken the surprise of the pain with it. After the ankles both wrists underwent similar incisions. I winced from time to time but my jaws were at least unclenched. I watched every move, even began to admire the neat, precision skill of the wielder of the knife.

When it was over, I disbelieved what a short time it had all taken. Outside, the sun was beginning to cast shadows on our doorstep. The stranger spoke in low tones in the corner of the room while Father

*A weird child, veritably weird.
**Sorrow knows neither child nor elder.

nodded and grunted in apparent agreement. Then the elder came back and began to pack his instruments, the boy rinsing out the dish just outside the door while the elder cleaned out his blades, poured the rest of the powders into small jars which he transferred to a bottomless bag which I now saw hanging by the door. Father saw them off, and shut the door.

He came towards me, sat on the vacated stool and said, 'Wole, you did—strong. You acted like a true Akin. And now listen to me. Listen very carefully, and this in spite of anything anyone, ANYONE tells you . . . If they tell you the contrary, tell them I said it . . .'

Unhurriedly, taking his time as if the taking of snuff was the most hazardous operation in the world, he reached sideways to the lower ledge of the small table, took out his tin of snuff, opened it, shook some into his left hand, replaced the cover, taking care to keep his left hand cupped to avoid spillage, replaced the tin on the ledge, then proceeded to take a pinch from the palm and treat either nostril to an equal amount of snuff. For some reason, probably because of the unprepared-for immersion I had just undergone, every sense was painfully tuned and the slightest detail of his motions took on a life of its own, so that I seemed to be seeing him for the first time.

My hearing also had acquired a wild tuning. When he sneezed I leapt up from the chair and my head continued to echo with the sound, even while he spoke.

'Whoever offers you food, take it. Eat it. Don't be afraid, *as long as your heart says, Eat.* If your mind misgives, even for a moment, don't take it, and never step in that house again. Do you understand what I have just said?'

I could only nod, dumbly.

'I said, anyone offers you food or drink, if your mind does not hesitate, go ahead. It is I that say so. If however, you experience even one moment of doubt, turn your back on that place and never go back. Next, don't ever turn your back on a fight. Where you are going, maybe next year, maybe the year after the next, I don't know. For all I know they may not let you back here before you go to that school but it does not matter. Wherever you find yourself, don't run away from a fight. Your adversary will probably be bigger, he will trounce you the first time. Next time you meet him, challenge him again. He will beat you all over again. The third time, I promise you this, you will either defeat him, or he will run away. Are you listening to what I am telling you?'

147

'Yes, Father.'

'First time, second time, never mind that he beats you. But keep going back. In the end you will put him to shame—either you will trounce him soundly, or he will run away.'

He rose. 'I sent your parents and the other children away to Sagamu. They should have gone by now, there are plenty of people there they haven't visited. So we are by ourselves.'

I turned towards the room. 'I thought Papa was in there.'

He smiled and shook his head. 'Oh no, this is just between the two of us. Now I must go to a meeting. Somebody will bring you your breakfast. Don't eat anything else. Don't eat anything today and tomorrow except what I send you. Do you understand?'

I assured him that I did. I felt drained, my head was in confusion and my wrists and ankles throbbed. There was a strange distance from my hands as if they no longer belonged to me.

Then I heard myself ask, 'Did Papa get his ankles cut too? I mean, when he was like me.'

Father raised his eyes to the rafters. 'They said it. Ayo warned me, and so did Eniola. When I said they should leave you with me today, they warned, Be careful. He will kill you with questions.'

He went into his room. I could still hear him chuckling to himself as he changed, letting out his single prolonged yell of wonder which had a neatly regulated tailing off at the end. For a long while I sat still, trying to work out if my ankles would take my weight or if they would fall off the moment I lifted my feet. It was as if my quandary had transmitted itself to him in the room because his voice came ringing out almost at once:

'Try walking on the outer edge of your feet, then on the inside edge. When both have failed, you might try walking as you normally do—squarely on both feet, only a little more gently. That usually works best.'

And then, as I stood up, I found myself grinning, because I was certain that Father did not think that I would understand.

X

The smells are all gone. In their place, mostly sounds, and even these are frenzied distortions of the spare, intimate voices of humans and objects alike which filled Aké from dawn to dusk, whose muted versions through the night sometimes provided us with puzzles of recognition as we lay on our mats resisting sleep. Even the least pleasant smell, such as the faintly nauseating smell of a smashed bed-bug, tinged with the whiff of camphor that should have prevented its appearance in the first place was part of the invisible network of Aké's extended persona; it was of the same order as the nocturnal rumblings of Sorowanke, the madwoman who lived by the mango tree, talking in her sleep. This was the mango tree in the square, nearly opposite the church. At night we would hear her distinctly exorcising her demons or bickering with her lunatic lover Yokolu. Even as the sizzle of the heated needle was heard from Wild Christian's nocturnal battles against the bugs, the crickets and cicadas engaged in their own challenge to the prolonged choir practice from St Peter's church, probably on the eve of a Church festival. Sorowanke punctuated the anthem in rehearsal with her sudden yelps and slaps against cracked, emanciated thighs as the tower-clock solemnly chimed the twelve strokes of midnight. Over it all, as we drifted asleep, coursed the pungent ferment of pulped corn from the dark corner of the kitchen, the smell of *ojojo* from the frying-pot of a woman who served the late night-farers, of palm-wine from the same night-stall which dispensed a late supper of *eko*-and-*ojojo* and, at week-ends especially, the sound of the lazy strings of Dayisi, the juju-band guitarist returning from an engagement, or simply serenading the night.

The smells have been overcome. And their conqueror, sound, is not even the measured chimes of the tower-clock or the parade of *egungun*, police band, market cries or bicycle-bell but a medley of electronic bands and the raucous clang of hand-bells advertising bargain sales of imported wares. The dusty road which once grandly intervened between our backyard wall and the church wall is now

149

shrunken; a half, pressed against St Peter's parsonage wall is shared among a variety of stores peddling the products of a global waste industry—fly-blown shawls, combs, mirrors, flaring radio antennae, chrome or foam-and-rubber motor-car decorations, ornamented flasks, drinking-glasses disguised as floral arrangements, oriental table-mats stamped Manchester, clocks, 'gold' jewellery, photo-frames with a backing of white voluptuous bodies . . . Raquel Welch, Marilyn Monroe, Diana Dors, Jane Russell, Greta Garbo. Sometimes the figures are mincing males, also stars of the celluloid world. They strike a pose of conscious masculinity but, even with their aggressive moustaches, the sum is—androgynous. Along the same midnight walk of Dayisi the guitarist now darts the young hawker, releasing into the faces of passers-by through his finger on the caller's button, the dulcet chimes of Made-in-Hong-Kong doorbells.

Along Dayisi's Promenade I also sang, but only on those occasional late evenings when I was sent on an errand to Pa Solatan or some other member of our parents' circle in the direction of Aafin or Iporo, or to our Auntie Mrs Lijadu. I sang to buoy up my spirits against the dangers of the dark, against figures who drifted past in the dark and who, for all I knew might be spirits or kidnappers. There had accrued to me a formidable weapon in my armoury of incantations against the unknown, after my role as The Magician on prize-giving day at St Peter's in Standard III. Even if most dangerous spirits did not converse in English, there was no way that they could mistake the ferocious will of the counter-force marching along Dayisi's promenade and singing at the top of his voice:

> For I'm a magician
> You all must know
> You'll hear about me wherever you go
> You can see my name in letters large
> You can see me perform for a poultry large
> For Anthony Peter Zachary White
> Is a man who always gives delight . . .
> My friends I bid you come and see
> What sort of wizard I may be
> Come one and all
> And join the crowd
> And lift your voice in praises loud . . .

150

Why poultry? It was one of the baffling details of that children's opera. The power of the magician was no stranger however, even though it belonged among the mysterious.

Centenary Hall was constantly host to a procession of magicians who were invariably 'trained in India'. They burnt incense, transfixed volunteers from the audience and sliced their assistants in half. Once there was a terrifying encounter between a member of the audience, a near duplicate of Paa Adatan. He had answered the call for volunteers from the audience on whom the magician would demonstrate his hypnotic powers. This aggressive, muscular volunteer had however refused to be hypnotized. The Doctor Magician exerted all his powers, burnt coils and coils of incense, muttered a hundred Abracadabras and recited the terrifying pronouncements of—someone whispered near us—the Seventh and Ninth Books of Moses; the volunteer simply turned towards the audience, half-rose from his crouch and sneered. The Doctor sprinkled his mystic water from Jerusalem around the couch, flicked his fingers at the recumbent form and fanned the air around the volunteer's face with down-facing palms; the stubborn Egba man refused to go to sleep. But finally the deed was done, the volunteer's eyes glazed over and the Doctor stood over his inert form, triumphant. But then, his face turned ugly. The confrontation had reduced his status and competence in the eyes of the audience and he began to prowl round the stage in a fury. He shouted words to the effect that the defeated man and he had been engaged in a life-and-death duel and thus the contest could only be concluded on those terms. The audience appeared nervous. Suddenly he dived on the sleeping figure, pulled up his *dansiki*. Sure enough, around his waist was a leather thong of amulets. This he ripped off and held out to the audience; we understood this to be the Doctor's explanation of the man's prolonged resistance. His next motion was the most terrifying moment of the entire evening. He pounced on the long sword with which he had sliced his assistant in half and, raising it, darted towards the couch with an intent that no one could mistake. Some of the audience fled, others covered their eyes and screamed. I was merely open-mouthed in horror, unable to believe that an evening's entertainment of magic could be about to end in such a violent manner. The commotion was so complete that I neither saw, nor could anyone explain to me how it all ended.

That contest unravelled itself for me, even as it took place, as a simple contest between the magician and the *osó*, the wizard or sorcerer. The magician was the agent of the mysterious Orient— India, Egypt, the Three Wise Men, Moses and Pharaoh and the Plagues. The wizard was our own challenger, armed with local charms against the alien forces of the orient. But he had been defeated and, for all I knew, had been vengefully cut in half by the enraged man of the Orient. The smell of incense hung permanently over my memory of that encounter, linking up in some undefined way with the aura of those three kings who had approached the infant child with gifts of gold, frankincense and myrrh. It was, without doubt, an evil, vengeful force, terrifying and pitiless in application. Playing the role of The Magician, self-declared both 'magician' and 'wizard' was therefore, a rather baffling contradiction but, the songs were all the more potent for that. It was the language of a dual force which the witches and the kidnappers would understand. Songs from that operetta became my regular guard whenever I had to brave the passage between our backyard wall and the churchyard where, to add to the menace of the dark, there was also a cemetery, not to mention the huge mango tree whose bole was large enough to house a hundred *ewèlè*, *òrò*, *iwin* and other *ànjònnú*!

But the seasonal anthems rehearsed by the choir also exerted my voice. The tunes came out clearly enough, but not the words. These emerged as some strange language, a mixture of English, Yoruba and some celestial language that could only be what was spoken by those cherubs in the stained-glass windows, whose mouths sprouted leaves and branches as they circled the beatific faces of saints and ar- changels. These indecipherable lyrics led to strange interpretations, and I was engaged in belting out some of these when I bumped into Mr Orija the organist who was just emerging from the rear-gate of the church compound. I was checked in stride by the apparition of the untidy man who always looked, wherever he was, as if he was still enveloped in his cassock and surplice and was racing towards the church with only seconds to spare before the beginning of service. I stopped, muttered a Good Evening sir in a panic and fled. I could no longer remember what jumbled version of the Easter Cantata I had been singing but I hoped that it had not sounded blasphemous enough to lead to a report to Essay the following day.

I was wrong. Mr Orija visited the house almost with the crowing of the cock the following morning. But he had not come to report any transgression, only to ask Essay if I could join the choir. There followed a somewhat prolonged discussion—I eavesdropped, from the moment I saw the lumbering figure of the organist approaching the front door. Essay thought that I was far too small but Mr Orija insisted that my voice was just right for the soprano. In the end it was agreed. Special robes would have to be made for me when the time came, but I was to join in the choir practices immediately.

Edun, who lived on the other side of Ibarapa morning market was inducted at the same time. We celebrated the occasion as yet another liberating step from the demands of our households. In addition to lessons, scouting, and a few fictions, there was now the legitimate escape through choir practice. And although I lived nearer to the church, it was somehow accepted that it was I who should go past the church, cross the street between Aké square and Ibarapa market, go through the market, pick my way through the intervening *agbole* and return with Edun through the same passages to the church for choir practice and, when we began to robe, for church services.

We varied the course. The evening market was normally out of our way since it lay on the other side of the road to Iberekodo, but the morning market was mostly bare and devoid of interest by the hour of choir practice. Going through the sister market only added some ten or fifteen minutes to the walk and I made sure that I set out early enough to make up the time for it. The flavours of the market rose fully in the evenings, beckoning us to a depletion of the *onini* and halfpennies which we had succeeded in saving up during the week. For there they all were, together, the *jogi* seller who passed, in full lyrical cry beneath the backyard wall at a regular hour of the morning, followed only moments later by the *akara* seller, her fried bean-cakes still surreptitiously oozing and perfuming the air with groundnut oil. In the market we stood and gazed on the deftly cupped fingers of the old women and their trainee wards scooping out the white bean-paste from a mortar in carefully gauged quantities, into the wide-rimmed, shallow pots of frying oil. The lump sank immediately in the oil but no deeper than an inch or two, bobbed instantly to the surface and turned pinkish in the oil. It spurted fat globules upwards and sometimes beyond the rim of the pot if the mix had too much water. Then, slowly forming, the outer crust of crisp, gritty light brownness which masked the inner core of baked bean paste, filled with green and red peppers, ground crayfish or chopped.

Even when the *akara* was fried without any frills, its oil im-

153

pregnated flavours filled the markets and jostled for attention with the tang of roasting coconut slices within farina cakes which we called *kasada*; with the hard-fried lean meat of *tinko*; the 'high', rotted-cheese smell of *ogiri*; roasting corn, fresh vegetables or *gbegiri*. *Akàmu*, the evening corn pap, was scooped into waiting bowls from a smooth, brown gourd sitting in enamelled trays on bamboo trestles, presided over by women who daily improvised new praise-chants. An *onini*, even a halfpenny did not fulfil every craving but the sights and the smells were free. Choir practice became inseparable from the excursion through Ibarapa's sumptuous resurrection of flavours every evening. When, a few months later, our apprenticeship was over and we became full-fledged choristers, I continued to leave early on Sundays and other church seasons to call on Edun for both morning and evening services. The morning market was not open on Sundays but, there was a woman who appeared to have converted all the smells and textures of both morning and evening markets in her pot of stew, a crayfish and locust-bean biased concoction which queened it over rice and a variety of yams. Apart from a few stalls of fresh vegetables, she alone defied the claims of Sunday to a market-free gesture of respect. The consequence was predictable. Breakfast at home was not niggardly, so it was not a question of hunger. It was even special on Sundays—yams, fish stew, omelette, bread, butter and the inevitable tea or lemon grass infusion. But it was not yet breakfast on Sunday until I had picked my way through the stalls of Ibarapa, cassock and surplice thrown over the shoulder, rescued Edun from his home and, robbing God to pay Iya Ibarapa, used up the pennies we were given for offering on the steaming, peppery, glutinous riot of liver, of chunks and twists of cows' insides served by the old woman as church bells signalled the half-hour before confronting God. Once or twice, probably a little oftener, we were struck by the fear that God might object to this weekly deprivation of his rightful dues, but I think I lightened our apprehensions by suggesting that we sang better after the richness of the markets in our throats than we ever did with the delicacies of the parsonage alone. In any case, we watched for signs of disapproval from the designated owner of those Sunday pennies, but received none.

When I asked Ibidun, Mrs Lijadu's niece, what our Aunt put in her stews to make it taste so peculiar she said, *pasmenja*. It was a strange word but one which was perfectly suited to the flavour of the meals we had with our Aunt who, we had decided, belonged to the vague

154

Brazilian side of some of our relations. An axis of tastes and smells was formed between her and our grandmother, Daodu's sister, who lived alone in Igbein almost on the other side of Abeokuta. We did not visit her much but, when we did, I would realize with a start—and not just at mealtime—that I was not at Mrs Lijadu's but in the home of our maternal grandmother, the mysterious elder sister of Rev A. O. Ransome-Kuti. It remained one of the mysteries of the family relationships over which Wild Christian spent so much time trying to educate us. Were the Olubi our cousins and did this mean blood or marriage relations? I listened, understanding none of the elaborate and intricate family history. Links were formed of far more tangible matters. Our Igbein grandmother had nothing in common, as far as I ever discerned, with her formidable brother Daodu. Equally stern and just as affectionate perhaps, but I was more ready to accept, and indeed continued to believe for a long time that she was Beere's mother. And I thought that she and Mrs Lijadu were sisters because they both cooked with *pasmenja*, both homes were constantly wreathed in the smell of *pasmenja*. Even their buns and *chin-chin* had identical flavours; as for food in both homes, it could only have been cooked, not merely by sisters, but by two people who had been sisters all their lives. Daodu's wife, Beere, I never associated with any form of cooking. Eating, that was a different matter.

Beere had a passion for *moin-moin* and she was so fond of *moin-moin* made by Wild Christian that she often sent one of her elder children, Koye or Dolupo all the way from Igbein to Aké for Wild Christian's *moin-moin*. When she came in person and joined our parents at table, a shriek of outrage was wrung from her if an over-zealous maid had unwrapped the steamed delicacy from the leaves. For her, the sublime parts of *moin-moin* were those wafer-thin truants which leaked into the folds of leaves and were now steamed into light, independent slivers, to be peeled leisurely from their veined beds and sucked smoothly through the lips in-between, or, as a finale to the chunky mouthfuls of the full-bodied *moin-moin*. The hapless maid produced *moin-moin* paraded in all its steamy, but naked glory and Beere would confidently insist that the leaves be retrieved. There was no danger; she knew very well that they had not been thrown into the dust-bin. We watched her glide meticulously through every leaf, prise through the stuck-together leaves with a skin-surgeon's care. She levered apart the baked veins of the leaf-wraps, casually picking up the oiled wafers along the way and licking her lips in ostentatious enjoyment. She acknowledged our unvoiced stares of protest by remarking loudly—if she happened to be in the mood—that anyone who really believed that such tidbits should be left to children was either a fool or an Englishman. Then, with a rougish look on her bespectacled face, she measured off a slice from the centre of the *moin-moin*, pushed it aside for us and winked, remarking afterwards that she would sooner forgo the main lump than lose those insubstantial slivers with their Wild-Christian flavour, sealed in secret corners cunningly pinched by her practised fingers.

The hawkers' lyrics of leaf-wrapped *moin-moin* still resound in parts of Aké and the rest of the town but, along Dayisi's Walk is also a shop which sells *moin-moin* from a glass case, lit by sea-green neon lamps. It lies side by side with McDonald's hamburgers, Kentucky Fried Chicken, hot dogs and dehydrated sausage-rolls. It has been cooked in emptied milk-tins and similar containers, scooped out and sliced in neat geometric shapes like cakes of soap. And the newly-rich homes stuff it full of eggs, tinned sardines from Portugal and corned beef from the Argentine. The fate of *wara*, among others, is however one without even this dubious reprieve. The vendor of milk-curds, floated in outsize gourds has been banished by chromium boxes with sleek spouts which dispense yellowish fluids into brittle cones. If it were, at least, ice *cream*! But no. The quick-profit importer of instant machines is content to foist a bed-pan slop of diabetic kittens on his youthful customers and watch them lick it noisily, biting deeper into the cone. Even Pa Delumo's Sunday school children knew better; the ice cream king of Dayisi's Walk would have been dethroned, through neglect, by the *wara* queen.

Our teeth were cut on *robo*, hard-fried balls of crushed melon seeds, and on *guguru-and-epa*, the friend and sustainer of workers on the critical countdown towards pay day. A handful of guguru was washed down in water, palm-wine or pito and hunger was staved off for the rest of the working day. Evening, and *konkere* department took over, a bean-pottage with a sauce of the darkest palm-oil and peppers, and of a soundly uncompromising density. Mixed with *gari*, it fully justified the name of concrete whose corrupted version it proudly bore. The Hausa women who sold *guguru* carefully graded their corn; we combined in our purchases the hard-roasted teeth-breakers, the fluffy, off-white floaters and the half-and-half, inducing variations into taste-buds with slices of coconut or

measures of groundnuts. Today's jaws on Dayisi's Walk appear no less
hard-worked, indeed they champ endlessly—on chewing-gum.
Among the fantasy stores lit by neon and batteries of coloured bulbs
a machine also dispenses popcorn, uniformly fluffed. Urchins thrust
the new commodity, clean-wrapped, in plastic bags in faces of
passengers whose vehicles pause even one moment along the route.
The blare of motor-horns compete with a high-decibel outpouring of
rock and funk and punk and other thunk-thunk from lands of
instant-culture heroes. Eyes glazed, jaws in constant, automated
motion, the new habituees mouth the confusion of lyrics belted out
from every store, their arms flapping up and down like wounded
bush-fowl. Singly, or in groups of identical twins, quad- or quin-
tuplets they wander into the stereo stores, caress the latest record
sleeves and sigh. A trio emerge with an outsize radio-cassette player
in full blast, setting up mobile competition with the already noise-
demented line of stores.

They move on to the trinket-and-cosmetic shop, their jaws im-
placably churning through the gummed-up troughs of synthesized
feed in every conceivable idiom, pause at McDonald's, bury corpses
of sausage-rolls in their mouths and drown the mash in coca-cola. A
girl decides at last on one of several competing brands of 'skin-tone'
creams, already picturing her skin bleached lighter, if the glossy
poster on the wall fulfilled its promises. There is a welcome intrusion
of a more localized noise, or so it seems at the beginning. Alas, it is
only yet another local imitation of foreign pop, incongruously
clothed in some pious, beatitudinal phrases and left-over morsels of
traditional proverbs and saws. But these musicians have the measure
of their audiences—the newly rich, importers and contractors, the
managers of 'groups of companies'. Bathed in the glow of such
instant piety, their minds and senses untasked by linear melodic lines
and the single all-purpose chord, they embrace and ostentatiously
patronize the new music, barely recognizing the identicality of the
new 'Fuji', 'Fuji-Rock', 'apola-disco' 'Afro-Reggae' with their
equally vapid precursors.

Their choices equally untroubled but tuned to distant mentors,
the children of the new professionals—doctors, lawyers, engineers,
bureaucrats and clerics—pass behind the parsonage along Dayisi's
Walk clutching the very latest cassettes from 'the abroad' and
congregate at Kentucky Fried Chicken to compare notes. A girl
pauses at the hair-dressers' and soon, the sound of sizzling joins the

157

disco sounds, followed by the smell of frying hair as the hot comb heats up the brain of the young consumer without firing her imagination. At the end of the operation the belle of St Peter's examines the magazine floss on her head, touches it lightly here and there and approves her new appearance. It is time to join the others at the Colonel's for a share of the 'finger-lickin' goodness'.

Sometimes Dayisi's promenade merged with strange cruelties. In the mango season Aké Square was particularly heady with smells. It was not just the fruits, though these gave off their own sticky perfumes, in addition to attracting a plague of butterflies swarms of flies and bluebottles once the sticks and stones began to fell the ripened fruits. The tree in season was however so lush with shade that food-sellers stayed willingly beneath it. All day, the workers, office staff from nearby local government offices, schoolboys and lorry passengers squatted among the roots of the tree, on improvised benches, or simply stood while they made combination meals out of a hundred varieties. Sorowanke was an additional attraction. Sometimes they would give her food, even occasional clothing, other times she was the subject of abuse, good-natured teasing, and the occasional anonymous missile.

Sorowanke had built her shack against bushes some distance from the mango tree—a few thin strips of corrugated iron sheets, some cardboard, rags and sticks were sufficient for the makeshift home. Yokolu her lover had no fixed abode; he patrolled all of Abeokuta and could be encountered at all hours in any corner of the town. One day, we saw him sharing a meal with Sorowanke. He came more and more frequently, until we noticed that among the rags which Sorowanke now spread out to dry after washing were some that belonged obviously to a man. Yokolu wandered off less and less, spending most of the day around the mango tree and sharing the food that was habitually given to Sorowanke.

The event created some consternation among the mango-tree population. Our own pupils at St Peters brought back daily news of the progress of this liaison between the two outcasts, and the reactions of the food-sellers and their customers. Imperceptibly at first, the crowd around the mango tree began to diminish in spite of the deep and broadening shade around the tree. The food-sellers who remained moved further away from the tree-trunk towards the church, opting for new positions almost on the perimeter of the shade. Sorowanke and her lover took over the abandoned space. Their tins, cans, frayed baskets began to appear among the roots where customers used to eat. Their laundry appeared on the lower branches of the tree. Soon, Sorowanke and Yokolu followed their possessions into the base of the tree. At high noon they could be seen dozing with their backs against the tree; their hearth was now permanently positioned in a convenient triangle formed by two exposed roots of the tree, the concoctions from their pots vying in pungency with the familiar smells of fried pork and yam pottage, *leki* and the myriad other delicacies of the regular food-sellers. There were grumblings, but it seemed as if the new demarcation of territory was now tacitly conceded.

And then, Sorowanke's stomach began to swell. It grew bigger and bigger and Sorowanke talked less and less, even at night, sitting on her haunches among the roots, drawing deeper and deeper into the shadows. No longer ranting to the universe as she was wont, especially when Yokolu went on his mysterious voyages round the world, she contented herself with muttering incantations which no one could decipher. One day, her consort disappeared. Sorowanke grew even more withdrawn from the world. Since she always looked downwards when muttering, it appeared that she was speaking to the swelling in her belly. Abruptly, one morning, we heard shouts, screams, the sounds of missiles clattering on iron sheets. I rushed to the ladder with others and there we saw some of our schoolmates pelting Sorowanke with stones and sticks. The food hawkers joined in while some men on their way to work simply stopped and watched, jeering and calling her witch. Only a few days before, she had returned from an unaccustomed absence—a few hours at the most— to find her shack smouldering, her belongings scattered, flung far from the base of the tree. Since then she would sit in the same position, muttering, barely eating. In any case there was not much food or money—perhaps it was this which took her away for a few hours in the first place. And now the stones were flying at her. A well-aimed cudgel knocked off her remaining tin-pot from the crude hearth beneath which she had lit a fire, spilling nothing but plain water. I saw her bleeding from the temple, waving a hand across her face as if she was trying to swat a fly. But they were hard stones, and sticks, and Sorowanke suddenly felt along the tree-trunk and staggered up. The children moved in, scattered her fire, threw the remaining rags and cardboard boxes into the bush where her shack once stood. The food-sellers completed the work, swept the grounds clean and moved back to their former stations. It took no more than a week before Aké completely forgot the pregnant madwoman, Sorowanke.

XI

All that I observed was that he kept more and more to his room, that he ate less often, and then, mostly in his room and that when he emerged, he appeared to look more keenly at us and shake his head sadly. Nothing changed in his appearance. Visitors came less frequently. When they did they stayed for only a short while, sometimes not seeing Essay, simply being told, 'Headmaster is resting.'

Wild Christian spent more time in the house, abandoning the shop to the maid and the cousins. She spent much of the day in and out of his room, taking him food, tea, conversing with him in low voices. Our little infringements went unpunished by either of them, and these in turn diminished so that there was really nothing to rebuke. A blanket of general somnolence hung over the house, a peaceful dispensation which repelled harsh voices. No one had to ask us not to raise our voices, to avoid knocking things over. We had no inclination to play truant, to dawdle on errands or join our other playmates in furtive dares. After school, I hastened home, unconsciously impelled by a need to be with the family, to share the quiet intimacy of touch, looks, a drawing together which was tangible in every simple action.

And yet I barely understood. Not even when I came upon him unnoticed among his flowers, his gaze more and more frequently floated on distances. I turned a corner of the house, and surprised him speaking softly to himself with an annoyed shake of the head.

'Oh dear, what a pitiful death.'

It happened a number of times. There was no mistaking the words. On his face played his smile of half-regret, half-annoyance, perhaps also, a touch of curious anticipation, but the words were unmistakable. Sometime he tossed his head, smiling with a touch of indulgence, as if he was chiding a wayward, precocious child.

'Yes, what a pitiful death.'

Then, one day, he called me into his room. He was sitting up in bed and made me sit down in his chair, by the window. I had never seen him smile so much, so insistently.

'You are not to let anything defeat you', he began, 'because you are the man of the family, and if you are not strong, what would you expect Tinu and the others to do? What you must pursue at all times is your education. Don't neglect that. Now you know I've always wanted you to go to Government College.'

Mystified, but now deeply troubled, I nodded yes.

'It is true you are now in the Grammar School. But you must continue to sit the exams for Government College. And not merely sit to pass, but win a scholarship. The government colleges have several scholarships for the deserving child, which is what you must strive to be. Aim for a place in Government College. You see, no matter what happens, the government will support its scholar—always bear that in mind.'

I promised to aim for a scholarship. It seemed so important to him and suddenly I was caught up in the feeling that I was making an important transition through a promise that was eternally binding. It was plain that I must let nothing come between me and the fulfilment of this promise, which was made between two people on an unfamiliar, hitherto unexplored plane. He nodded, as if he had recognized my own act of recognition, and was content.

'Things do not always happen as one plans. There are many dis-appointments in life. There is always the unexpected. You plan care-fully, you decide on one step after another, and then . . . well, that is life. We are not God. So you see, one cannot afford to be weighed down by the unexpected. You will find that only determination will bring one through, sheer determination. And a faith in God—don't ever neglect your prayers. You are the man of the family, remember that others will look up to you. You must never let them down.' He shook his head for emphasis, 'Never, never let them down!'

That evening, I developed a high fever. It raged throughout the night and through the following day. Not until the third day did it begin to abate. Throughout the delirium I was conscious of only the two faces—father and mother—bent down anxiously over the bed. And the voice of Wild Christian saying, when the fever began to drop,

'What is the matter? Is it because of the talk you had with your father?'

I said nothing, knowing that what she had suggested was the truth, but failing to see how one thing could possibly have led to the other.

162

When I recovered, I found the photographer hovering around the house. My illness had, it seemed, delayed a planned fiesta of photography which now commenced with a kind of calm intensity. Essay had turned out his wardrobe for his finest *aso oke*. He was photographed singly, with every shrubbery of his garden, the crotons and the roses, he was photographed with Wild Christian, with each one of his children, then with all of us, then in several family groupings. He went back to his room and changed, was photographed against the setting sun, against the walls of the bedroom, seated, standing . . . but always with that wide smile on his face. He moved about cheerfully, giving the photographer instructions, positioning each of us exactly as he wanted us, first on his knees, then standing beside him—I wondered what the photographer made of this sudden orgy of portraiture. Essay's last instruction to him that evening was that he should hurry the results. Over the photographer's amazed protests, he insisted that the plates must be developed, printed and brought to the house the following evening.

I went back to bed, fatigued, suffering a mild relapse of the fever.

Then, so gradually that I did not really notice it, the shadow passed. Little by little I began to observe a return of the old routine, an increase in noise, cheerfulness, jokes, front-room visits and the normal shop-keeping absences of Wild Christian from the house. When the house was normal again, I began to think that it had all been a hallucination of my fever. That inert spell of seeming to wait—for what I did not know—had lifted. The days regained definition and pattern. A sense of liberation, a deep psychic relief, a sense of a lasting reprieve took over. Beyond a few times when I caught myself watching Essay with a baffled intensity, beyond the evidence of the photographs which had been framed and now hung on the walls, I accepted the new dispensation as a matter of course, with perhaps a sense of gratitude to an unseen Force for a deliverance from the suspected but unnamed Menace.

XII

Grandfather was right, they were not all men at Abeokuta Grammar School—AGS to most of Abeokuta—but there were numbers whose only distinguishing feature from teachers was that they wore the blue shirts and khaki-khaki uniforms of the schoolboys. In every other aspect they were ready to be heads of their own households, and some of them already were.

Nearly half of my beautiful new text books, exercise books, pencils, rubbers, blotters and other equipment vanished in the first week in AGS. The deepest loss however was a gleaming mathematics set, the first I had ever held or seen. It opened up vistas of a totally new form of scholarship and promised great excitement. That it should vanish before I even had the time to understand what the dividers, the compasses, the set square and the translucent half-circle with strange markings were meant to impart was far more painful than the punishment which accompanied their loss. Not even the replacement—with an equally new set—could compensate for the loss of that first flat metal box to which I had accorded such reverence that, I ignored all advice and refused to deface it by carving my name on it. The big boy who had stolen it, who everybody knew had stolen it and who knew that we all knew, had already scratched his name across the box inside and out. It established his ownership and there was little that anyone could do, not even the class-teacher to whom I reported the loss, and my suspicions.

There were a few more acts of initiation into the new world and, before the year was out, I did not need to overhear Wild Christian's remarks to acknowledge that I was now inclined to day-dream far less and was responding with some enthusiasm to a noisy environment. My mathematics set had been stolen right under my nose, even as a lesson was in progress. Such an event would have been unthinkable at St Peter's. I began instinctively to study my new companions very closely and devise ways to survive among them. I looked forward to my next visit to Isara: even the prescient old man, I felt, had something to learn about the natives of AGS who moved in and out

164

of its mansion in pursuit of knowledge.

Daodu was away when I joined the school. He had joined a mission of educationists selected from all over West Africa to England; in his absence Mr Kuforiji, a mathematics teacher acted as principal. His nickname was Wẹẹ-wẹẹ, a name which meant nothing until one encountered the thin, piping-voiced Acting Principal in his tight-fitting gabardine suit, spectacles which placed his gaze above the head of whoever he conversed with, and a gait which suggested a hen interrupted in the act of pecking scattered corn. When he went on his rounds of the school, appearing suddenly in the classroom where he remained for minutes to monitor the lesson, he was never without his cane. Apart from whatever report the class-teacher had to make on individual performance and conduct, Wẹẹ-wẹẹ also made his own on-the-spot assessment of appearances and application, picked out those who fell short of his requirements and administered his corrective before the class.

Even so, he was considered only an average disciplinarian. He could be managed, even manipulated, and many succeeded in getting away with close to murder with him. Even the dramatic height of his Acting career, a scandal which involved a prefect, ended with the wrong climax, and not even with a whimper.

AGS was justly called a toughening school, a training ground for later survival in life. It appeared often to be managed, not by the teachers but by a combination of anonymous forces which were located somewhere in the huge dormitory of the boarding school, in the cellars and corridors of the arched stone mansion and along the perimeter of trees and bushes and copses round the playing fields. Transactions of an obscure nature took place over those fences with the outside world during sports periods, during breaks in lessons and after classes. I obtained the feeling early that it was in these places, not in the schoolrooms or assembly hall, nor in the principal's office, that the real running of the school took place. School bounds did not exist for some of the boarders who had perfected a system for con-founding any housemaster who found, on his nightly rounds, an empty bed that remained empty until morning. At the end of the enquiry he more than often became uncertain that he had ever seen such a bed, or that the bed which he saw so starkly empty had been in that particular row of beds.

It was not uncommon to see a senior boy dispensing fortunes to his friends; he had simply broken into his father's strongbox and

165

emptied it. An agitated father would arrive, the future Public Enemy No. 1 was summoned into Wèé-wèé's presence for the commencement of a moral siege. When the father was lucky, the remainder of his fortune was recovered in the stuffing of his son's mattress, in one of the individual 'safes' within the walls of the various buildings or buried in a termite-proof box beneath a tree on the school farm. Once, the entire savings of a cocoa-farmer were stolen in this way. The bereaved man arrived in a state of collapse, and had to be carried up the stairs into the principal's office. On learning that his father was in the school, the son simply packed his box and fled. He never returned to the school and neither, we learnt, did he return to his home. He disappeared to Lagos, took a job and paid occasional visits to his old school dressed in the latest fashionable suits, dispensing largesse to his former classmates. One day he came to say a final good-bye. His father had saved up again and was now sending him to England for 'further studies'.

But the real scandal came when a Senior boy, and a prefect, made a girl pregnant. It was not unusual, but it was the first time that the girl's parents had insisted on the offender's dismissal from school. Normally the matter was taken up and settled by the parents of the two people concerned. The prefect was popular. He had a game leg which did not inhibit him in any way. His firm handling of the school was so full of humour that no one bore him any resentment. Always fastidious even in his school uniform, he had even developed a way of walking with his handicap so that it looked more like a dandyish 'style' than a disability. Some of the junior boys actually tried to imitate, in a milder form, the unique swank which he gave his body as he walked up to the platform to cries of his nickname—A-Keenzy—to make announcements, or to prepare the assembly for the arrival of the Acting Principal. It was sheer bad luck that he had to pick on an 'important' family in Abeokuta who demanded their pound of flesh. Mr Kuforiji was reluctant to blight the career of any student by dismissal, especially in his final year, yet the offence was grave enough to merit some exemplary punishment. He hit on public caning—before the entire school assembly. For a school prefect this was, even for AGS, a serious humiliation. And the number of strokes was an unprecedented—thirty-six!

A special assembly was summoned. The staff filed solemnly into the front row of the auditorium and Mr Kuforiji mounted the platform. In appropriately formal tones, he announced the purpose

166

of the meeting, expressed the shock of the entire school community at the disgrace brought upon us, and the unhappiness visited on the girl's family by the thoughtless act of one of our own members. He then named the offender, ordered him to rise and come to the platform. Kuforiji turned to him and intoned that he had resolved to give him another chance in life by offering him a choice. He could leave the school in dismissal, with his name tarnished for ever, or he could receive thirty-six strokes of the cane before the assembly. The young man chose the latter.

Three canes had been laid on the table. The prefect was ordered to 'touch his toes' and the punishment began. One of the teachers was appointed to keep count.

Wèé-wèé changed canes at the end of the first twelve; Akeenzy did not move a muscle. Halfway through the second dozen, Wèé-wèé had begun to sweat. When he changed canes at the count of twenty-four, we noticed that he took longer before he resumed, and that his strokes had begun to lose their bite. There was stillness in the hall, punctuated only by the falling strokes. I sensed that history was being made. All eyes were glued to A-keenzy's body, unable to believe that any man could absorb twenty-four strokes on his back and buttocks without once shifting position, without the slightest noticeable twitch of a muscle. I began to wonder if A-keenzy had padded himself in some way when I recalled that Wèé-wèé had first pulled back the prefect's trousers and peeped down them to ensure that there was no cheating. Kuforiji administered the last six strokes through sheer will-power. Sweat covered him profusely. A-keenzy rose, calm, unruffled, bowed with impeccable grace and intoned the ritual response to the administration of correction:

'Thank you, Principal': and then the roof of the assembly hall was solidly pounded with a thunderous applause. In vain did the principal, having first recovered from the shock, bang on the table for order. His assistant grabbed the bell and swung it furiously. It only added to the sounds of jubilation. All staff joined in the attempt to staunch the spontaneous outburst of applause, it went on and on, wave after wave until it wore itself out. For minutes after the silence, Wèé-wèé was too scandalized to speak. He glared over the heads of his wayward charges, looking for appropriate words. Finally he spluttered,

'Eyin ọmọ Satani!* Shameless incorrigible idiots, you really think

*Satanic children . . .

167

that that was something to applaud? Awon omo alaileko!* Your souls must be corrupted in and out—Get out! Assembly dismissed!'

Wèé-wèé sank gratefully back into the mathematics classroom when Daodu returned from his mission in England. He was welcomed back into Abeokuta by crowds which must have emptied every home in the town. Daodu rode on a white horse into Aké for a Thanksgiving service at St Peters Church, flanked by royal buglers, drummers, and a column of boy scouts. His agbada looked, if anything, more voluminous than usual, as if it had been designed specially to arc outwards on the broad back of a horse in contrast to the leaner girth of the motorped which had put him in hospital two or three years before. His exploits in England had become known largely through word of mouth—how he had forcefully ranged himself against the British plans to establish only one university for all of their West African Colonies, he insisting instead on one university for each country. His stubborn, nearly isolated opposition was highly acclaimed; only our Daodu could have done it.

For most of us however the implication went over our heads, though it was not difficult to grasp the principle that more schools were better than one. What mattered however was that Daodu had braved Hitler's submarines which, from all reports, did not discriminate between warlike and peaceful ships. Daodu had survived Hitler's demon bombers, had safely crossed the seas, twice, in spite of the infamous mines which dotted the shipping-lanes. He rode into Aké, a towering ebullient presence which—it was rumoured—had frequently overawed even the District Officer of the colonial government and the Alake of Abeokuta before whom, in his own turn, men prostrated themselves as he passed and women knelt. An anthem of welcome was composed by the music-teacher; I sang it constantly at home.

A week after his return, I began to wonder why Hitler had committed the unforgivable blunder of letting the Rev A. O. Ransome-Kuti escape, unharmed, when he had him at his mercy. I did not go so far as to wish him at the bottom of the seas but, we had heard of prisoners being taken after merchantships were bombed or intercepted. Surely there was no reason why the same fate should not have befallen Daodu. From all accounts, he had neglected his priestly profession for the sake of education; I felt that God had missed an

*Lacking in home-training.

168

opportune moment for redress, that he should have arranged Daodu's itinerary to include a few years' spell as chaplain to a prisoner-of-war camp.

Mowing the grass of the compound at Aké was an integral part of schooling, as indeed it was in any school of our knowledge. It was a simple, regulated occupation with fixed hours, with demarcated plots for every class. From time to time also a student might earn extra hours of grass-cutting as a punishment. Exceptionally, the entire school population was turned out, *oja agba** in hand, to crop the school compound from end to end, moving like a well-drilled army in straight lines and leaving nothing behind that could flutter to the heaviest movement of the wind. The teachers followed afterwards, looking out for patches that had not been cropped close enough to the ground.

True, I had done less of grass-cutting than most in the formative years but this had been due to the unlucky accident which had nearly taken off my right eye. It had left a permanent scar, a visible reminder to every teacher of what, to everyone, was nothing short of a miracle. Overawed by this singular mark of divine protection and, reluctant to tempt fate all over again, the teachers simply ordered me back into the classroom whenever it was time for mowing the grass. I had therefore a retarded education in the art of the *oja agba* but, I did catch up in my last year in the primary school when the incident had become all but forgotten.

Grass mowing was as it should be—without any mystique. The blade had to be kept sharp, stones must be avoided in order to keep the edge even, the mower bent low to the ground, knee flexed, the arm swung the *oja agba* in a smooth, unbroken arc and the stroke ended on the opposite side of the body, slicing through the measured space and leaving its batch of green slivers at the mower's feet. The masters of the art were of course prisoners. I had often watched them at work on the lawns before the Alake's palace. One, sometimes two of them would be appointed the song-master. Using a piece of metal and a can, or a long nail on his *oja agba*, he provided a rhythm to which the rest wielded their blades:

> N'ijo itoro—Gbim!
> N'ijo i sisi—Gbim!
> O o ni lo l'oni—Gbim!

*Cutlass made from barrel hoops.

169

O o ni se b'emo—Gbim!
Won gba e l'eti—Gbim!
Ewon re d'ola—Gbim!
Tin tinni gba tin tin tin gba
Tin tinni gba tin tin tin gba . . .*

In AGS however, grass took on 'good' and 'bad' definitions. It was
not just a question of weeds or dangerous kinds of grass with thorns
or with sharp or stubbly roots. Grass, ordinary smooth, green luscious
grass which I had taken for granted on the lawns and playing-fields of
Aké was now split into two categories—good, and bad. The care of
our fields was therefore carried out, not with *oja agba* or hoes, but
meticulously with one's fingers. Every clump of bad grass had to be
uprooted one by one. Recognizing good and bad grass was easy
enough after a while, but discriminating between them, and
therefore acting upon them as required proved increasingly difficult
for me. I could not understand it! What was more, the effect of this
strange procedure, which was not complemented by the re-planting
of good grass in the stripped areas had turned every lawn and field
into a patchwork of grass and desert. Looking down from the upper
floor of the building, the football field especially appeared to be
under the attack of a fungoid growth or some other kind of com-
municable skin disease.

Invisible lines criss-crossed the football field, dividing it into plots
for every class. Then further divisions within each plot marked the
allotments for each group of three or four. It was evident that Wéé-
wéé did not share Daodu's unique obsession in grasses; his inspection
on Friday afternoons consisted of walking through the fields like a
brisk sleepwalker, looking above the head of all the students, certainly never down at the grass. With the announcement of Daodu's
impending arrival however, attitudes changed. Class teachers were
given instructions. Many hitherto neglected chores and rituals were
re-introduced. Leaning on walls, especially with one's hands brought
down unaccustomed punishment. Most of these were irritating, some
irksome, but none produced that special block which the treatment

*On the day of threepence
On the day of sixpence (i.e., stolen)
You are tightly held
You won't ever repeat it
You are soundly slapped
Your sentence begins tomorrow.

of grass had constructed in me. I infected a few others in my class and, my own group dawdled while others clawed into the ground for their lives. We were new to the school, had never encountered Daodu professionally and we sensed much exaggeration in all of this. No monster could be as thorough as he was made out to be—was he not the same Daodu who had fallen off his moped, been carried into my father's bed and then hospitalized? I could not see him being so ill-occupied as to go sniffing the ground for every single blade of so-called bad grass and creating a fuss because of a stray one here and there.

Ransome-Kuti resumed his duties as if he had merely gone away a day or two. This created my first misgiving—that a man who had just run the gauntlet of bombs should move straight to presiding over the school assembly, inspecting ceilings for cobwebs and complaining of the singing. And his first Friday found him also routinely on the open grounds, doing just what no man fresh from international adventures should be expected to do. Followed by the entire staff, Daodu was carefully criss-crossing the field and, while he did not actually get down on all fours, he walked slightly bent forward, his hands folded behind him, his alert eyes sweeping yards to the right and left like a searchlight. Abruptly he would stop, look more intently. Then he gave his signature chuckle, which I now heard for the first time. It was, I discovered too late, a world of meanings apart from those beefy Daodu chuckles to which I was accustomed. This began in the region of his lower chest, rose to his lower jaw and stayed there, to be released throatily, in deep contented measures through lips that were parted in a mirthless half-melon smile. It was a chuckle which said,

'A-ah, they thought they could get away with it but they simply do not know me. After all these years, they still do not know the one and only Daodu!'

It was apparently also a cue for the school. When the sound of that chuckle was heard, I was astonished to hear also, from all corners of the field, a chorused response. It took the form of just one word lengthily intoned. 'Dao-o-o-o-o-o-o-o-o-o!'

Beyond a mere glance in his direction to see who the victim was, Daodu's schoolboys paid no further attention. He had in the meantime pounced on the offending spot, uprooted and held up the 'bad' example.

'And who was in charge of this?'

171

The criminal stepped forward. Daodu looked around to see if there were any further oversights in the same area, nodded satisfaction and announced,

'Three!'

The boy knew what to do. He bent over, Daodu stretched out his hand and a cane was placed in it. The *Ta-a, ta-a, ta-a* of the switch over a tautened skin menaced our ears, followed by the boy's mandatory, 'Thank you, Principal', and the tour continued.

The desperate efforts which my group now put into extracting Daodu's unfavourite grass came too late. We uprooted what we could, stuffed our pockets with them, tried to smooth the blades of the 'good' grass over its objectionable bedfellows but finally had to stop as the entourage came closer. The lenses of Daodu's glasses positively twinkled with delight when he came on our plot. The chuckle rose from its usual starting-point, came up to his throat, then descended into his stomach and bubbled there for a while before it travelled back for its sadistic release through his half-melon, mirthless smile. From every spot on the field the salutation rose in the air:

'Dao-o-o-o-o-o-o!' On and on it went, as if it would never end, measured out in proportion to the intensity of Daodu's own chuckle. He had no need to ask who were responsible for the offending plot, guilt was written unmistakably on a group of four freshers who stood apart, waiting for the worst. When he announced it, I felt ready to bolt. I was convinced that this man was a potential murderer and could already see me being carried off the field, dead.

'Twenty-four,' he said, and we all gasped in disbelief. He paused, looked along the line of the four of us. His eyes came to rest on me, then moved to the biggest boy of the four who was almost twice my size. 'Now,' he resumed, 'here we have four partners in crime. How do they normally share their things—may we know? Equally? Or according to size?'

Such was my relief at discovering that we were not to receive twenty-four each but share it between us that I did not hesitate to insist,

'Equally.' Stepping forward at the same time. One thing I was not prepared to share with the others was the agony of watching and awaiting my turn. The bigger boys could have it to themselves. By keeping my eyes and my mind on the grass and reflecting on the absurdity of the distinction I was required to make between them, I was able to take my mind off much of the pain, apart from the first

172

which sent a shock through my body. Daodu clearly wielded a massive stroke. I allowed myself to hear only the count, not the strokes themselves. It was soon over, I straightened up and remembered just in time to say,

'Thank you, Principal', feeling anything towards him but gratitude.

It was the only time Daodu would flex his cane against my back and the last I would wish him in Hitler's concentration camp. Not even a week passed after this before he resumed his usual place in my admiration. Everything that Daodu did was not merely larger than size, he made trivia itself larger than life and made drama of every event. 'Discipline' was turned into an adventure. Sometimes it seemed that the code, 'Innocent until proved Guilty' was created specially for him or by him—he carried it to the lengths of absurdity. It was not enough to admit an offence; it had to be proved against the accused. Or else the accused was required to prove it against himself, arguing extenuating circumstances along the way. If he made a forceful plea, he not only went scot-free but his accuser might earn what would have been his punishment, especially if his presentation of the case was adjudged inept.

Once, the principal himself caught three boys red-handed in one of the many copses at the bottom of the field. One was the notorious 'Iku'. They were roasting a freshly killed chicken over a small fire. The head and feathers lay beside them, so Daodu had no difficulty whatsoever in identifying the source of the chicken. Daodu kept the most massive poultry I had ever seen anywhere and I had heard the bigger boys say often how they would love to get their hands on one of them. These three had obviously managed it at last.

Court was held in the usual place, the diningroom-corridor which ran the full length of the front of the mansion. The corridor which opened into this at ninety degrees served as classrooms for what appeared to be the primary section of AGS but was in fact an in-dependent section run by Mrs Kuti and known as Mrs Kuti's Class. The Kuti lived in the part of the building which began halfway down the front corridor, the earlier half serving as diningroom for Mrs Kuti's own boarders. The boarding and teaching sections, and the living quarters of the Kuti thus flowed into one another, a screen separating the boarders' diningroom from the dining section of the Kuti.

Preceded by the evidence of offence, the head, feathers and half-

173

roasted chicken, the accused tapped on the screen and were admitted. The screen was then moved aside so that any interested watcher could observe or participate in the proceedings from the dining section of the boarders. Since Daodu was himself the principal accuser, the boys were required to present the charges themselves, prosecute themselves and make their own defence.

'Iku', as we expected, was the spokesman. The nickname, Death was one of the most appropriate nicknames coined for any boy in that school. Iku constantly defied death by his choice of routes for nightly escapes from the dormitory, any one of which could have resulted in a broken neck. He looked confident.

'It was this way, principal. There was I at the lower perimeter of the fields principal, with my friends about to engage in a scholastic experiment, Chemistry to be exact, principal, relating to the phlogiston theory of spontaneous combustion. It succeeded, principal. To our scientific delight a small fire erupted among the twigs and *oguso**
which we had gathered for the purpose, principal. We were about to put out this fire, it having served its purpose of proving a scientific point when along came a cockerel, whose patination and regal bearing identified it beyond doubt as having emerged from no other place than from the private poultry yard of Mrs herself.

'The second accused, Bode here, principal, said to me, "Iku, there promenades a chicken belonging to principal's Mrs. How did it get here?" To which I replied, principal, "I am as ignorant as you are on the subject matter". Upon which the third accused—Akinrinde, principal—said, "Ours not to reason why, but to act; using our initiative as the principal himself constantly teaches us." I concurred principal, and there being no time like now because action speaks louder than words time and tide waiteth for no man opportunity once lost cannot be regained a stitch in time saves nine, principal, and finally, one good turn deserves another so, with these thoughts for our guide, we spread out, closed in on this cock in order to catch it and restore it to the poultry yard from which it had escaped.

'Principal, it was a frisky cockerel. It was not one of those mangy, timid fowl which one meets in most houses. It was a spirited cockerel principal, a well-nourished, aggressive, independent minded cockerel principal—how could it be otherwise when it was raised, reared and nurtured under the very hands of the principal and his wife, Beere?

*Fibre kindling.

That cock flew against the second accused, knocking him down—you may like to examine his battle-scars, principal. That fearsome cockerel simply batted him with his wings, scratched his outstretched wrists—second accused, will you please step forward and exhibit your scratches.'

Bode stepped forward, held out his wrists to Daodu and turned them over. They were indeed marked by what appeared to be long scratches which could have been inflicted by talons. Daodu inspected them solemnly, nodded to Iku to resume.

'Now principal, upon the second accused falling backwards to protect himself, the impetus with which the deceased had launched itself naturally carried it forward, inflicting, as we have said principal, the aforesaid wounds on the outstretched wrists of the second accused. Now principal, it is possible to conjecture what would have happened if this had been an ordinary fire. But it was not, principal. This was a fire built on the phlogiston theory of total, spontaneous combustion. It followed therefore that it was extremely, and evenly hot. The cockerel's impetus carried it right into the centre of that inferno, where it instantly lost consciousness, overpowered by the intense heat, and itself contributing to the validity of the experiment which had taken us to the seclusion of the field in search of scientific truth, thus leaving us without any outside witnesses, principal.

'Our offence therefore principal, lies not in any wilful, overt act, but in the passive misdemeanour of concealment, principal. But the deed was done, there was no use crying over spilt milk, in every cloud there is a silver lining and like thoughts, not to mention our fear to report ourselves and maybe, be misunderstood, kept us back. For this slight error of judgement, speaking for myself the first, and the second and third accused here principal, we throw ourselves on the mercy of the court.'

All was silent. The accused awaited their fate. Daodu sipped at his now tepid tea and thought hard. I thought I had never heard such an impudent rigmarôle and waited confidently for a series of punishments to be pronounced which would begin, at the least, with eighteen strokes apiece. I had much to learn from Daodu's schema of evidence and guilt. It was not enough to dismiss any defence, however fantastic or derisive as a piece of impudence: the onus was for the accuser to *disprove* it. Even the explanation for the existence of the fire—what was the phlogiston theory anyway? I doubt if principal knew himself; physics was not his field. He looked up finally without a trace of a smile.

'Case dismissed.'

'Thank you prin-ci-pa-a-a-a-a-a-a-l.'

He interrupted by holding up his hand. 'I refer however only to the case with which you were originally charged, which was . . .?' He waited.

'Unlawfully stealing a chicken, property of Rev and Mrs Ransome-Kuti and knowingly roasting same with the intention of secretly consuming it, principal.'

'Good. But you raised a new charge in your defence. Concealment, failing to report an accident.'

'Correct, principal.'

'To which you also, at the same time, pleaded guilty.'

'The principal is again correct.'

'So that it now remains for me to pass judgement.'

'Yes, thank you principal.'

'Then this is the sentence. You will all three take back the chicken and complete what you were doing with it. That will be your entire diet—for all three of you—for the next week.'

'Thank you principa-a-a-a-a-l.'

'The kitchen should be instructed accordingly. Court adjourned.'

'Thank you prin-ci-pa-a-a-a-a-l!'

One chicken between three fully grown boys for seven days? It sounded inadequate. I wondered if they wouldn't have preferred to be beaten and given other tasks to perform. However, I did not think he really expected them to starve, he knew only too well that they would live by their wits and with the aid of others. Iku, I later discovered, was a veteran of many argued cases. Indeed, he would never plead before any teacher, insisting on his right to be heard by the principal. The teachers had long given him up and left him to do pretty much as he liked. The other two were his regular accomplices in hundreds of escapades, some of which took place in the town, leading to identification parades which never succeeded in picking him out.

Daodu was manic in his treatment of music. When he conducted the school in one of the many anthems we performed periodically, his massive frame was galvanized, and a patch of wetness emerged beneath the armpit of his jacket, widening its circle until it reached his chest. His ears picked up unerringly the source of a wrong sound.

176

I was mystified however by his failure to simply weed out those who were obviously tone-deaf. Instead, he picked out the offending row, or class, and caned them after a faulty performance. The solution was obvious, very simple, but he never seemed to consider it. The school was required to sing; any portion of it which could not sing well had to be punished. I spent my lunch-hours with the family, upstairs, eating with the boarders at meal-times. One afternoon I was tinkering with the piano when Daodu asked my why I did not learn the piano properly, offering to give me lessons. I hurriedly assured him that my father had already begun, dreading the impact of his cane whenever I fluffed a note. This was less than a half truth but the cause justified it even if it had been an entire lie. I had now assumed a definite position with regards to the rational shortcomings of grown-ups, marvelling how, for instance, an educationist and ex-perienced traveller like Daodu could behave like Wild Christian who obtained all her authority from that section of the Bible which said, 'Spare the rod . . .'

Before Daodu's return, a group had grown up around Mrs Kuti. It was an informal gathering which began with three of four women, then increased in numbers. They met, discussed problems which had to do with the community and matters relating also to their homes. Wild Christian was a member of this group and whenever she came to the Kuti for a meeting, I simply waited after school and later returned home with her. They ignored my presence near abouts as they chatted and drank tea. They were all Christian, wives of 'professionals'—teachers, pastors, pharmacists, and so on. When they were not discussing problems of sanitation, the shortages or rise in price of some commodity, plans for some kind of anniversary, their absorbing concern appeared to centre on the plight of young women who were just entering a phase of domestic responsibility. Over and over again came the observation that 'they don't know what to do'; 'they seem not to understand how to take their place in society'; 'They don't know how to receive visitors'; 'even the wedding of such and such was a deep embarrassment'; 'some of them don't know about sanitation or even child care'; and more in that vein. Attempts to help individually often met with abuse, they complained. It was suggested that they could jointly visit the homes of such newly-weds and discreetly offer advice. Another suggested that such 'problem' ladies should be invited casually to their meetings and duly instructed.

I felt I knew just the sort of women they were talking about. My mind went back to the saddest wedding I had ever witnessed at St Peter's, Aké. It was a white wedding—gloves, veil, hat, bouquet, gown etc. Itemized, there was nothing missing in the colonial ensemble of the occasion. The bridegroom wore a matching suit with his best man, pocket handkerchief and carnation in place. The chief bridesmaid, pages and other bridesmaids were spread out on either side of the bridal pair in all the correct attire, shoes gleamed and stockings were spotless white. The bridal train spread a long way behind them on the cobbled yard of St Peter's as they stood on the steps for a photograph. There was only one thing wrong—not one item of attire fitted anyone. The clothing appeared to have been picked off an assortment of shops and dumped on the backs of a random choice of children, men and women who had never set eyes on a city or heard an organ peal. The bride looked as if she would deliver her child any moment, her pregnancy stuck out before her like an explanation of the misery on the face of the bridegroom, and of the bored, uncomfortable stance of the pages and maids. There was a shabbiness about the spectacle which went beyond the ill-fitting clothes; it was the lack of joy anywhere, a guilty furtiveness in spite of, indeed reinforced by the depressing attempt to impose an outward covering—and an alien one—on a ceremony that lacked heart or love or indeed, identity.

I seriously hoped that the group of women had this on their mind, I waited for them to refer to it specifically, to make their disapproval felt for a scene which had troubled me for days afterwards. No one brought it up however, and I had to be content with hoping that they all had it in mind. They were however equally concerned with the problems of infant deaths, how to get women to use the post-natal clinics more, rely less on patent medicines picked up at random. They also, in some vague, general way, wanted women to involve themselves in more civic activities, such as philanthropic work.

Daodu was strolling past the 'Group' one afternoon when he stopped to listen. Then he interrupted:

'You know, you women have quite good aims but you don't seem to know how you want to implement them. You've been meeting now for some time and all I see all the time are *onikaba*.* The people

*Gown wearers.

178

who really need your help are the *arósọ*,* yet they are not here. Forget the problems of social graces for newly-weds. Concentrate on the *arósọ*. Bring them in on your meetings. They are the ones who need your help.'

And he continued his stroll.

The white-haired lady, the most venerable looking among them was the first to speak after he left them.

'Daodu has just spoken a truth of the first importance. We are incomplete. The next time, let each one of us bring at least one *arósọ* to the meeting.'

*Wrapper wearers.

XIII

Wild Christian took her friend, Mama Aduni, to the meeting of the Group. The meetings had now outgrown the dining-room of Mrs Kuti's Class and shifted into the courtyard below. On the faces of the women who now flocked to the meeting, market women who dealt in peppers, gari, palm oil, and homemade wares, I identified the same inward tiredness as I had seen in our itinerant traders from Isara, our chaperons who, in their own homes, placed their meagre resources at our disposal. The wide arched balcony windows looked directly on to the yard.

On the days of their meetings I went upstairs, listened and watched. There was always some little drama going on, some dispute which had to be settled—usually by Beere, the White-haired Lady whom I now knew as Ma Igbore, or Wild Christian. Sometimes, one of the women would burst into song or tell some ribald story. The meeting might take on the atmosphere of a Counselling Court, or a spontaneous festival. Some of them arrived early to prepare the food.

The movement into the courtyard began after another suggestion by Daodu. He now made it a routine to stroll past the group and listen for some moments. His bedroom and study were within earshot in any case, and I suspected that he took his 'casual' stroll only after the discussions had reached a point which gave him an idea, for he hardly ever passed without contributing something. One day he said,

'Do you know the real trouble with the *aróṣọ*? They are illiterate. They don't know how to read and write, that is why they get exploited. If you set aside half an hour at these meetings, you could end up making all the women in Egbaland literate by the end of a year!' He chuckled at his own wild optimism, strolled on.

The idea was taken. Mama Aduni and the handful of *aróṣọ* who had by now joined the Group were told to spread the word. Slates and markers were bought, pencils and exercise books. When the trickle became a flood, they shifted into the courtyard. Each *onīkaba* took on a group which she coached intensely for half-hour to an hour at each meeting. Then, while the discussions continued on hygiene, community development, self-help programmes, market and commodity prices, they continued to copy the letters, the figures, pausing only to join in the talking. From the top of the balcony, one saw only a series of backs humped in concentration, topped by head-ties which showed in some cases, wads of white hair. For that first half-hour they worked in almost total silence with sudden outbursts of laughter, laboriously making one stroke, then another. Often it was Wild Christian's bantering voice which caused the laughter. She would for instance, seize an agonized hand in hers and guide it along the slate, instructing loudly:

'Like this. Look, put down this stick, no no, make it a straight piece of wood like an electric pole not a crooked one. Or do you think it's your husband's leg you are drawing? Now, put something like a curving road on it—no, no, not like that. Don't you even know what your belly looks like when you and your husband have been getting up to God knows what? En-hen. I knew that would do it. Now that is a "b". One electric pole, and your big belly resting at the bottom of it—"b" bente-bente . . . asikun bente-bente . . . bente-bente, asikun bente-bente . . .'* moving smoothly into an improvised song-and-dance.

The courtyard erupted with laughter while Mama Aduni or the white-haired lady went and dragged her away complaining, 'For a teacher's wife, you are remarkably good at disrupting the concentration of pupils!'

They were keen pupils, mostly young, and it was these keen ones who set in motion in Igbein, the Great Upheaval that ended in Aké. They were always the first to arrive, they helped in setting up the benches and chairs, sweeping the yard when necessary, getting in an extra hour of practice to themselves before the others arrived. I accidentally became a proud teacher at those pre-meeting sessions. Dolupo and Koye, the two eldest of the Kuti children, had long been conscripted into service. I was already in my usual place on the balcony when I saw them struggling with words—they had reached the stage of putting the letters together, mostly in the wrong order. I shouted a correction, they shouted back, asking if I was too lazy to come down and show them. I was down the stairs in a flash. I found that they were mostly from outlying villages, not from the main town of Abeokuta itself; perhaps that explained their eagerness.

And then they stopped coming; even to the main session they would come late. Sometimes they never turned up at all. It was not

181

only the eager pupils, there were others too, and not only from the suburbs. It was harvest time; these were mostly farmers' wives, so the leaders assumed for a while that the chores of the farms kept them away. They took their places with apologies, tried to catch up on their lessons as the meeting progressed. Finally however the right question was asked, or the leaders listened more keenly to those excuses that the late comers mumbled through an ongoing debate. The gatherings of mutual self-improvement changed character from that moment when one voice followed the other to explain:

'I was arrested by the Tax people.'

'The *Parakoyi** took half of my farm produce for market toll. I went to the local councillors to seek their help.'

'We were waylaid on the way to the farm. The Local Police asked us to contribute one-fifth of every item as duty.'

'I tried to dodge the uniformed men. I turned into a path I thought I knew and got lost. Only God saved me or I would still be wandering in the forests.'

'They have no heart, those men. They look at you like they have no flesh and blood until you give them what they want.'

'We spent the night in a police cell. They seized all our goods and will continue to hold them until we bring them our Tax papers. But we have not even been to the market, how can we pay when they have taken the goods we are going to sell?'

'It is those chiefs. They are in this together. They set the *adana*** to do their dirty work because they daren't levy a toll on farm produce.'

'No, it's the Alake; I heard one of the *adana* say we shouldn't complain to him. "Go to Kabiyesi who sent us," he said.'

'Our own tormentors said it was the white man. He said the order came to the *ajele**** from his fellow white man in Lagos. They are just servants of the white man in Lagos.'

'ENOUGH!'

The voice was none other than Kemberi's. The junior 'wives' of a household and a mischievous lot, I reflected, to so name a woman whose real name, and a Christian one at that, was Amelia. To the women's gathering this highly feared, fearless and voluble woman might be Madame Amelia, but about the time that I became a limpet on the group, I heard both Wild Christian and Beere refer to

*Market wardens.
**Agents who waylay farmers or market women.
***An administering agent, thus, the District Officer.

182

her as Kemberi. When I delivered a message soon after and referred to her as Madame Kemberi, my head nearly flew off from a swipe from Wild Christian's backhand. Beere protested, pointing out that I could hardly be blamed for repeating a name I had heard. Only then was it explained to me that Kemberi was a special nickname given to her by the 'wives' of her compound. Only really close comrades such as Beere and Wild Christian ever called her by that nickname, and only when they were all by themselves.

'Enough!' Kemberi repeated and the murmurs of indignation began to subside. 'What you are all saying in so many words, is that the women of Egbaland are no longer free to walk the streets of their own land, or pursue their living from farm to home and farm to market without being molested by these bloodsuckers—am I right?'

'What else have we been saying?'

She held up her hands, then turned to Mrs Ransome-Kuti. 'Beere, you heard them. What are we doing about it? You said, teach them ABC; we have been doing that. And we also said to them, give your children a clean home, and strain every bone in your body to give them a good education. And they have been doing that. It is because of these children that they refuse to sit at home, waiting for some idle drunkard of a husband to learn the same lesson. After all, the women of Egbaland are not unaccustomed to hard work. But now we gave them a new reason—their children. And they began to work and they gave their little savings to the education of their children. And because of the little we have learnt together, these good-for-nothing children no longer come home and lie that they have come first in class when all they have been doing is staying away from school and scoring the round, fish-eye of Zero. At least, some of us now know the difference between 100 and Zero, between 1st and 34th. When the school report comes home, even if some of our women cannot read everything, they can read enough on that card to know if that child is wasting their money. And if they cannot read, they know where they can bring the card—right HERE!

'Now these same women are telling us that they can no longer come here freely. The streets of Egba are blocked by the very people against whom we have tried to give them protection. Tax! Tax on what? What is left after the woman has fed children, put school uniform on his back and paid his school fees? Just what are they taxing?'

A roar went up from outraged voices. Kemberi again commanded silence. 'It is time we told them, No more taxes. They want to bleed us dry, let us tell them, No more Taxes.'

A tumult of approbation overspilled the courtyard. Order was resumed. Mrs Ransome-Kuti was empowered to give notice of a demand for the abolition of tax for women, both to the District Officer and the Alake of Abeokuta and his Council of Chiefs. It was the longest meeting so far of the women, and the 'Group' remained upstairs long after the crowd had departed. There was no question of my going home that night; I sensed the beginning of an unusual event and was gripped by the excitement. On a par with the Sanitary Inspector, the Tax Officer was perhaps the most feared individual in Abeokuta—without however the tolerance which generally attached to the former. The Tax Officers had invaded our house on occasion. Although their conduct was polite, even routine, they did succeed in conveying such an aura of power that I was constantly relieved when Wild Christian opened one of the smaller top drawers and produced the yellow receipt. Once, in a sweep of the petty shops, an over-zealous type had even accompanied her home to verify that she had indeed paid her tax. The bigger cousins wanted to chase him out. Kemberi's pronouncement therefore sounded like an ally's declaration of one of those civil wars which appeared to make up both Yoruba and English histories in the text-books. There was also the memory of the women from Isara, trudging the forty plus miles from Isara laden like *omolanke*,* the push-carts which had begun to compete with the human *alaaru*.** I saw them waylaid by the *adana*, forced to disgorge a portion of their merchandise at the gates of Abeokuta, after carrying them an inhuman distance. And of course the immediate outrage against my own prize pupils who could no longer come early to their lessons because of the taxman's harassment became a personal affront. Before I fell asleep, I had made up my mind that when I grew up, no khakied official was going to extract one penny in tax from my hard-earned salary.

The Group met till late. I had long fallen asleep on the bench in the dining-room and woke up the following morning in a bed in the dormitory of Mrs Kuti's Class. On the following morning at breakfast I heard, for the first time, the expression Egba Women's Union. There appeared to be some further bandying around of alternative titles but, finally, a new movement appeared to have emerged,

*Push-cart.
**Porter.

184

formally, with that name—Egba Women's Union.

Beere left for England shortly after this—war or no war, there appeared to be conferences to attend; if it was not the Christian Mission, it was the Colonial Mission. Wild Christian's shop at Aké became a focus for women from every corner of Abeokuta. Mama Aduni became a kind of Roving Marshal, showing up at all hours with women of every occupation—the cloth-dyers, weavers, basket makers and the usual petty traders of the markets—they arrived in ones, twos, in groups, they came from near and distant compounds, town sectors and far villages whose names I had never heard. They smelt of the sweat of the journey, of dyes, of dried fish, yam flour, of laterite and the coconut oil of their plaits. Some were tatooed on arms and legs, with cicatrices on their faces. In addition to the head-tie, their shoulder shawls, neatly folded were placed lightly on their heads for additional protection from the sun.

Far from dodging the chore of keeping shop, I could now hardly be kept away from it. Some of these women came first to the parsonage, as this was easier to find than the shop. Before they had even stated their business I had jumped from my books and was escorting them to the shop. In the distance between the house and the shop, freed from the usual reproving glances to check the 'compulsive' questioner, I shamelessly indulged my curiosity. Only one of them unwittingly betrayed me. Unable to take my eyes off her stooped shoulders which, I was convinced, had been caused by carrying merchandise through distances as far as Isara, I suggested,

'Why don't you take the horses of that chief at Itoko? They can carry your loads for you.'

The woman laughed and promised to ask Mama Aduni to put it forward at their next meeting. But she told Wild Christian within minutes of their meeting. To my surprise she only shook her head saying, 'I should have known.'

There was a long lull. No one could tell me whether the women had actually stopped paying taxes or not. I now listened, without any attempt at subterfuge to discussions between Essay and Wild Christian—she sought his advice on many of the problems which the women brought to her. The daily routine at the parsonage increasingly revolved around the new Women's Movement. Wild Christian travelled, addressed groups, received her womenfolk at all hours. Sometimes their visit to the shop lasted no longer than a minute: the next moment, Wild Christian had picked up her shawl,

185

flung a head-tie over her head snatched up her bag with an 'O ya', and to me, 'Mind the shop,' ushered out the complainants before her to the source of the trouble. Invariably I locked up the shop as it fell dark. She often returned late, yet, even then, over a late meal that lasted hours, she and Essay would discuss her tactics on the immediate problem and a further strategy for resolving it definitively in favour of the victimized women.

Essay became a grass widower though, from what I could see, he thrived on it. He would mull over a new approach to some problem, then send a note to Wild Christian in the shop. I could always tell when it was a 'crisis note'. If she was away from the shop at the time, I opened it and read it. If I knew where she had gone, it provided the perfect excuse to keep the courier in the shop while I went after her, remarking in as off-handed a manner as I could manage that I considered it urgent. Sometimes I tried to recollect how I had slipped into the habit and wondered at the fact that Wild Christian never raised any objection. However, she never voluntarily took me along to these trouble spots while my curiosity was uncontrollably aroused whenever she made her lightning departures with the complainants. Simply by paying close attention to the brief conversation, I easily located these trouble spots after their departure. When there were no notes from Essay, any *arόṣọ* visitor provided an even better excuse. I simply locked up the shop, took them in tow, and went after her.

For the first time, I travelled out of Abeokuta without either parent. In spite of his increased involvement with the Women's Movement, father had never lowered his sights on GCI, the government college in Ibadan where he had scheduled me for a scholarship. I scored him surprisingly insensitive for his attempt to prise me off Abeokuta at a time of such absorbing events. However, he had taken good care to see that my homework preparations were never interrupted. In between trailing Wild Christian to her crisis points, there were pages of exercises to be completed and brought home after shop. I sat the examinations, weeks passed, then the letter arrived summoning me for an interview in Ibadan. I gained a new acquaintance in Oye, who had also qualified for an interview, and, we planned the Big Adventure together, only to have my parents reduce its dimensions by insisting on a chaperon for me. In vain I reminded them that I was now ten, a veteran of six months survival course at AGS—nothing would budge them, not even my record as Oddjob man with the Women's Movement. The other boy was admittedly older, but Oye's parents had consented to his travelling alone only when they learnt that he would be going together with the Headmaster's son. I argued the lack of sense of it with Joseph who had been appointed my guard. If I was considered by this boy's parents sufficient guarantee of his safety, wasn't that all the greater proof that I could be trusted to look after myself?

Joseph looked at me with something akin to pity. 'I hope those white men at your new school like argumentative brats.'

When the final results were published, my name appeared on the list. I had won admission but no scholarship. It meant waiting another year for another try. Joseph took it to heart, he brooded for a long time, then went to Wild Christian. 'Mama, please beg him not to argue with the white man. You see, they had to admit him, they know he is clever. But do you think the white man will give food to a native who will only get strength to chop his head off with a cutlass?'

I was disappointed. Before I attended the interview the idea of Government College was no more than a curiosity which lurked in the back of my mind. Winning an interview and travelling on my own to Ibadan would have been a satisfactory climax, but I had not counted on the physical lure of the school. My parsonage was dwarfed by its sheer expanse, so was AGS. What it lacked in Abeokuta rocks was more than made up with woods, orchards, brooks, farms and small game. The candidates were drawn from every corner of the country—at least, so it seemed. We arrived as instructed, with our own blankets and pillows, were housed together in one long dormitory where friendships developed fast and lasting from first encounters. Appalled by my ignorance of such a diversity of names, facial types, places and temperaments, I became tongue-tied and for once, asked no questions. And again, Father was right—they were mostly MEN. But the proportion of those nearer my age was comfortingly high. This group instinctively banded together, eyed resentfully by the 'papas' among them. One of them had a moustache.

Two other boys had travelled together from the same town. They were also Ijebu, but not from Isara. We were hardly two hours old in Apataganga, the suburb of Ibadan where the school was sited, before we were cautioned by others to beware of them. They had come with *oogun** which was designed to throw all others into confusion while

*Medicine (supernatural, magical)

187

they took, uncontested, the top places. A boy from Edo swore that he had seen them burying something in the corner of the schoolroom where we would sit the exams. A further proof of their sinister intent was that they had arrived one day earlier than required. While this was to be expected from those who had to travel long distances—Benin, Awka, Makurdi etc., there was no excuse for someone from the near Ijebu province to leave his station on any day other than the day before the Interview. There could only be one reason—they had come to 'spoil the ground' for others!

This last argument was exceedingly persuasive, and there could be only one response. Someone proposed that we search their luggage during their absence and was vociferously cheered. I had not really believed we would, but we found an assortment of strange objects—amulets, black powder wrapped in a piece of paper, the kind of rings which I had seen on Paa Adatan and, a sheet of paper with strange diagrams and words which seemed to me distortions of some biblical names from the Old Testament.

It was a grim reception awaiting the boy in whose luggage these items had been found. While I was a willing participant in the search, I was rather dubious about the rightness of actually confronting the pair with our trophy. I *knew* we had no right to search their luggage, yet I accepted that we *needed* to do it. Confronting them with our discoveries was another matter—for a start, what did these things mean? Why shouldn't anyone be in possession of amulets, black powder and a paper filled with cabalistic signs? I thought of Bukola, the *abiku*, and my fingers went round my own wrist where Father's visitor had incised mysterious potions into my bloodstream. There did not appear to be a qualitative difference between these varied 'possessions.'

The two boys saw the grim circle of accusers, but only one pair of eyes flew directly to the corner to behold the laid-out items on the bed. His face worked, enraged, he ended up spluttering.

'You can all go to gaol for this. You are robbers, thieves. When I report you to the police you will see.'

The Edo boy who had alerted us in the first place said, 'My father is a police officer. Last month he arrested somebody for using bad juju against another man. That man nearly died.'

The beleaguered boy reacted this challenge by turning to his townsman, as if for help. His friend looked confused, not quite knowing what to do. The next moment the juju-maker spun round

188

and walked fast into the night.

'Don't let him escape!' his main accuser shouted and they all sped after him. I did not move. The pace of events left me in as great an uncertainty as the other Ijebu boy with whom, apart from two or three others, I found myself alone in the room. I walked up to him.

'Do you believe in this juju?'

He shrugged. 'He does,' nodding toward the exit through which everybody had just departed.

'But what about you?'

'I don't know. I swot hard. I need a scholarship or I'll never get any education.'

'But your father doesn't make you any juju?'

He shook his head. 'He used to be a Moslem. Now he is a Christian. As far as I know he has never used juju. Maybe that's why he is so poor.'

He had picked up a book, preparatory to reading. I decided to risk bothering him with one more question. 'What did he bury in the corner of the classroom?'

'Oh, so they saw us.

'You mean you buried it with him?'

He shook his head. 'No, but I watched him.'

'And you didn't try to stop him?'

'Why should I? Do you believe in it?'

I shrugged in turn. 'I am not really sure.'

'Well, there you are. Nobody is sure.'

They trooped back later, having lost him in the dark. I told the Edo boy what the fugitive's friend had told me.

'Right' he said, 'We'll get a priest to say prayers over it tomorrow morning.'

I looked at him in surprise. 'What will that do?'

'It would destroy its power' he replied.

I was not satisfied. 'How will he know what kind of prayer to say? He doesn't know what kind of juju it is.'

Someone else offered, 'There are only two kinds of *oogun*—the bad and the good. Any prayer can undo the power of the former.'

Then another voice suggested that it was safer if we dug it up altogether and threw it on some rubbish heap.

There were voices raised in terror. 'You don't know what you are saying. Who is going to take such a chance? Go near a thing like that and have your hands wither? Count me out'.

189

Before I knew what I was saying, I had boasted, 'My hands won't wither.'

'Yes?' came back the sneer. 'I suppose your father has "baked and seasoned" you?'

'No, not my father. My grandfather did.'

I immediately earned some strange looks. Some of the boys drew further away from me, while others crowded round in curiosity. 'Are you serious or joking?'

'Let's go and dig up that thing and you'll see.'

I felt quite light-headed as I picked up the lantern. The Edo boy followed and soon I was heading a procession of five or six boys to the schoolroom. The Edo boy directed us to the corner, we picked up some sticks and dug.

We had hardly scraped down to three inches before we came on the white bundle, about the size of an orange. I picked it up by the tip of its tie and took it over to the pavement in the middle of the lawn.

Someone asked, 'What do we do with it?' to which the Edo boy promptly replied, 'Burn it of course. That's what they do in court with the bad juju which gets seized.'

So we unscrewed the cover of the lantern, soaked the bundle in kerosene and threw a lighted match on it. The cloth caught fire immediately, burnt for a while and then commenced a series of small explosions from within. A particle of something was flung out, landing quite close to the feet of one of the boys. While the rest of us simply drew back instinctively, he panicked and shouted,

'Epe lo fo ja'de yẹn!' *

and fled. The infection was instant. We all turned and raced back to the dormitory, some screaming 'Jesu' 'Jesu Gbami' all the way. Even through the tumult however, I heard the Edo boy muttering, repeatedly, 'S.M.O.G., S.M.O.G. . . .' like a mystic incantation. When we had all regained some measure of sanity back in the dormitory, I asked him what he had been reciting.

'S.M.O.G.' he replied. 'Have you never heard it? It stands for Save Me O God. When you are really in a hurry, it is quickest to use the initials.'

The cause of all the excitement must have returned during the night. When morning came his luggage was gone and his bed was

---

*That's dangerous spells spurting from its mouth.

not slept in. We never saw him at the interview. Good riddance, was all I thought to myself, but the Edo boy sat up in his bed, both hands clutching his head. I asked him, 'Were you still thinking of having him arrested?'

He shook his head in a most troubled manner. 'You don't see. Just see what careless fools we were, going to sleep like that. He could have killed us with his juju during the night! If my father got to hear of this. . . .'

'Why, what would he do?'

'He would beat me for carelessness. That is how to get yourself killed. Or maimed for life.' He looked round slowly, sank into utter despair and even turned to broken English,

'Look how we sleep like munmu.* We no even sabbe wetin that bastard done leave behind.'

'What are you worrying about? Keep saying S.M.O.G.'

He brightened up, nodded eagerly and we went out for our showers.

Ransome-Kuti's curiosity knew no bounds. He admired the government schools for some things but was, in the main, dubious about the ability of the white teachers to impart a worthy education to an African.

'For one thing' he said to me, 'they cannot impart character to a pupil. Not the right *character*. What a school like AGS does is to give our boys character. No other school can touch it. What did you think of those white teachers?'

I reminded him that we had not been taught, only interviewed and made to sit further examinations.

'Yes, yes, but they spoke to you. You spoke with them. What opinion did you form?'

'They seemed nice enough. But I still found it difficult to understand them all the time—we all did. This speaking through the nose . . .'

'You'll get used to that. I got used to it myself. Hm. I know the white man at home, which is really where to get to know them. I am glad I went to England. Makes one better fitted to cope with the small boys they send here as their colonial officers. Some are not bad though. But as teachers . . . no, I still don't know why Ayo wants to send you to their school.'

Disloyally, I blurted out, 'I like the place now.'

191

His eyes widened, 'You really do? You prefer it to being here.'

'I think I am going to like it uncle.'

He looked at me as if he was seeing me anew. 'Amazing. Now that is amazing. You really prefer . . .' And then he recovered quickly, 'But then you haven't even completed a year here. You haven't really become a Grammarian.'

'I like the school,' I insisted. 'I hope I can get a scholarship.'

'Now that's it!' he exploded. 'I was trying to remember the one advantage which could possibly speak for that school. Yes, they do award scholarships. Right, if you obtain a scholarship, all right, that will be good for Ayo. But you must see me every holiday. I want to know how they go about their teaching.'

I promised I would.

'They teach you to say "Sir" in those schools. Only slaves say Sir. That is one of their ways of removing character from boys at an impressionable age—Sir, sir, sir, sir, sir! Very bad. So you must come and see us during the vacation . . .' Another shortcoming struck him and he looked rather wistful, shaking his head. 'And they hardly ever use the cane there—now that is a serious mistake.'

'I don't think so principal.'

'No. You don't.believe that caning is good for character?'

'No, principal.'

'Oh dear, oh dear, oh dear. You of all people, Eniola's son?'

'No, principal.'

He sighed, shook his head dolefully once more and continued down the corridor.

Beere was on the high seas, heading home. One morning the newspapers were filled with denunciations of her activities in England. At a conference—or a public lecture—she had claimed that the women of Egbaland led a pauper's existence. They were wretched, underprivileged and ruthlessly exploited. The four-page newspaper carried a long letter contesting her statements and upbraiding her temerity in telling such lies against the noble women of Egba. It was a disgrace and Beere was a traitor to her own countrywomen. The letter invited the British people to visit Abeokuta for themselves. There they would see prosperous women, even the average Egba woman lived in comfort and splendour. There were hospitals galore, the town was spotlessly clean and housing was sumptuous. Mrs Ransome-Kuti was advised to stick her nose in whatever business took her to England, and leave the concern for the welfare of Egba womanhood to the one man who had always made it his benevolent concern, the father of all Egba himself—the Alake of Abeokuta.

Even as the women were gathering for a meeting arranged by the Group to decide what reply to make to this attack, the same journal published a letter in her defence by someone who signed himself 'Onlooker'. This writer confirmed Beere's claims in detail, referred his readers to the numerous hovels hidden away in Ikereku, Iberekodo, Ago-owu etc, where the women burrowed like rats to eke out a miserable existence. At the meeting, the new copy was passed from hand to hand. Even those who could not read wanted to see it. Finally, Ma Igbore, the white-haired lady took the paper and read it out, translating the contents. Shouts of approval rent the air. Then Kemberi took the floor.

'The other letter, that one which says that you are all millionaires, was signed by Atupa Parlour and some of those prostitutes of the Alake. Because a mere handful of them have accumulated some *jibiti** wealth and mince in and out of the palace dripping with gold trinkets, they forget that they are still living among those who cannot even give their children two square meals a day. Well, Beere is on her way. When she arrives, Egba people will know who is the real *odale.*** But there is one thing you must all keep in mind—the hand is the hand of Jacob but . . . we know who Esau is!'

Another rose. 'Of course. I can confirm that. The Alake put them up to it and it was the D.O. who put it in the Alake's head. The D.O. was still at the palace when Kabiyesi sent for Atupa and her wealthy friends. The letter was waiting for them when they arrived, all they had to do was put their fingerprint at the bottom—Atupa can't read A from B. They did not write that letter themselves. Since when has Atupa Parlour been able to put two words together except to say, "Wait, let me take off my wrapper."'

In the midst of the gales of derisive laughter which followed, Daodu strolled in, holding also a copy of the Onlooker's statement.

'What you women should do,' he said, 'is print a hundred copies of this. Take them with you when you go to meet Beere and distribute it at the port.'

The idea was acclaimed. Daodu resumed his stroll while the

*Fraudulent.
**Traitor.

193

meeting continued. He was back ten minutes later.

'Make it a thousand. Yes, one thousand. Hand them to all the people just disembarking and distribute them among those who have come to meet them.'

Again the women chorussed their approval. Daodu did not reach the end of the path before he turned back yet again, his face set, and walked briskly back to the meeting. 'Make it ten thousand. Yes, print TEN THOUSAND. We'll find the money somehow. Scatter them in the air, spread them right under the nose of the colonial government in Lagos. Yes, print ten thousand!'

There was no time to lose. Daodu now took over the direction of arrangements for welcoming back his Beere from England. He overlooked no detail. He ordered huge water-pots, the same size as ours in Ake, to be bought, buried all over the compound and filled with water. He conferred with Wild Christian and the other leaders in the Group over the feeding of the crowd of well-wishers who were bound to descend on the compound. I caught, I believed, a glimpse of the workings of his mind—Daodu wanted his wife's homecoming to be an even greater triumphal entry than his, beginning in Lagos and swelling in magnitude to envelop her detractors and overwhelm them completely.

XIV

Mrs Kuti's return changed the AGS compound into festival grounds. In addition to the water-pots, Daodu had ordered hundreds of oil-lamps. Bamboo poles were cut in four foot lengths and buried along the paths, round the fields, in the kitchen compounds and the oil-lamps were placed in their hollows. The corridors of the vast mansion, the ledges on the arched pillars, benches, garden tables also had their quota of lamps. When they were lit at night, the compound looked as if it had been invaded by millions of giant fire-flies. Huge trays, pots and basins and baskets moved in and out of the rows of light, loaded with food. There were songs, sudden roars of 'Dao-o-o-o-o-o-o-o . . . Bee-re-e-e-e-e-e-e . . .' as one or the other of the couple appeared in some part of the compound. Groups of women poured endlessly into the compound, some of them preceded by their own drummers. They had no sooner passed than another entered from a wholly different direction. Two or three would meet along the same path, there would be a medly of rhythms and melodies, then they would merge or simply separate again, retaining their own identities, filter through the crowds or dance upstairs to greet the newly arrived. From time to time a group would fall silent. Above the sounds of singing and shouting in other areas of the compound would rise the voice of a priest, offering yet another prayer of thanksgiving for Beere's safe return. I had never seen Daodu so proud, a big man already, he was visibly bursting with satisfaction and pride at the occasion. I watched him closely whenever I came close to him; it seemed to me that I was looking at a rare event—a grown man who was unabashedly happy. His barrel chest was, if anything, thrust further outwards than I had ever seen it. His shoulder appeared to have gained a few more inches, he rolled from side to side, filling out the huge *agaada* which he had selected for the occasion. He remained mostly upstairs, but would often look out of different windows, his eyes taking in everything, turning to give orders and point in a particular direction. It was clear that the Women's Union had a truly formidable ally in Daodu.

Towards midnight the crowd appeared to diminish; strolling through the compound however, I found that what had happened was that the women had reduced their activities. They were seated or sleeping in every nook and corner, in every corridor, resolved to keep vigil till daybreak. I went to sleep sometime later but was soon woken up by a commotion at the gates. I heard shouts, and rushing feet. When I leapt out of bed and rushed to a window, I found a man already there, swathed in a big dressing-gown. It was Daodu. His eyes were trained on the crowd just outside the gate where the trouble was taking place. He called out. The crowd turned, then parted. In the middle, helpless in the grip of other women was a young woman, stark naked. Her captors began to lead her towards the building, heaping abuses and blows on her. On her head was a calabash of *ebo*.* In the flickering lights I saw that it contained the body of a dog, cloven in two from head to tail. It was covered in a mess that could have been made up of blood, palm-oil, ashes or some kind of powder. Around it were kola-nuts, some coins—mostly pennies and *onini*,** cowrie shells and palm kernel husks. The woman's body was already covered in weals where she had been beaten. But it was her face which held me riveted. There was an unearthly quality about it so that, just as her body did not appear to take any notice of the blows, her face registered nothing of the pain. It shone vividly in the light of the oil-lamps but it registered nothing. Her luminous eyes stared straight before her except once, when a screaming woman moved directly in front of her and screamed:

'Dahun! Tani ran e?'***

Then she stopped, turned her eyes on the woman and rested them on her, without expression, until the procession moved on again towards us.

When they were below the window, Daodu asked them again what the matter was, ordering them to stop further blows on the woman. He reminded them that Beere was fatigued after her journey and the strain of the welcome, and urged them to keep their voices down. The male night guard provided details of what had happened. He had found the woman inside the compound, with the *igba ebo*****

*Sacrifice, a ritual offering.
**A coin, equivalent to a cent, no longer in use.
***Answer! Who sent you?
****Calabash of sacrifice.

on her head. He had actually found her close to the house, not far from where he was then standing—he pointed out the place. When he challenged her, she fled, escaped through a gap in the fence and ran to the front of the gate where she tried again to deposit the *ebo*. By this time his shouts had aroused the other women and they helped him capture the intruder. That was all.

Daodu turned to the women. 'Does anybody know her?'

The women looked at one another, at the captive, shook their heads. They struck their palms across each other, hissed, sighed and cursed. The mystery of her sudden materialization had disconcerted them. The path was broad, was more than effectively lit. There were people everywhere one stepped in the compound that night. Yet this woman, stark naked, with a conspicuous *igba ebo* on her head had penetrated right up to the walls of the mansion where she would have deposited her evil load but for the vigilance of the night guard. No one knew her, and she would not speak. I noticed in fact that no further effort was being made to make her speak. It was as if, at some moment, all the women knew for certain that the woman could not be made to speak.

One woman said, 'Atupa Parlour must have sent her.'

The suggestion became an accepted fact even before the utterance was completed. Voices were raised in execration of this diabolical plot to injure Beere through satanic means. The Alake also came into it at some point but the general verdict was that Atupa Parlour had sent the woman.

Daodu looked nonplussed. It was only four o'clock in the morning and he had not quite solved what to do with the naked woman standing below him. I could see that there would be no more sleep for me that night, so I hoped that he would decide to hold court as he normally did with his school offenders. I tried to phrase the charges but they all fell short, incomplete. I had never known any case of a naked woman caught prowling in AGS with an *igba ebo* on her head. I wondered how Iku would handle her defence.

Finally Daodu ordered them to keep her under close guard until daybreak, then send for the police.

The women led her away to the lawn behind the kitchen. They formed a ring around her and made her stand, the calabash on her head, until daybreak. Then they prodded her forward and led her through the streets, still naked, to the police station singing,

Atupa Parlour on ngb'ebo ru
Gbogbo oloye n'tagbure*

Obviously, before dawn they had also decided that the Egba chiefs had something to do with the attempt. Even with the coming of daylight, the neutral expression on the woman's face did not change.

Explanations were numerous throughout the following day and for days afterwards. The commonest appeared to be that the carrier had been bathed in a potion which rendered her invisible—it was for this reason that she had to be naked. The potion must have been defective however, making its effect wear off before her mission was completed, hence her sudden appearance from nowhere at all in front of the walls of the mansion. What the *ebo* was meant to do, no one could say, except that it was directed against Beere and was certainly not a friendly, welcoming gesture from whoever had sent it. On their way back from the police station the women made a detour past Atupa Parlour's house at Ikereku. They smashed more windows there and threw debris through the windows into her famous 'parlour'. She herself was rumoured to have now taken permanent refuge at the Aafin.

The meetings of the women, probably as a result of the attempt on Beere's health—or even her life—became galvanized by a new sense of urgency. Leaflets were printed almost every other day on one subject or the other. Wild Christian drafted some or, to be more accurate, she spoke her ideas aloud to Essay who then made notes, re-wrote everything in his neat longhand, then pushed the sheets of paper towards her saying, why don't you get the women to discuss that tomorrow? I had now settled fully into my role as Special Courier, moving swiftly between Igbein and Aké, the shop, Mama Aduni's, Mama Igbore and Kemberi, settling down longest wherever there appeared to be some promise of action. The general meetings continued, the reading and writing lessons had been resumed and I had begun to wonder if one of my pupils would not make a better wife than Mrs Odufuwa. She was younger, lively and teased me incessantly. She was also unmarried, which, I had then discovered, was rather important in the making of such decisions. And she also had the habit of saying that she was eager to learn, so that she could speak grammar to me when we were married. Since I had not

*Atupa Parlour is carrying round offerings
All titled chiefs are selling vegetables.

198

mentioned the subject to her, I felt that this was a point in her favour, responding without any prompting to what was already going on in my mind. Unfortunately some of the others had also declared their intention to marry their 'young teacher'. Wild Christian was constantly urged by them to feed me properly so that I could grow up quicker and catch up with them and continue their lessons in a secure, matrimonial home. They had a habit of gesturing in very secretive ways when they said this, so that the women around roared with laughter. They would look wise and knowing, including my favourite pupil, in ways which my first wife-to-be would never have permitted herself. It was at once embarrassing and intriguing, I never quite knew what to make of them and yet I guessed that they were referring to the secret rites that went on between husband and wife. They had inexhaustible energy and appeared to be intimidated by no one, not even Beere, Wild Christian, or Daodu. In the 'classroom' however, they were transformed. When one of them became too high-spirited, the others were quick to reprove her, the favourite proving the most constant ally. I decided that we would get married after I became a doctor.

The Group now held their own regular meetings apart from the general one. At one such meeting it must have been decided that, just as an hour had been set aside for reading, writing and arithmetic, another for health questions and so on, a period should also be set aside for the airing of tax problems. I arrived at my observation post one day to find the gathering engaged at one of these sessions. It started out like any other, but culminated in the first of the women's marches on the Aafin.

Several women had spoken of their experiences with the Tax officers. The women's original resolution had been turned down, it seemed, or simply ignored. At every meeting a report was given about the course of the No More Taxation demand. It was hardly necessary; reality was manifested in their continuing harassment on the roads, in the markets, in their petty businesses. These were recounted in great detail, to cries of indignation. New texts were drafted. New delegations were chosen. The District Officer was bombarded with petitions, demands and threats. Mrs Kuti had travelled to Lagos countless times and toured the country to gain support for the women's demands. At some point, much later, we heard of the formation of the Nigerian Women's Union. The movement of the *onikaba*, begun over cups of tea and sandwiches to

199

resolve the problem of newly-weds who lacked the necessary social graces, was becoming popular and nation-wide. And it became all tangled up in the move to put an end to the rule of white men in the country.

For suddenly there was Oge-e-e-e-ed!*

And there was Ze-e-e-e-ek!** His oratory, we learnt, could move mountains.

Some young, radical nationalists were being gaoled for sedition, and sedition had become equivalent to demanding that the white man leave us to rule ourselves. New names came more and more to the fore.

A new grouping was preparing to visit England, just as Daodu and Beere had done. They would demand, not just higher institutions for all the colonial countries, but an end to the white man's rule. Their people were going round the whole country to collect money for this purpose. The Women's Union threw its forces behind the efforts. Concerts were held. We surrendered our pocket monies, knowing somehow that even our half-pennies mattered in the great cause. Oged, Zeek, Tony, Ibiam, Ojike—these were simply names, but in Abeokuta, everyone knew Beere and the Women's Union. And both their *onikaba* and their *aroso* had said Yes to a certain movement with the longest-winded name any of us had ever heard—The National Council of Nigeria and the Cameroons. We were anxious to speed them on their way.

But the Women's Union still faced the Tax Problem. At the hour for the recital of experiences, an old woman got up to speak. She was so old that she had to be assisted up. The meeting was her first, and she had dragged her feeble body to the assembly as a last hope for the menace now hanging over her head.

'I come from near Owu,' she began, 'I heard that some people here are doing something about the suffering which the Tax people are putting on our heads. Perhaps you can help.'

She began to rummage in the folds of her wrapper, at the end of which a knot was tied. Her fingers fumbled at the knot, obviously incapable of fully untying it, so other hands rushed to help her. The knot was unravelled and a piece of paper was taken out.

'There it is,' she said, 'that is the cause of the whole trouble. I have brought all the disaster on my own head . . . I will tell you. I had a

*Ogendengbe Macaulay, nationalist leader.
**Nnamdi Azikiwe, nationalist leader.

200

son, my only son, and he died about three years ago. He left thirteen children do you hear? thirteen children from different wives. They are all young children. When the children were brought to me, I said, what am I to do with these children? I have no husband, and that was my only surviving son. Even I now have to think of how to live.

'Well, to cut a long story short, it happened that my son had a farm, that was where he derived his livelihood. So people said to me, Iya, don't just sit there and watch these children suffer. Go and take over the farm. Take with you those of the wives who are not afraid of hard work, get help from anywhere, cultivate the farm and use its produce to educate the children. So I said, well, it is better to work than to beg. I went to the farm. We have just been managing to make a living from it, just a living, nothing more. Even the education of the children is stop and go. They can only go to school one at a time.

'Well, I thought that life was hard enough on me at my age. That was until two weeks ago. The Tax people brought this paper, they say that, because I have a large farm, I am to get a special assessment. They say that I am *Gbajumo** because I have a large farm, but they say nothing about the thirteen children and four women who depend on the farm for *gari*, no. They say I am *gbajumo* with a large farm. So, that is the paper before you. Where am I supposed to get the money they have written on that paper? I want you to tell me where. Just tell me where the money is so I can go and look for it because I tell you, in the three years we have been taking our food from that farm, I have never seen that kind of money. Me, my 'wives', my children, none of us has ever seen that kind of money in our lives.'

In the hush of the gathering, the old woman was helped down on her seat. Among the Group who sat at their usual table facing the assembly, there was no deliberation, just the piece of paper moving from hand to hand, then being laid on the table and smoothed flat slowly by Mrs Kuti, a frown on her face. The silence went on and on, mocking the spate of resolutions, delegations, consultations, the high-sounding organizations in and around the existence of the gathering. Not unpredictably, it was Kemberi who erupted into the silence. She was suddenly up behind the table, pushing back her chair with her body. Mrs Amelia Osimosu, known to the junior wives

*Well-to-do, well-known.

201

of the Osimosu compound as Kemberi looked round the table, and forced her way out from behind it:

'Enough! We've heard enough. O ya, e nso l'Aké!'*

The women rose in a body. Hands flew to heads and off came the head-ties, unfurling in the air like hundreds of banners. The head-ties flew downwards, turned into sashes and arced round the waists to be secured with a grim decisiveness. Kemberi leading the way, they poured out of the grammar school compound, filled the streets and marched towards the palace at Aké.

There is a public frontage at the palace of the Alake; it consists of a broad field which is almost square in shape and runs the entire length of the palace. The field acts as a kind of buffer between the palace walls and the public street. Wild Christian's shop was situated opposite the Aké end of this field, on the other side of the street. The field was well-kept, bordered by the usual white-washed stones and shaded by trees which stood at precise intervals along the perimeter of the field, and on either side of a broad drive from the arched gate to the palace building itself. Over the arch was the figure of an elephant in repose, the symbol of royalty of Egbaland.

Bordering the field at right angles on the Aké end was a long, low structure of wood and clay. It was broken at neat intervals by uneven archways which were sealed two-thirds way up by wooden crosswork and topped by a low-slung corrugated iron roof. One side ran along the same public road as the palace field; the other, at right angles, simply vanished into a warren of mud houses and compounds. These two walls hid, from the streets, the corridors of the *ogboni* enclave. From the shop we saw them pass at all hours of the day on their way to attend a meeting of chiefs at the Aafin or their own periodic sessions within the ogboni compound. Age appeared to be the condition for this numinous society, yet a number of them also strode by in crude, vigorous health, called out their greetings in robust voices, looking more like warriors than participants at sessions of cunning, experience and wisdom.

Each *ogboni* was invariably to be seen in a single broad cloth which he wore like a toga, one shoulder covered by the end loops. On the other shoulder, otherwise bare, was thrown the distinctive shawl, a narrow piece of cloth of coarse weave, tasselled at the ends, with a

*It's time. Let us march on Aké.

mid-section of fluffed-out multi-coloured patterns. Some, especially the older *ogboni* wore a *buba* beneath the covering broad cloth. Some passed barefoot or bare-headed, some in leather or woven slippers, in the casual headgear of a soft cloth-cap whose pouch fell over one ear. An iron or brass staff of office was carried in the right hand or borne before them by a servant. The broad, circular stiff-leather fan appeared to belong to their formal attire, but the most distinctive feature of the Egba *ogboni* was the broad-rimmed hat, usually of stiffened leather, decorated with coloured leather or raffia strips, cloths or beads. The *ogboni* slid through Aké like ancient wraiths, silent, dark and wise, a tanned pouch of Egba history, of its mysteries, memories and insights, or thudded through on warriors' feet, defiant and raucous, broad and compact with unspoken violence. We were afraid of them. Among other furtive hints and whispers we heard that they sent out child kidnappers whose haul was essential to some of their rites and ceremonies. Certainly they controlled the *oro** cult whose bull-roarer sent all women into the first available indoor refuge. It was unusual for the bull-roarer to be heard in daylight, and without warning, but it happened once when I was in the shop with Wild Christian. She quickly locked the shop doors on us until the danger was past. Their weird chants drifted many evenings into the parsonage, punctuated by concerted thuds which, we learnt, was the sound of their staffs striking the clay floor as they circled round in their secret enclave. There was no formal teaching in such matters, but we came to know that in the *ogboni* reposed the real power of the king and land, not that power which seemed to be manifested in the prostration of men and women at the feet of the king, but the *real* power, both supernatural and cabalistic, the intriguing, midnight power which could make even the king wake up one morning and find that his houseposts had been eaten through during his sleep. We looked on them with a mixture of fear and fascination.

To reach their own enclave however, the *ogboni* had to pass through the central elephant-topped archway, then turn left into the private path which led into their sector. The central driveway led directly into the palace complex, through a passageway under the long, two-storey building which formed the outer line of the palace structures. This building housed the offices and council rooms of the

---

* A secret male cult with the task of carrying out sentences.

Native Administration, presided over by the Alake. And at the inner wall of that building, emerging from the tunnel beneath it into a courtyard, the outer world stopped.

This brief, low tunnel, roofed by the upper floor of the offices was a time capsule which ejected us into an archine space fringed by the watchful, luminous eyeballs of petrified ancients and deities. For this was my first impression on emerging from the brief shadow of the tunnel into the sunlit courtyard. From the humane succession of bookshop, church, cenotaph, sewing academies, bicycle repair shacks, barbers' shops, petty trader stalls, the stone and concrete bulk of the Centenary Hall, stray goats and noisy hawkers, tree-lined field and office buildings, we were thrust suddenly on this arc of silent watchers, mounted warriors—single and clustered, kneeling priestesses, sacrificial scenes, royal processions. Knowledge of the names came later—the eyes of Ifa, Sango, divination priests, Ogun, Obatala, Erinle, Osanyin iron staffs with their rings of mounted divination birds . . . even the *ogboni* in procession, frozen in motion. They surrounded the courtyard on a low wall which formed the half-circle of the courtyard and was shielded by an outjutting roof held up in turn by houseposts, elaborately carved in human and animal figures. The low wall was only the outer line of a curved passageway whose inner wall housed grottoes filled with more carved denizens of the ancestral world. Passageways opened into it from various interiors of the palace, radially, and these were again filled with intervals of votive presences, progressively shadowy as the passages receded.

One of these passages, to the left, facing inwards from the tunnel, was broader than others. It rose on wider, staggered planes and vanished into a pillared space over which rose an independent unit with a wooden fretwork verandah which overlooked the main courtyard—these were the living quarters of the Alake. At his hour of public audience the crowd gathered in the courtyard below. When the Alake appeared up in the verandah, men prostrated themselves flat on the ground and the women would *yinrinka*, a motion which involved getting on their knees with their elbows on the ground, then tilting until they touched the ground with one side, then the other before returning to their half-crouch position. The petitioners· or complainants were then called upon in turn by one of the Alake's clerks or chiefs, judgements were awarded, advice given, settlements and arbitrations recommended or instituted on the spot.

204

I had witnessed the scene several times. We were first taken to visit the Alake, Tinu and I, one day after church. I had hardly begun school then, and the lasting impression was one of a cemetery with no headstones, no marbles and whitewashed graves, only wooden figures which did not quite conform to the usual shapes of angels and cherubs such as filled the graveyard beside the church. But there had also been the familiar surrounding of the Alake's private garden which was nearly as luxuriant as Essay's, but boasted a number of plants that I had not seen before. Most memorable of all however was his aquarium, the first I had encountered. It was at the bottom of a series of flagstones, in a kind of indoor courtyard, and contained both grey and coloured fishes. One of them, we were warned, would give an unpleasant sensation if touched. At the first opportunity I slipped out from the parlour and went and touched it, nearly falling in. The sensation was a frightening one; I had no choice but to keep it to myself for fear that I would never be allowed inside the palace again. The Alake made much of the Headmaster's family, largely on account of our mother, of whom he was very fond. During later visits, he held Tinu and me by either hand, pestered us with questions and referred to us as his 'yekan'. When I asked mother what 'yekan' meant, I was most unprepared for the news that it meant that we were his relations. The world of the parsonage and the Aafin were so far apart, I could not see how the two could be linked in any way. The king, in spite of his periodic appearances in church where he had his own pew, was compelled by his position to follow the *orisa*. Becoming a king was to 'je oba', and this, we informally gathered, was to be taken literally. When the old king died, his heart and liver were removed and the new king was required to eat them. Nothing upset me more than to learn, so casually, that the man who had taken me on his lap and claimed I was his *yekan* had actually eaten human flesh, even for the sake of kingship. For some time after this I would watch the Alake on our visits, wondering if I could detect the stain of human blood on his lips, and doubly puzzled to find there nothing but a warm, crinkly smile. I never found the courage to ask him directly; it seemed to be one of those very few things in the world which one dared not ask about, I could not find the courage to do it!

I knew the hour of the Alake's audience and sometimes when we were two at the shop, I risked going over to watch the various petitioners. Once he saw me and beckoned to me at the end of the

audience. Afraid that he perhaps wanted to send a message to Wild
Christian, thus exposing my presence there, I fled. After that I went
very rarely, taking great care not to be detected. The cases were
varied, and many of them were filled with comic drama. Some had
nothing of the humorous about them, except for the retainers or
some attendant chiefs who seemed to quarry belly-laughs out of any
situation. It was at these sessions also that I found, for the first time,
that one of those passages which led away from the arced corridor was
lined with detention cells. I had seen 'native' police around the
mouth of this passage but assumed that they were merely part of the
palace guard. At one of these sessions however, a door in the passage
was unlocked and a group of offenders—men and women—were led
out by the policemen. They were flung down in the dust of the courtyard below the Alake whose thin, plaintive voice then floated down
from the balcony asking them,

'Why is it you people always have to be made to pay your tax?'

It was this scene that came most clearly to mind as I turned aside half
a mile before the CMS bookshop to take a short cut which took me to
the rear of St Peter's parsonage, through the cemetery, then through
the school compound, through BishopsCourt, emerging by the
nearer gate opposite Pa Solotan's house, then round the back of the
church to Wild Christian's shop, stopping to pass the news to Bunmi
who was on duty at the time. I secured myself a good observation
position a full five minutes before the advance-guard of the women
crowd burst on the palace and into the courtyard to demand an
immediate audience with their 'Baba'. The *akoda* at the tunnel
entrance began by confronting them with an attitude of extreme
haughtiness.

'Who are you? Who sent you? What do you mean? Have you ever
known Kabiyesi grant audience at this hour? Go back and warn those
noisy people coming behind you that . . .'

When the 'noisy people' swarmed through the gates and spilled
into the fore field of the palace, filling it completely, the rest of the
akodas' questions and commands stuck in his throat. He goggled and
began to walk backwards into the palace, to be replaced by a hurrying
squad of junior chiefs. I recognized them as the retainers, some of
them with some minor palace titles, who usually lounged on mats in
the courtyard before the passage that led to the Alake's quarters.
Some of them I had also seen as functioneers during the king's

audiences, selecting the next petitioner to be heard and running errands like clerks of a court. Their urgent mission seemed to be to persuade the advance-guard to keep the women from entering the main courtyard of the palace. The women replied that the crowd would remain peacefully in the field as long as Kabiyesi emerged to receive the delegation of women who were then on their way. The chiefs thanked them, returned to deliver their message to the king.

Not long after, the formal leaders arrived—Mama Igbore who astonished me by keeping pace with the others to arrive so quickly, Wild Christian, Mama Aduni, two or three other women and of course—Kemberi. When the Alake appeared, they curtsied, going down on their knees, but no more. The Alake had obviously resolved to receive the emissaries courteously. He spoke to them with urbane fatherliness, his high-pitched voice coated with a persuasive concern, addressed them as his own daughters, friends or relations, inviting them to share their civic concerns.

'Ah-ah, Moroun, *yekan mi* . . . And Mrs Owodunni . . . I see Igbore is here too, not to mention the clergy . . . well, the matter must be heavy. But even the very composition of you here, who in effect make up the city, assures me that there is nothing we cannot solve. Nothing can be beyond solution with the group I see before me, so let's get to it. What is the matter in our beloved Egbaland?'

Kemberi knelt again, greeting him, 'Kabiyesi o, Kabiyesi', shifted from one knee to the other, then stood up. 'Kabiyesi, the message which I bring you today, is the message of all the women who have left their stalls, their homes and children, their farms and petty affairs to come and visit you today. They are the suffering crowd who are gathered on your front lawn—you can see them yourself Kabiyesi, they are all the womanhood of Egba, and they have come to say— Enough is Enough. The voice with which I speak is the voice of our Beere, Mrs Kuti. The words which you hear from me are the words of Mrs Kuti. She asked me to tell you, on behalf of those women you see outside, that the women of Egba have had enough. They are starving, their children are starving, they are diseased, they have no hope of education or a better future, and yet their mothers have more and more burdens placed on them. Now the women are saying, Enough.

'Once upon a time Kabiyesi, the *parakoyi* in the markets formed an honoured, revered institution. They kept the peace, their presence gave us a sense of security, even a sense of being in our own homes during the long hours of keeping market. What we gave, we gave

207

gladly. We set ourselves a toll which we contributed to keep them fed and clothed. Now, in these past years, they have grown beyond the level of greed. They dip their hands in our *gari*, in our *elubo*, our salt, vegetables, in our corn and oil, right up to the elbow and do it as of right. They say they are empowered to do this by the chiefs, by the council or whatever comes into their minds. It doesn't matter where they get this new power, we say Enough is Enough. We don't want them in the markets any more. We want them moved out. They bring *akoda* and police to arrest our women, lock them up and even flog them. We don't want to see them in the markets any more.

'And then, after the *parakoyi* have filled their fat bellies, in return for which they do nothing, the Tax people waylay our women on the roads, raid them in the markets, in their homes, carry them off—even nursing mothers—to lock-ups until they pay their tax. Mrs Kuti says I am to tell you that we have written petitions, held meetings, protested everywhere about the injustice of many of these assessments which are used to oppress our women. She says we have told the council to keep their officers in check, to look into this matter of demanding tax where the breadwinner has nothing with which to feed the family. Now, the matter has reached *gongo*. Special o, ordinary o, levy o, or poll o, our Beere says I am to tell you—no more. The women of Egba say, NO MORE TAX. Of any kind! Simply—NO MORE TAX. Beginning from today, we reject all forms of taxation!'

Her voice had risen at this point, carrying to the nearer women in the field. Immediately they took up her cry which gathered volume and rolled through the field, filling all of Aké with that one cry:

'No more tax! We women say—No More Taxation!'

The Alake waited for a lull, sitting thoughtfully, weighing the problem in rapt concentration as if it was the first time he had encountered it. Finally he spoke:

'Enh, it is a matter you have put very capably, Amelia—I thank you very much, I thank all of you and I thank Mrs Kuti who is not here.'

'She herself is on the way' Kemberi assured him.

'Is she?' And I thought the Alake looked momentarily worried but recovered quickly. 'Ah well, then we will have even more heads to put together over the issue. But right now, let me ask you women—do you think it can be done? Taxation is as old as human society, can one simply do away with it just like that?'

Wild Christian replied him, 'Kabiyesi, over this matter, I wish to implore you to reflect very carefully. *Very* carefully. The women are saying, No more Tax. It is no time to start asking whether taxation began with our forefathers or not. Our women today, those women whom we meet everyday, they are the ones we are talking about. They cannot afford the tax.'

'That may be true' the Alake replied. 'I am not saying that I am not in sympathy with their plight. But my question still remains— can it be done? Is it really possible to have a society today where women will not pay tax? In any case, this is not a decision which I can take. It is not the Alake who imposes taxation, it is a council of government. The matter has to be laid before them. And what I am asking all of you is—do you really see a body which must run a community, using not sand but money—do you really think it can be done, abolishing tax just like that?'

Kemberi burst in, shaking her head vigorously. 'Ngh-ngh, Kabiyesi, ngh-ngh. We have come to you as our Baba, as the one we know. We do not know any council of government other than you. You are the government and the government is you. It is you we have come to talk to, not to any chiefs or council. It is you who must reflect on this matter very carefully, As *Aya* Headmaster has said, reflect *very* carefully.'

'I will, I will', Alake assured her. 'But I have to summon a council meeting. I have already done so. I have even sent for the *ajele* because you see, that is all part of what I am saying—this matter extends beyond the palace, it is not a thing we can do alone. And it cannot be done overnight. So, give us time. Tell your people, I have promised to look into it. The council will meet, and we will consider everything.'

He sighed then turned, somewhat wistfully I thought, in the direction of Wild Christian. 'Moroun,' he said, 'let me ask you something. You are the wife of a teacher, the Headmaster of a school. He is in charge of the school, he supervises activities, he decides policies and so on. Now imagine a situation which calls for a decision which will profoundly affect the normal direction of the school. I mean, not just a question of changing the style of marching or of holding the morning assembly or even whether to declare a school holiday or not. I am speaking of something which goes to the root of administering the school—increasing or decreasing school fees, changing the education curriculum—things like that. I want to ask you, can the Headmaster do it alone?'

My mother replied, 'No, Kabiyesi. He would call a meeting of his staff.'

The Alake nodded carefully. 'We are all in agreement so far. Now comes the more difficult one. Suppose, at the meeting, whatever measure is proposed by the Headmaster is opposed by all his staff. This is something he believes in very much, something he sees as necessary, perhaps a demand by the pupils' parents which he believes in wholeheartedly. The meeting goes on all day, continues into the next, goes on for a whole week. He argues his points carefully, he tries to win them over but they won't agree. Nothing he says can make them change their minds. True, he is the boss, but he is only one. He has done his best, his conscience is satisfied. Well, what should a wise man do at that point?'

Wild Christian kept her eyes on the ground and shook her head sadly. 'Kabiyesi,' she said, 'this question you have asked me is one which should really have been put to *agba-igba*,* not to a child, which is what we are before you.'

'But I asked it as a question between husband and wife,' the Alake said.

'Well,' said Wild Christian, 'in that case, and since you have spoken of satisfying one's conscience, I would say to him, if you cannot follow your conscience, then the job is not worth clinging to. That is what I would say to the Headmaster.'

All the women in the Group nodded, gravely. The Alake stared ahead in the absolute stillness of the courtyard. An endless moment elapsed and then he sighed, rose and entered the house.

The end of the audience was separately signalled from the outside by the arrival of Beere which let off the familiar cry 'Bee-e-e-e-e-e-re' from the multitude on the fields. She was hemmed in on all sides and, for a while, passage into the main courtyard was impossible. As if to complicate matters the District Officer arrived, accompanied by policemen who vainly tried to clear a path for him. The women at the outer fringe, that is, near the arched gate recognized him and, in a good-natured way, began to tease him. In fact, their attitude was extremely friendly, as if they felt that, with his arrival, the sinister operations of the Alake's oppressive agents would be fully exposed. The young Englishman however grew redder and redder in the face, recognizing that he was being made fun of and resenting this slight

* A well-seasoned elder.

210

to his authority. He ordered the policemen to clear a way forcibly through the crowd, which they did easily because the women co-operated. But then he came to where Mrs Kuti was, surrounded with anxious women who plied her with questions.

Those women around Mrs Kuti were not as patient as the earlier ones. They remained stolidly where they were, evidently expecting the District Officer's group to do the same. When the policemen tried to exert pressure on them in order to clear the way, they turned angry, let up a continuous shout of derision at the officer. His face and neck now approaching the colour of camwood, he ran the gauntlet of insults until he gained—and only through Beere's intervention—access to the palace courtyard. It was, I felt certain, this lingering sense of humiliation which made him, once he had gained the security of the palace, mount the balcony of the offices which overlooked the field and shout to Mrs Kuti:

'Look here Mrs Kuti, we are trying to hold a serious meeting here. Will you kindly keep your women in order.'

Mrs Kuti replied, 'So are we, holding a serious meeting. Or do you think we are here to play?'

Further infuriated, the man shouted, 'Well, tell them to shut up!'

There was a pause. Mrs Kuti blinked through her glasses upward at the man, then inquired, 'Excuse me, were you talking to me?'

'Yes of course I am. SHUT UP YOUR WOMEN!'

In the sudden silence which fell over the shocked women, Mrs Kuti made the response which flew round Abeokuta for weeks afterwards, as the 'grammar' which hammered the ill-starred District Officer into submission. It was referred to sometimes as the grammatical TKO of the entire uprising, sometimes the episode was simply described as one in which Mrs Kuti 'fi grammar re l'epa' or 'o gba n'stud', 'o gbe fun' and a number of other variations. It was undeniable that the District Officer was rendered speechless by Mrs Kuti's angry riposte which rang through the hush:

'You may have been born, you were not bred. Could you speak to your mother like that?'

The District Officer's open-mouthed retreat was accompanied by a welling of the women's angry murmur. There were shouts on the Alake to get rid of the insolent white man at once, within minutes. If he was not out, they would come in, cut off his genitals and post them to his mother. Chiefs appeared on the same balcony, were hooted away with only one demand—that white man was to leave the

211

precincts of the palace immediately as his very presence was an abomination not merely to the women but to the palace which belonged to the people of Egbaland. The mood was now violent, the Group was lost amidst the multitude, vainly attempting to placate the women.

What would have happened next, was impossible to predict. I had retreated to the edge of the field but remained close to the office blocks, fearful now of being trampled to death. I passed Mrs Kuti once in the crush and saw her smile for the first time that day saying,

'Hm, l'oogun, o ti ya de'bi.'*

She asked me where my mother was, little realizing that she and Mama Aduni had been within arms length of her during the exchange, before the surge of the crowd prised them apart again.

The tension was not immediately relieved, but its focus was shifted away—fortunately for the white man—by the arrival of one of the *ologboni*. They had been arriving in ones and twos to confer with the Alake on the crisis and their passage had been quite uneventful. Now came the Balogun of one of the Egba districts, an arrogant, puffed-up individual, or perhaps it was simply that he felt it his duty to act in accordance with his title, which was that of a war-leader, in face of this civil disturbance. Undaunted by the sheer mass and mood of the gathering, indeed, probably provoked by it, he decided to assert his manhood authority, hissing as he strutted through the rear section of the crowd, accompanied by his retainers. In a voice as burly as his figure he hissed:

'Hm-hm-hm, pshee-aw! The world is spoilt, the world is coming to an end when these women, these *agb'eyin-to*,** can lay siege to the palace and disturb the peace.' And he raised his voice further, 'Go on, go home and mind your kitchens and feed your children. What do you know about the running of state affairs? Not pay tax indeed! What you need is a good kick on your idle rumps.'

What happened next constituted the second high point of the uprising on that day. After that, no one could doubt the collective psychic force of the women and, specifically, of the Beere. She was now rumoured to exert supernatural powers—to which indeed was already credited the exposure of that carrier whose invisibility had worn off as she was about to set down the evil load at Beere's doorstep. For something happened to the Balogun's thigh as he

*Hm, man of strife, here already?
**Who urinate from the rear.

212

suited action to his threat and delivered a kick in the general direction of the women. As he set that leg down, it simply gave way under him and he collapsed. Embarrassed, he very quickly scrambled up, only to half-collapse again as he attempted to set his weight on it. He had come with about six retainers—perhaps it was this also which gave him so much daring—and they now rushed about him in a practised way and bore him off. It happened very quickly and smoothly, like a familiar exercise, reminding me of the accounts of civil war in Yorubaland when the war-leader's attendants would rush to rescue him, when wounded, even in the face of fire. The women were of course also spellbound—momentarily at least—by his collapse. In fact, those nearest to him had shrunk back, not knowing the nature of his sudden seizure. By the time they had recovered, the Balogun had been swept away, leaving his brother *ogboni* in trouble.

For from then on, any figure in an attire which remotely resembled an *ogboni* was set upon. His shawl was snatched, shredded, his wrapping cloth was stripped off him—fan, office staff, cap all had long disappeared. The *ogboni* were flogged with their shawls, fans, and were left only with their undershorts when finally let through a gauntlet of abuse into the palace or back in the direction of their homes.

And then I heard the ultimate challenge of the women, for this was not just a rallying-song, even an ordinary war-song, but the appropriation of the man-exclusive cult—*oro*—by women in a dare to all men, *ogboni* or not. I could not be sure whether the women would regard me as a 'man', or that, if they did, they would at least recall their 'young teacher', courier extraordinary, scout and general factotum. When I saw stocky, middle-aged and elderly, grizzled men, the fearsome *ogboni*, abandoning their hats, shawls, staffs of office and run on the wind faster than I ever saw Osiki perform, and beheld even the non-*ogboni* men skirting the palace environs, moving deeper into their shops, and finally picked out the wording of their new chant:

> Oro o, a fe s'oro
> Oro o, a fe s'oro
> E ti'lekun mo'kunrin
> A fe s'oro*

* *Òrò*-o, we are about to perform *òrò*
Lock up all the men, we are bringing out *òrò*.

I decided to move closer to the sanctuary of Wild Christian's shop without further delay!

I found her already there, issuing instructions about closing up the shop. She looked worried, very worried. Since the beginning of the women's movement I had never seen her so downcast. Only then did I make an incredible discovery—Wild Christian deeply abhorred violence! It was an astounding revelation. Her entire temperament, her violent outbursts on our hapless heads had led me to assume that she would be in the midst of the tumult—which I had myself very reluctantly abandoned, and only for fear of my own safety. Indeed I had expected her to return home with trophies gathered from the comic apparitions of those deflated terror figures. She mentioned then that she had been looking for me in order to send me to Bunmi to lock up the shop and, speaking more to herself than to me, remarked that the situation had got out of hand, the women no longer distinguished between the Balogun type, and those other *ogboni* who had actually given them help, had encouraged their fight against taxation and were going to the palace to speak on their behalf. But it wasn't just those friendly ones she was concerned with, the entire scene of violence sickened her.

Even as she supervised the packing up of the wares which were laid out in front of the shop, a late *ogboni*, completely unaware of what was going on, marched confidently past the shop towards the Aafin. Wild Christian stared at him, unbelieving, for some moments, then cried out:

'Baba! Baba, where are you going?'

The leader stopped, assured himself that he was the one spoken to and announced, 'To the Aafin. We have been summoned to sort out some trouble there—yes, I can even hear it from here.'

'Baba, get back quickly. If they catch sight of you . . .'

Something in the renewed noise from the palace gate made me realize that the women there had seen the old man. Wild Christian heard it too. She rushed out and dragged him into the shop, shut one half of the door on him and said, 'Quickly Baba. Remove your robes, remove all your *ogboni* gear.'

The urgency in her voice only made him more confused. 'Enh? Enh? Ewo lo tun de yi? Enh?'*

She reached behind the door, snatched off his shawl and hat and

*What new development is this?

threw them behind the counter. 'Baba, kia-kia, your wrapper—take it off. Throw it behind with the rest. Leave only your shorts.'

The women arrived moments later, about twenty of them. There was only one direction in which the *ogboni* they had seen so clearly could have disappeared and this was Wild Christian's shop. They gathered in front while we continued packing up goods from the display mats and trestles. Wild Christian did not attempt to deny that the man was in the shop.

'If it is that old man you are looking for, he is inside changing. He is not an *ogboni*.'

There was a chorus of disapproval. 'Ah, Mama Wole, how can you tell us that when we saw him with our own eyes.'

'Well, when you saw him, he was, but now he is changing. I've told him to take his *ogboni* things off because the *ogboni* are no longer wanted here today. What more do you want?'

'They are still enemies,' interjected one of the women, 'in or out of their silly shawls they are our enemies. Are they not the ones who have been taxing us? Mama, let's apportion this one his own *seria* before we let him go.'

The rest raised shouts of support. Another added, 'Today is the day of reckoning for all of them, Mama, bring him out.'

And yet another voice, 'We are the *agb'eyin-to*, not so? They forget that they were all born by these same *agb'eyin-to*. Including the very oldest among them! Well, let their mothers teach them something today.'

Wild Christian burst out laughing. 'Is that all that is paining you? Because one stupid *ogboni* called us *agb'eyin-to*! Listen, did we come here for that or for weightier matters? The man who insulted you has been carried home, half-paralysed—that is heaven's justice for you. I don't know this man, one of you can go inside and ask him. At the most I know only two or three of the *ogboni*, so don't think I am protecting him because he is my *ibatan*.* But I do not like trouble, I don't like all this violence. It is not what we set out to do.'

They looked a little mollified, in any case, their initial ardour had cooled somewhat. Still one of them demanded, 'Let him take off all his paraphernalia. We don't want to see any of it on the streets of Abeokuta today or tomorrow, even forever.'

Wild Christian pushed in her head, 'Baba, fold all your attire

*Relation.

215

neatly and tie it up in this cloth and go home.'

The man sighed, 'Ah, I'm in no hurry. I will stay here until all is quiet, then go home exactly as you say.'

Wild Christian turned to his pursuers. 'You see, what more do you want? The Baba is still suspicious of you. Go on. I'll see him off when you have gone.'

Still they insisted, 'We want to see his face. There are a number of them for whom we are specially on the lookout. Let's see his face and make sure he is not one of them.'

So the old man had to show his face, introduce himself, and swear that he had never done a thing against women, was going to cast his voice on the side of the abolition of tax and the women could count on him on any measures they wanted. As for the *parakoyi* he had told Kabiyesi times without number that they were leeches and parasites—and this was no hearsay, he had gone by the evidence of his own wife who was a market trader like most of those he was then talking to . . .

They left at last, the old man prostrated himself repeatedly, thanked and blessed Wild Christian profusely. He sped off in his shorts, bundle in hand, leaving his staff behind. He would fetch it the following day, he said.

Calm began to descend as it neared dusk. At some point, a decision had been taken that the women would lay siege to the palace until all their demands were granted. The calm was hastened by what seemed an orchestrated movement from all roads and byways which led towards the palace. This movement contrasted deeply with the earlier violence and chaos, yet did not appear to be a separate event; one thing simply flowed into another, affected what it replaced and gave birth to a new mood, a new atmosphere of communion and cohesion.

They came from the direction of Iporo, Iberekodo, Ibara, Lantoro and Adatan, from other byways within the heart of the city itself. The lines of humanity curled through hidden *agbole* to swell the other throngs on a final approach along the road that led to the gates of the palace. They were like the caravans from Isara, laden with stocks and foods, only there were streams and streams of them. From about an hour before sunset, as if they had been signalled in, processions of women brought food and greetings from outlying villages, market women arrived, having closed their stalls for the day, hastening to partake of the events at the palace. The cries of welcome

216

began to overcome those of outrage and pursuit. The newcomers recognized faces, reported their arrival to the leaders who, by these means, now began to regain control of their followership. Mats arrived on the heads of the women. There began a transformation, not only of the physical terrain, but of the shapes and motions of the gathering. Fires were lit; for the first time, water and food were thought upon. The younger women were rounded up and assigned to different chores.

Evening had settled on the field when, as if to further enhance and consolidate this new mood, word came that a woman was in labour. Wild Christian, who had by now dispatched Bunmi home with the shop basket and returned to the field, hastened there with her lieutenant, Mama Adunni. They examined the woman and decided that she must be rushed to hospital. It was too late. The excitement of the previous hours, the rush, the noise, the shoving and pushing, had been too much for the baby which, no one was at all surprised to learn, was a girl. It was nearly my first chance to watch a live birth but, after being ignored in the panic and excitement Mrs Kuti, who was hurrying in after news had reached her, saw me standing placidly among the ring of women and chased me off. Still, I watched them bury the after-birth under one of the trees on the lawn. Nothing could have happened of such a profound propitiousness as the birth of the child—and a female! The mood, which had already subsided into one of quiescent in-gathering now became radiant with joy. The baby was cleaned, the umbilical cord tied—I was allowed to see none of this but the running commentaries, instructions, advices were more than enough vivid transmission—and finally, both the mother and child were taken to the Catholic Hospital a hundred yards away—Oke Padi.

And yet more and more caravans arrived. As yet another group was welcomed, Mama Igbore shook her head and said,

'It is as if the heavens themselves have opened up, as if the graveyards have opened and all the dead and forgotten peoples of other worlds are pouring to join us here.'

From a swiftly shifting point in the various groupings, a voice would rise in song, but now it was all rapture and plain festivity. The outwardly religious songs—inspired by the *orisa*, by Allah or Christ—were begun by the adherents of the particular religion but were taken up by everyone irrespective of their leanings and chanted into the night.

217

La—illah—il—allah
Anobi gb'owo o wa
On'ise nla gb'owo o wa
Anobi gb'owo wa
A te'le ni ma ya gb'owo o wa
Anobi gb'owo o wa*

*La-illah-il-allah
Lord, take our hands
Doer of great deeds, take our hands
He who follows without deserting, take our hands
Lord, take our hands.

XV

The women now dug in for a long siege. Shock squads roamed the city, mobilizing all womanhood. Markets and women's shops were ordered closed. Those who defied the order had their goods confiscated and sent to the field before the palace. Even before the concession was formalized, the *parakoyi* had vanished from the markets, the tardiest only catching a glimpse of the approaching militants before abandoning their positions and seeking other predatory grounds. The men became more fully involved, at least, they became more openly involved. At every step, they had shouted their encouragement of the women's actions and even in some cases, driven their hesitant wives from the home, angry that such wives did not know that the cause concerned them also, and that its victory would bring them much-needed relief. One physically dragged his wife to the palace one morning, gave her money to spend on food and assured her that he would look after the children until the strife was over. There were also many women there with their young who camped out in the open with them and shared the hardship. But the movement of laden lines towards the Aafin now included men. They stopped by on the way from their farms; many had even journeyed to the farm to bring the women yams, fruits, palm wine. A hunter or two stopped to drop the day's catch of bushmeat and share jokes with the women.

Beere and The Group negotiated with the new District Officer, the former having been recalled. They held meetings with the Alake's Council, most of which ended in deadlocks. At the end of each meeting they reported back to the assembly who responded with songs and dances of defiance.

Reinforcements of armed police had been sent from Lagos the morning after the initial riots. They stayed away from the palace but within sight, camped in the Centenary Hall and drilled ostentatiously on its grounds. A group of young women moved on to the road next to the drill grounds and mimicked their actions in comic formations. Crowds gathered and turned the police 'showing the flag' exercises into a farce. The drill-major sweated in the morning sun, striving in vain to retain some dignity and cower the women with his authority. He gave up finally, gave the order and the police dispersed and retreated to the other side of the hall, keeping only an observation post on the steps of the hall to monitor the activities of the women.

And yet another shock squad had moved to Ikereku, to the two-storey building of Atupa Parlour. They sacked it completely, having first put to flight the half-dozen policemen who were posted there on guard. Fortunately Atupa had not returned to the house since the episode of the *ebo*. They returned to the camp waving a few underwear looted from her house and singing with coarse relish yet another song:

> Obo Atupa lo d'ija s'ile
> Alake oloko ese.*

Obviously, some time since the first courteous exchanges, the women had cast the Alake fully in the role of the arch-villain; there was to be no more diplomacy. When the raiding team arrived, they were joined by the massed camp who milled round the trophies borne aloft on poles, laughing and slapping palms, punctuating the song with obscene gestures. I tried to picture their prisoner, the Alake, sealed up with his aquarium and electric fish, unable to stop the sound of this and other derogatory songs which the women had made up about him and saw a frightened, lonely man. I could not imagine him eating the heart or liver of anyone and failed to understand why he refused to take the simple course of granting every single request of the women. I concluded somehow that he was perhaps as much the slave of the District Officer—if not the present one, at least of the earlier, insolent one—as he was a prisoner of the women.

The gathering now moved to isolate him further. At some point a decision was taken and announced loudly so that everyone, including casual passers-by could hear it: no woman must be seen, for any reason whatever, within the palace. Even The Group did not exempt themselves, having, as I later discovered, taken the step of appointing a male chief as their future go-between. The truth was, Mrs Kuti and her colleagues had now reached a point where they felt that there was nothing further to be gained from future discussions with

---

*Atupa's vagina started the strife
Alake, with penis of a poison rat.

220

the palace. It had now become a war of wills.

And the negotiations went on, but they now took a form in which the results could only be known afterwards. To my disappointment, I could no longer be present at any of these meetings, even of those taking place among The Group by themselves. The veteran messenger continued to run errands between Beere and Wild Christian especially, but was now only left with vague notions of contacts being made, negotiations and draft agreements being signed to be put later to the entire assembly, processes which took place at unstated hours and places. For instance, The Group and some of the chiefs held a meeting with the new District Officer at his office. It was at this meeting, it was later revealed, that the abolition of the Special Assessment on all women was first proposed by the 'other side', also that the *parakoyi* were to be disbanded. The Group announced these to the assembly even while assuring them that they considered the concessions derisive.

And there was another secret session, a report of which was not shouted from the rooftops but which nevertheless percolated through the rank and file within minutes of the session. It had taken place in the *ogboni* enclave. The elders had sent a message to Mrs Kuti, their humiliations at the hands of the women forgiven.

'Come and talk to us' they said. 'We consider ourselves the sons of Majeobaje;* we cannot sit back and watch things get worse and spoil totally in our hands. Come and see us with a list of all the things the women want. You'll be surprised how closely our minds agree.'

At the meeting, the *ogboni* assured them that everything was happening as it had been written, nothing was strange to them, the elders, because Ifa had seen and spoken it all. Wild Christian recited their speeches to Essay during dinner on the following day, the first dinner at home at which I had been present—with her and Essay—in days, even weeks.

'They were very nice, very courteous. They didn't even want us to apologize over their rough treatment at the hands of our wild ones. They only warned us to be cautious, to know where we were going, to be sure where we actually wanted all this to take us. "As for us" they said, "we are not surprised or alarmed. Ifa said it all before and, when it started, we went back to consult again and Ifa said—now is happening what I told you before." Those *ogboni* said it comes in

*Let-things-not-come-to-ruin.

cycles—every fourteenth king—or was it thirteenth? I've forgotten—
I feel so tired. They said that after every thirteenth or fourteenth king
to sit on the throne of Egbaland, it always comes about like that.
They said so many things, so many strange things. But the main
thing they wanted to say to us was that we should rest assured that
they would not allow things to spoil in Egbaland. They didn't want
us to think that they were sitting down doing nothing.'

They were locked up together a long time that night, speaking in
low voices. I did not really think that Wild Christian was physically
tired. Something had happened at the *ogboni* enclave to move her
profoundly—it showed in the manner in which she recounted the
events. Her weariness appeared not to belong to the body but to her
mind, to some new form, or hint of understanding or maybe simply
of viewing events. I reflected on the little I had heard, and concluded
that the *ogboni* must be very careless or forgetful people. If everything was already predicted and they knew it—as they claimed—then
why had they not anticipated their treatment at the hands of the
women? And I wondered if the Balogun had anticipated his fate—
matters were worse for him, he had become fully paralysed on one
side and was now receiving treatment at the clinic of a traditional
healer, far from Abeokuta. I did not think much of the claims to
prescience of the *ogboni*.

It was time again to make another assault on the broad fields and
orchards of Government College. During the turmoil I had again sat
the examinations; once again I was summoned for an interview. Essay
coached me relentlessly—but for the thought of the consequences, I
would have said to him, Don't worry, I shall win that scholarship this
time—I know it. But he had already begun to upbraid me for over-
confidence, wrongfully I thought. There was no way of explaining to
him that there were certain things of which I would, without any
reason, suddenly become assured. For instance, as the women's
struggle wore on and Essay pinned me to the front desk of the house
after returning from school, I often sat there and studied without
feeling that I was missing anything of importance. When he
returned, looked at me with a glint of mockery in his eye and asked
how the women's war was getting on without me, I often replied
without thinking,

'Oh, nothing is happening right now. Nothing will happen for the
next two days.'

I never knew just why I had said that, but I was more often proved right than wrong. I had a feeling that this used to irritate him immensely.

After a week-end closing assembly at school, I went upstairs to say good-bye to Daodu and Beere as I was to leave for Ibadan the following day. Formerly, the assembly alternated between two anthems as the final song—one was the Egba National Anthem, the other was a kind of 'God Save the King', the king being the Alake of course, not the other one on the other side of the ocean. For some weeks now, the latter anthem had been abandoned. As we trooped out of the hall however, I heard it being rendered unofficially by several independent groups. For a moment I thought that it was an act of defiance against Daodu, then I heard the words. A different verse had been substituted for the former words of salutation and loyalty:

> Kabiyesi, oba on'ike
> Ademola k'eran
> Omo eran j'ogun ila
> Omo ote lo l'obe
> Kabiyesi, baba eran
> Kabiyesi o
> Kabiyesi oba iwin
> Kabiyesi o*

Poor Alake, I thought, his rout was really complete!

When I came upstairs, Beere was at the telephone, one of the three or four telephones in the whole of Abeokuta. Her tone was angry, I had never seen her so furious with anyone.

'Let me tell you Mr District Officer, we are not impressed. We are by no means impressed—no, not surprised either. I knew it was coming and when I heard it on the radio all I could think was, just like them, just like the white race. You had to drop it on Japan, didn't you? Why didn't you drop it on Germany? Tell me that. Answer my question honestly if you can—why not Germany?'

*Hail, king of hunchbacks
Ademola has carried trouble
Son of a beast who inherits okro
Child of intrigue who takes the soup-pot
Hail, father of beasts
Hail, king of wood daemons.

223

There was a pause while she listened to what the other speaker had to reply.

She laughed—a dry, bitter sound. 'I give you credit for intelligence, but not for honesty. That was a merely clever answer, it was not honest. You know bloody well why. Because Germany is a white race, the Germans are your kinsmen while the Japanese are just a dirty yellow people. Yes, that *is* right, that is the truth, don't deny it! You dropped that inhuman weapon on human beings, on densely populated cities. . . .'

Her face became more and more agitated as she listened, then broke in again, 'Yes, you know damned well what you should have done if you sincerely desired their surrender. You could have dropped it on one of their mountains, even in the sea, anywhere they could see what would happen if they persisted in the war, but you chose instead to drop it on peopled cities. I know you, the white mentality: Japanese, Chinese, Africans, we are all subhuman. You would drop an atom bomb on Abeokuta or any of your colonies if it suited you!'

This time I heard the laughter of the other speaker over the earpiece. He spoke for a long time while I watched the various changes of expression on Mrs Kuti's face. It relaxed, smiled, then became taut, even grim again as she resumed speaking,

'No, I did not ring you up for that, I just wanted to pass a message to the so-called Allies, and you were their nearest representative. But now, since you bring the matter up, let me tell you this. Your king— this one here I mean . . . no, don't interrupt me, I have a right to say he is yours because you saved his head this time. As far as we women are concerned, he is already gone. But listen to me, there really isn't much to discuss. I have sent you our list of complaints. He has gone back on every word, every promise and agreement which he signed before we decided not to press on for his abdication. Well, just tell him from me, that if he hasn't learnt his lesson from Hitler . . . comparison or not, never mind that now . . . just tell him he should take his lesson from Hitler. As for you, that is, as for the Colonial Government, better get your atomic bomb ready because the next time round, he is going. Tell them Beere said so, his days are numbered. He is GOING!'

I saw her listen some moments longer, shrug and simply add, 'Well, I've warned you. Good-bye,' and she replaced the phone.

She turned to me and stared for a long moment. 'Yes, I remember you are leaving us for Government College. Wait here, I have something for you.'

She disappeared into the bedroom, returned with a small, flat parcel—it looked like a shirt but I never got to see what it was because I had to correct her at once.

'I am not leaving yet. I am only going for an interview. Schools don't start a new year until January.'

She thought briefly. 'Of course. How could I have made such a mistake? In that case I can't give you this yet.' And she replaced the shirt on the dining table.

'Suppose I don't get selected after all?' I asked.

Smiling, she pretended to give that also some thought. 'Hm, that would be a difficulty. I've been keeping this for your departure. Well, let's see . . . all right, let's begin from the beginning. How long will you be away for this interview?'

'Three days.'

She fished out a sixpence. 'That's for you to buy something with. Now, suppose you are admitted . . . wait, aren't you also supposed to win a scholarship?'

I nodded, and she resumed. 'Good. If you gain admission but no scholarship I shall give you the shirt. Right? Now, if you win a scholarship, guess what.'

'A pair of shoes,' I replied promptly.

She exclaimed, 'What!' and then remembered and laughed. 'Oh yes, I remember now. All right, a pair of shoes.'

One day I had tackled our parents over the fact that we were never bought shoes. It was particularly galling at Harvest, Christmas and New Year when special outfits were made, to find that shoes were one item most resolutely omitted in the HM household. This I could not understand, since both parents wore shoes and slippers as a matter of course. I picked the occasion of a festive meal-time when the dining hall was full—Tinu, Femi and I, the various cousins and even some of the neighbouring children. 'Why,' I asked loudly, but of no one in particular, 'does no one ever buy us shoes?'

Essay blinked, turned on his deaf ear while Wild Christian simply declared:

'Children do not wear shoes.'

I felt the eyes of both on me, expectant, for some time afterwards but I said nothing further. Eventually, Essay said,

'Wole, don't you even want to know why children do not wear shoes?'

225

I shook my head. 'No,' knowing full well that he must have thought up a good answer to be so persistent. I much preferred the grounds which Wild Christian had carelessly selected and only awaited my opportunity.

That moment came not long after, at the Kuti residence, on a Sunday where we had gone visiting. Wild Christian was sitting to lunch with Daodu and Beere while, at a table across from them, Tinu and I sat with our cousins who had just returned from church and were still variously attired in jackets, long dress, ties, shoes and socks. I picked a moment of silence in the brisk conversation—which was difficult, because Daodu was an incessant conversationalist—and said loudly,

'Mama, I thought you said that children do not wear shoes?' and continued eating.

Conversation died for some moments. Then Daodu threw back his head, slapped his thigh and let out the most deafening roar of laughter the corridor had ever heard. He laughed and wiped his eyes, spluttered, took a sip of water and continued chuckling sporadically for a long time after. Mrs Kuti simply smiled and said,

'Eniola, owo ba e l'ote yi.'* She then added, to me, 'Wole, any time you find a pair of shoes you like, come and tell me. I shall give you the money for it.'

Koye immediately offered, 'I have some which I have outgrown. I'll take him to my room after lunch and we'll see if any of them fits him.'

Dolupo offered also to take Tinu along. I looked at Wild Christian. The smile on her face looked more like a trapped scowl but I was past caring at that moment. In any case, even if we returned home with bags bulging with shoes, I knew that we would never wear them. Essay was inflexible on that score—to him, shoes on the feet of children was the ultimate gesture in the spoiling of the young. The children of relations and acquaintances who had been packed off to the Headmaster's house for 'training' discovered that, to their intense unhappiness. Their shoes gathered mould in their boxes, and eventually they outgrew them. In his school, a new pupil who had transferred from Lagos turned up one day in a pair of canvas shoes. He was not merely suspended, his real parents had to travel from Lagos and plead for the entire day before he was taken back.

*Eniola, you have really caught it this time.

226

Mrs Kuti delighted in small conspiracies; she understood very well what I meant and so we went into the strategies of the operation. Clearly, the shoes could only be worn during term at Government College; they would have to remain there during vacations and would never be produced at home. And of course I had to ensure that they were kept out of sight in Ibadan whenever my parents came to visit me—at least at the beginning. She was confident that it would no longer matter once I became a senior boy.

That problem out of the way, I asked her why she had been angry about the bombing of the Japanese. Were they not Hitler's friends?

'The white man is a racist,' she said. 'You know your history of the slave trade, well, to him the black man is only a beast of burden, a work-donkey. As for Asians—and that includes the Indians, Japanese, Chinese and so on, they are only a small grade above us. So, dropping that terrible weapon, experimenting with such a horrifying thing on human beings—as long as they are not white—is for them the same as experimenting on cattle.'

Daodu returned from the office during the conversation, deposited some files on a shelf and, catching the trend of the animated lecture, came over and poured himself some tea, nodding at several of Mrs Kuti's points. He stabbed the air in my direction:

'I would never send Koye or any of his brothers to a school run by white men. But you must understand this, it is not merely because they are white, it is also because they are colonizers. They try to destroy character in our boys . . . remember what I told you last year when you were going off for your first interview?'

'Yes, Uncle.'

'Right. Was I right or not?'

'But I told you Uncle, the school was on holidays, it was empty. All we did was sit exams.'

He turned to Beere. 'Do you know what I found out? Those teachers don't allow pockets in their shorts!'

Beere was clearly startled. 'Is that true?' she asked me.

I confirmed it.

'Now, why do you think they do that? Why on earth should a young man not have pockets in his shorts? You know,' he shook his head in a really worried manner, 'the white man is a strange creature. In his country, in his own schools—and remember, I visited a number of public schools during our conference—Eton, Harrow etc.— well, their boarders wear suits, all with pockets. From the most junior form. And the question I ask myself is this—why should one of them come here as a principal and forbid pockets in the shorts of his black schoolboys, WHY!'

I gave it some thought. Something which I had remarked about the pair of them—Daodu especially, struck me all over again. With them, I never needed to ask so many questions. They were always ready to talk to me—or indeed to any willing child—as they would to their fellow adults. Daodu would often collar me, even if I was quietly reading in the parlour or dining-room and ask me if I had heard some recent item of news from Lagos or elsewhere, and ask my opinion. It could be labour unrest, the formation of an association, some projected alliances as the war progressed, a new scientific invention . . . if I had not yet encountered the item of news he would shake his head reprovingly,

'You must take an interest! Don't just stick your nose in that dead book you are reading. Don't you see, if Mussolini could undermine the independence of Abyssinia, what chance has the new National Council of Nigeria and the Cameroons got with their demand for some measure of self-government? These people who have managed to defeat Mussolini, is it likely that they will ever surrender what they already have? What do you think of Winston Churchill?'

I blurted out on that occasion, 'Actually, you remind me very much of him.'

I had not really considered it before but a strong resemblance did strike me at that moment, very forcefully. He stopped in his stride, folded his arms across his chest and tucked his hands under his armpits as if he was hugging himself. I could see the inside of his head working out all the elements which must have combined to make me give such a forceful declaration.

'Amazing, amazing. I have always found children's powers of observation remarkable. Now you have to tell me *why* you hold such an opinion. No, not right now. But you must remind me. I want every single detail of what has given you that opinion.'

It was that persistent, bulldog expression on his face again as he asked—why? Why would a white principal forbid pockets in the shorts of the GC boys? I had some ideas on the matter but first I had some good news to give him:

'We learnt that Powell will be leaving shortly. He's retiring. The new principal may let us have pockets.'

Daodu turned to his wife and explained, 'Powell is the present principal. A very keen Boy Scout. A-ha! Now that is an even greater indictment. A boy scout needs as many pockets as he can use. Have you ever been a boy scout?'

'Well, I was a cub at St Peter's. We had a teacher who was a keen scoutmaster. His name was Activity.'

They both laughed. I added, 'But he left, and no one else took his place.'

Daodu nodded approvingly. 'Now scouting also develops character. It would be interesting to see if this scouting enthusiast, who does not provide pockets for his schoolboys, at least encourages scouting in his school.'

I was able to fulfil his worst fears—GCI had no scouting programme. At my previous interview, I had marked down Scouting in that section of our questionnaire which required us to state our hobbies. One of the white faces who sat on the panel had smiled and regretted that there was no scouting in the school. When I passed this information to Daodu, he raised his arms in genuine concern, looking at me with something akin to commiseration.

'See? Do you see now? This Powell, Mr V. P. V. . . . no, what are those peculiar initials of his again?'

'V.B.V.P.'

'That's right, V. B. V. Powell . . .' He shook his head. 'Heaven knows what those letters stand for . . .'

'Very Bad Very Poor,' I briskly announced, and he and Beere chuckled loud and long. I told them that one of the candidates who already had a brother in the school had informed us of that secret interpretation of Powell's initials.

'A fair enough judgement,' Daodu commented. 'He is always posing at the head of the national scout jamborees with his scout uniform stuck all over with labels and decorations. So, there we have the keen scoutmaster, yet he does not encourage scouting in his school.' He pursed his lips and looked me up and down as if I was walking into some mortal danger. Even Beere seemed to be equally infected by the sudden pessimistic outlook on my future. She commented:

'Double standards of course. It's just what I was telling that District Officer before you came in—dropping the atom bomb over Hiroshima but not over white Germany. There is a racist in every white man.'

Reverend Kuti sighed. His countenance was really doleful and I

229

began to wonder if I had not made a mistake in wanting to go to Government College. Then he brightened up somewhat, asking, 'You are now what? How old, how old?'

'Eleven,' I replied.

'Mm . . . . well, that's not too bad. You'll be eleven and a half when you join them in January. And you've had two years as a Grammarian . . . that ought to have done it I think. Don't you think so?' Turning to Beere for confirmation.

'Oh yes, yes,' she assured him. 'Not forgetting the fact that he's been brought up by Ayo and Eniola. I think he'll be able to cope with them over there.'

Daodu nodded. He was visibly cheering up, and he gave a defiant snort. 'Yes, we'll see. An ex-public schoolmaster who sews up his students' pockets and makes them say Sir-Sir-Sir, like slaves. A scoutmaster who discourages scouting. And no caning either—at most maybe two or three instances in any year—oh yes, so I've discovered. Mostly ceremonial caning—I doubt if any pupil from that school has ever taken home a single scar on his back! How on earth do they hope to train our boys properly that way? Oh . . . I nearly forgot—no shoes.'

It was my turn to be startled. 'Are you sure Uncle?'

Firmly, he repeated, pressing his lips, 'No shoes. Since your first interview I have become very interested in that school. They have very strange ideas of character building. No shoes. Except for the senior prefects—they are allowed to wear tennis shoes. Or sandals. Otherwise, No pockets, No shoes . . . aha, there is yet another one, no underpants. Why it should be a school policy I don't know. As long as the uniform is clean and neat, I fail to understand why the housemasters should concern themselves with making sure that the boys wear no underpants. Especially the bigger boys . . .'

I was no longer paying attention. My eyes had swivelled slowly to encounter Beere's who was grinning with her eyebrows raised in mock distress. The sight was so comical that I burst out laughing and she joined in, leaving Daodu glancing from one to the other, frowning in his attempt to recollect what he had said that was so funny. Tilting her voice in sympathy Beere queried,

'No shoes?'

'No shoes,' I sighed, feeling the oppressive weight of my years. It was time to commence the mental shifts for admittance to yet another irrational world of adults and their discipline.

ABOUT THE AUTHOR

Internationally acclaimed as a playwright, poet, novelist and critic, WOLE SOYINKA is currently professor of comparative literature at the University of Ife, Nigeria. He holds an honorary Doctorate of Letters from Yale University and has been accorded major literary prizes in England, including the prestigious John Whiting Award. His previous works published in America are, among others, *Collected Plays*, the memoir *The Man Died*, and the critical study *Myth, Literature and the African World*.

DATE DUE

OCT 3 1 1991

FEB 2 4 1992

APR 1 8 1992

NOV 0 9 1992

NOV 1 1 1993

JUL 2 2 2004

GAYLORD   PRINTED IN U.S.A.